Y0-CBA-736

UNLOCKING THE MEANING OF

LOST

AN UNAUTHORIZED GUIDE

2ND EDITION

LYNNETTE PORTER & DAVID LAVERY

SOURCEBOOKS, INC.®
NAPERVILLE, ILLINOIS

Copyright © 2007 by David Lavery and Lynnette Porter
Cover and internal design © 2007 by Sourcebooks, Inc.
Cover photo © Punchstock
Sourcebooks and the colophon are registered trademarks of
Sourcebooks, Inc.

All rights reserved. No part of this book may be reproduced in any
form or by any electronic or mechanical means including information
storage and retrieval systems—except in the case of brief quotations
embodied in critical articles or reviews—without permission in writing from its publisher, Sourcebooks, Inc.

Published by Sourcebooks, Inc.
P.O. Box 4410, Naperville, Illinois 60567-4410
(630) 961-3900
Fax: (630) 961-2168
www.sourcebooks.com

Library of Congress Cataloging-in-Publication Data

   Unlocking the meanings of Lost : the unofficial guide / David
Lavery
and Lynnette Porter.
      p. cm.
   2006 ed. has authors in reverse order.
   Includes bibliographical references and index.
   ISBN 978-1-4022-0917-8 (trade pbk. : alk. paper)   1.   Lost
(Television
program)   I. Porter, Lynnette R., 1957- II. Porter, Lynnette R.,
1957-
Unlocking the meanings of Lost. III. Title.

PN1992.77.L67P67 2007
791.45'7--dc22
                                      2007012398

      Printed and bound in the United States of America.

            VP   10   9   8   7   6   5   4   3   2   1

TABLE OF CONTENTS

Acknowledgments...v
Introduction: Getting *Lost*...1
Part One: Creating *Lost*..13
    Chapter 1: The Making of *Lost*.....................................17
Part Two: The Many Meanings of *Lost*................................43
    Chapter 2: *Lost* Within and Without..........................45
    Chapter 3: Finding *Lost* Meanings...........................103
Part Three: Spirituality..139
    Chapter 4: Spiritual Practices on the Island...............143
    Chapter 5: Formal Religion as a Way to
              Unlock Meaning....................................179
    Chapter 6: Larger Spiritual Concepts 203
Part Four: The *Lost* Fandom 237
    Chapter 7: Cult(ivating) a *Lost* Audience:
              The Participatory Fan Culture of *Lost*.........239
Epilogue: *Lost* in the Future...271
Appendix A: Character Sketches 275
Appendix B: Character Connections......................................285
Appendix C: Similar Names 295
Appendix D: Episode Guide...305
Appendix E: *Lost*'s Awards and Nominations, 2004–2007 311
Bibliography 321
Works Cited 329
Index...335
About the Authors..341

Acknowledgments

The original idea for doing a book on *Lost* was Lynnette Porter's, and it is to her that I owe my greatest debt in making this project work. Thanks for being such a knowledgeable and wonderful collaborator.

Thanks to Uwe Stender for hooking us up with Sourcebooks. Thanks to Peter Lynch for your interest in our project.

Thanks, as always, to my wife, Joyce, with whom I have gotten *Lost* since the first episode. After over a quarter century, she is still the woman I would most want to crash on a desert island with.

I also want to thank Hillary Robson. In many respects this book's third author, she wrote much of the fandom chapter. As I learned in many conversations even before this book began, her knowledge of *Lost*, especially the *Lost* fandom and conspiracy theories, is second to none. Lynnette and I are in your debt; it's hard to imagine this book coming together without your help. Thanks, too, for your excellent website at http://www.unlockinglost.com.

—David Lavery

Having an insightful collaborator is always a gift, but having fun while working with a knowledgeable colleague is even better. Thank you, David, for your valuable ideas and good humor throughout this project.

Hillary Robson also deserves my thanks for her hard work and for sparking my interest in even more areas of fandom. She maintains our website at www.unlockinglost.com, but more importantly, she assists in the development of the book and provides editorial assistance. Thank you, Hillary, for your dedication to this project.

Thanks to Uwe Stender for bringing us to Sourcebooks.

Peter Lynch, Whitney Lehman, and Tony Viardo at Sourcebooks, thank you for your enthusiasm for *Lost* and this project. I appreciate your feedback and support.

As always, thanks, too, to my family—Jimmie, Bart, Nancy, and Heather.

I couldn't get *Lost* with better people.

—Lynnette Porter

INTRODUCTION

GETTING *LOST*

"At the pit of exhaustion from directing Mission: Impossible, all I could think about—all I wanted to do—was write or direct another episode of Lost. Put it this way: If I hadn't helped create it, I would be a fan— and I'd be absolutely furious with myself for not thinking of it first."

J. J. ABRAMS

In September 2004, the ABC network series *Lost* debuted on U.S. television. Within a year, the series had gone international, running in Canada, Australia, Brazil, Colombia, France, Germany, Greece, Iceland, Israel, Italy, Malaysia, New Zealand, the Netherlands, Norway, Spain, and the U.K.; North America, South America, Europe, Asia, Africa, and the Middle East were all watching *Lost*. Everywhere the series is broadcast, *Lost* brings in high ratings, and it frequently is among the top three programs. By September 2006, *Lost* was second behind *CSI: Miami* as the most-watched program internationally.[1]

The popularity of *Lost*—a godsend for ABC, a network that had not had a hit show in years—makes it more than just another series from the United States sold around the world. During the second season in the United States, the series again topped ratings charts, not only winning its time slot on Wednesday nights but frequently the entire night's programming. Early

Season Two ratings actually increased (episodes averaging 17.8 million viewers, up from Season One's 15.9 average). However, the news wasn't quite so positive—at least on the surface—at the beginning of Season Three. Ratings for the first episode pulled only 18 million viewers, down from the more than 20 million watching the first episode of Season Two. Nevertheless, *Lost* was the second-highest-rated program of the week, and its number of viewers was higher than the Season Two finale. Although viewership for most, if not all programs, new or returning, is down, *Lost* still maintains its core fan base and brings in more viewers for new episodes than most series hope to attain.

Lost continues to do exceedingly well, not only in the United States but worldwide, even though it's its own tough act to follow. Beyond the wildest expectations of ABC executives, the cast and crew, and even series creators, *Lost* has taken on a life of its own. Millions of people around the world still look forward to getting *Lost*.

THE PHENOMENON

In the United States, the series has consistently been in the Nielsen Top 20 and almost always won its timeslot in the tricky Wednesday 8:00 p.m. (7:00 p.m. Central) time period in the first season and the 9:00 p.m. (8:00 p.m. Central) timeslot during the second and third. It became the second-highest-rated new show during the 2004–2005 U.S. broadcast season. With the order for a full season of shows in October 2004, the number of episodes was upped a few times until a three-hour finale in May 2005 ended *Lost*'s first season with twenty-four episodes, an unusual number in modern television practice. Long before ABC announced the rest of its schedule for fall 2005, *Lost* had won renewal for a second season. A second-season move to the 9:00 p.m. timeslot (8:00 Central) allowed writers to introduce more adult themes, including the island's first (albeit brief) sex scene. Season Three introduced even darker themes in the first six episodes, which were aired as a "mini-season" in October and November 2006. Faced with stiff competition and returning in February, after competitors became established in their timeslots, *Lost* moved to a 10:00 p.m. timeslot (9:00 Central). ABC hoped to please fans by placing *Lost* an hour later than the popular *American Idol* and to gain affiliate support by giving local news a strong lead-in. Even with the introduction of new characters and the demise of favorites, ratings wars, and different timeslots, *Lost* has continued to maintain its ardent fan base.

In addition to its prime-time hit status, *Lost* became noted for several innovative firsts in broadcast media:

- By late 2005 *Lost* had become the most frequently down-loaded series for iPod, and in late 2006 it remained one of the most frequently downloaded series, despite a number of new entries to compete with it in the market.
- It is one of the first U.S. series to be simultaneously broad-cast in Spanish and English.
- Episodes became available for viewing on mobile phones, and during the hiatus between the first wave of new episodes in autumn 2006 (in the U.S.) and the remainder of the sea-son, beginning in February 2007, *Lost* stories continued through a series of brief "mobisodes." These mini-stories featured the cast and offered fans a chance to view side sto-ries; it provided fans with their *"Lost* fix" during yet another hiatus. *Lost* is trendsetting not only as a television series with intriguing plots and characters, but as a successful product available via many types of media outlets.

The marketing for the series branches into many directions and reaches fans and prospective viewers in sometimes unexpect-ed ways. During August 2005, the pilot episode was popular among passengers on Virgin Atlantic's Britain-to-U.S. flights. How unusual for a graphic depiction of a plane crash to be viewed (repeatedly) by air passengers crossing the Atlantic! The first-season DVD set, complete with extras such as actors' auditions and episode commentaries, sold well; its release in September 2005, just prior to the beginning of the second season in the U.S., encouraged more people to catch up so that they would understand new episodes. Following the success of the first DVD set, the second set, released in September 2006 before the October launch of new episodes, also proved a bestseller. This set offered more interactivity for fans, who were told by Dr. Marvin Candle of the Dharma Initiative to look closely at the information on the Extras disk in order to learn even more. Even the structure and style of the DVD set, complete with its many "Easter eggs," made something as passive as DVD-watching more of an interactive, clue-finding game.

Fans who like to read as well as watch *Lost* storylines could buy a series of novelizations beginning in late 2005; a mystery written by the doomed author on Oceanic 815, Gary Troup, was published in 2006. Fans' imaginations (and purchasing power) were inspired by *Lost* conventions at which actors and the creative team behind the series answered questions, posed for photo ops, and shared inside secrets. (Creation Entertainment presented the first official convention in June 2005 in California; actors participated in a Grand Slam convention in March 2006, and Creation Entertainment hosts the Official *Lost* Fan Club.) Either individually or collectively, *Lost* people appeared at such fan venues as San Diego's Comic Con and at other science fiction, comic book, collectible, and television conventions. The actors, writers, directors, and producers seem as eager to talk with fans as fans are to attend these events.

Lost has been popular with critics as well as fans. During its first season alone, this difficult-to-classify, multi-genre series was nominated for or received awards for such diverse criteria as visual effects, family programming, scriptwriting, directing, acting, and themes involving the accurate portrayal of drug use. In

December 2005, *Entertainment Weekly* named the cast of *Lost* its "Entertainer of the Year." In 2005, *Lost* won an Emmy as best drama series, a feat repeated at the Golden Globes in January 2006. The number of prestigious nominations and awards is highly unusual for a series in its first or even second season. The shocking absence of major nominations for *Lost* at the 2006 Emmy Awards provoked a backlash among many very vocal television critics, who protested the new rules to determine nominees and continued to praise *Lost*'s writing, acting, and production value. Even with a lack of flashy nominations for acting and best series, *Lost* did receive nine nominations for writers, directors, technical specializations, and best supporting actor. It also garnered nominations from such "specialists" as the Producers Guild of America and the Writers Guild of America, who included *Lost*'s creative teams in their lists of nominees for 2006–2007. (A list of *Lost*'s many nominations and awards is included as Appendix E.)

What initially made the series so successful? It takes more than a beautiful cast or a tropical island to attract viewers. The diversity of awards and nominations and the fervid enthusiasm of its fans demonstrate that many people discover multiple strengths in *Lost*. Successfully bending genres and combining the best aspects of storytelling from classic television and movies, *Lost* provides intriguing action and plot twists to keep audiences hooked from week to week. Perhaps most importantly, however, it pulls viewers into the personal stories of a group of human beings with a broad range of experiences and different worldviews representing at least a half-dozen cultures and countries. Audiences watch *Lost* because they care about the castaways.

The basic premise of *Lost* seems simple: Forty-eight people survive a plane crash on a supposedly deserted tropical island. When no one comes to rescue them (at least during the forty days of the first season), the individuals learn that they must pull together in order to survive. What happens to them individually and collectively during that time makes riveting television. The castaways learn to fend for themselves, finding fresh water (in caves housing the bones of "Adam and Eve"), hunting boar, fishing in the surf. They bicker over luxuries as they build temporary shelters; they forge alliances but question others' motives. Important turning points for individual characters shape the story: Claire gives birth; Charlie kicks heroin; Jack struggles with his ghosts. A young man dies; love is discovered (or reclaimed); and destinies are realized. In short, life (at least for most) goes on.

The castaways' lives are further complicated, and the drama thickened, by the introduction of the "Tailies," a small group of survivors from the plane's tail section. The newly enlarged society attempts to understand the information revealed in the Dharma Initiative's research projects in the Hatch and other abandoned stations the survivors discover on the island. The Others, whom many viewers might label terrorists, appear and bedevil the castaways.

During the second season, the mythology deepens, especially with the backstory of Desmond, found in the Hatch early in Season Two, and the arrival of the ambiguously written Henry Gale. The popularity of these characters, and the actors' brilliance in their roles, brought them back as regulars in Season Three. Juliet, yet another new Other, quickly became a fan favorite. She, like Henry Gale/Ben Linus, is much more complex than most television characters and leads the viewer to question whether she is good or bad.

Lost continues to astound critics and fans three years into the story because it maintains an intriguing story, with plenty of plot twists, new characters, and multiple ways to interpret scenes. All the reasons why *Lost* initially achieved success still hold in Season Three. The creators and writers find new ways to introduce characters and build on a mythology once reserved for "cult" series. Those fans who thought the mythology too confounding or twisty became pleasantly surprised at the mixture of character development and plot conundrums during the first six episodes in

Season Three. Not only were fans' ideas about the nature of the island and the Others turned upside down, but those who longed for a good "Skate" (Sawyer–Kate) snog were rewarded. In true *Lost* style, however, the writers took beloved characters to dark, dangerous places for that character development. *Lost* continues to re-create itself each season so that there's something new, as well as something familiar.

We're often asked whether people new to *Lost* can make any sense of it by just jumping in. Of course, the more fans know about the series, the more they are to enjoy new episodes that build on a more than two-year-old foundation. Our answer is this: As with any serialized program, *Lost* may seem confusing on a first viewing. However, the characters are so well drawn that by the time a viewer has seen a few episodes, the large cast of characters has been introduced and certain assumptions about relationships can be easily deduced. Even fans-from-the-first receive new and often surprising information in each episode, and what they thought was true may not be, or may be only part of the "whole truth." In that sense, all viewers are equally *Lost*. This series succeeds because it doesn't present the same old thing each season, or each week.

Even the frustration arising from *Lost*'s second-season scheduling, full of repeats and long absences, didn't destroy the fan base. Fans complained—loudly—in person, on blogs, through email—and critic-fans wrote about these complaints and provided their own. In response, ABC offered a compromise. It wanted to show first-run *Lost* episodes early in the new television season, but it also needed to keep fans happy with few to no repeated episodes. ABC thus created a new schedule in which a six-episode block was shown toward the beginning of the new 2006–2007 season, with a long hiatus before the final block of episodes began nearly three months later. ABC also made the new episodes available free at its Website on the day after they first aired. iTunes also provided downloadable episodes.

The series' creators and writers, and even ABC, still appear to court the fans while retaining their autonomy. Fan input is important, but *Lost*'s creative team and the network still control the series' fate. Despite their grumblings at certain plot points, characters, or schedules, millions of fans return each week a new episode is shown, and Internet buzz remains high.

This Book

What makes *Lost* more than popular, but cultlike in its fandom? Why do so many millions of viewers worldwide tune in each week or grouse about a hiatus between new episodes? Most importantly, why is *Lost* significant to Western culture? How many layers of meaning can be unraveled in each episode, and what do those meanings indicate not only about a television series but about our larger world?

These are some of the many questions we explore in *Unlocking the Meaning of* Lost: *An Unauthorized Guide*. It has been written for anyone seriously interested in the show:

- Those who study television programs and their cultural impact, including teachers, students, and critics
- Long-time fans of the series who want a closer look at the many influences on *Lost*'s storylines and characterizations, as well as the way that *Lost*, in turn, is influencing popular culture
- New fans of the series who want to catch up with the *Lost* phenomenon

This second edition provides a complete, if unauthorized, analysis of Seasons One and Two and the first six episodes of Season Three. Much of the first edition has been completely rewritten to build on new information learned by careful and multiple viewings of episodes airing since the first publication. Completed at the end of 2006, the book's seven chapters cover the immediate and potentially long-term significance of this immensely popular series. The first season's fourteen major characters and twenty-four episodes (twenty-five including a summary episode shown in the United States) are summarized, with increasing attention paid to Season Two's new characters and twenty-four episodes (twenty-seven including summary episodes and a pre-Season Three teaser). Season Three's new and now full-time characters (e.g., Desmond Hume, Ben Linus, Juliet), developments between the Others and the Oceanic 815 survivors, and the introduction (and new perspective) on the "outside" world are emphasized. The book has been re-structured to emphasize key themes while keeping discussions about plot and character coherent and as linear as possible.

The first chapter, "Making *Lost*," examines the creative team behind the series and also contemplates the extraordinary challenges faced by them in sustaining its suspense while retaining good faith and credibility with its deeply inquisitive viewership. Chapter Two, "*Lost* Within and Without," illustrates how many ways the characters (and viewers) may be lost in life. In the third chapter, "Finding *Lost* Meanings," we explore the many ways to make meaning from clues and symbols found within episodes. The spiritual elements of the castaways' lives on the island, as well as individual characters' quests for redemption and enlightenment, are examined in Chapters Four through Six; hope, faith, and destiny, for example, bridge specific religions and help the castaways find meaning in their lives. *Lost*'s international, influential, indefatigable, and highly imaginative fans are the focus of Chapter Seven, "Cult(ivating) the *Lost* Fandom." Where do we go from here? What should *Lost* do or become to keep its ardent fan base? We explore that question in the Epilogue, "*Lost* in the Future." *Unlocking the Meaning of* Lost's back pages offer a plethora of supplementary materials including an episode guide, character connections, a list of similar names, sketches of each major character, a list of awards and nominations, bibliographies, and an index of people, places, and key themes in the book.

As new information about the series is revealed, please check our website at http://www.unlockinglost.com for updates.

As we discovered, being *Lost* can be an exhilarating ride in participative television viewing. Three years into the journey, we're still enjoying the ride, even if we've learned to keep our hands inside and to wear our seatbelts. We hope that you also will find yourself as you enjoy getting *Lost*.

NOTE TO THE INTRODUCTION

1. "CSI Show 'Most Popular in World.'" *BBC News*. July 31, 2006. Retrieved August 1, 2006, from http://news.bbc.co.uk/2/hi/entertainment/5231334.stm.

PART ONE:

CREATING *LOST*

"If [Lost] *works at all, it's because the audience and the characters want to know the answers to the same questions. The mysteries that we're grappling with while watching the show are the same ones they're grappling with, and that's part of the fun."*

—J. J. ABRAMS

After "I Do," during the two-month Season Three hiatus, *Lost* was in the headlines without being on the air. Media outlets all over the globe announced that, in an unprecedented step, the series' masterminds (Carlton Cuse and Damon Lindelof) were in negotiation with the ABC television network to set an end date for their ongoing narrative. To know precisely when *Lost*'s creators would need to resolve the show's myriad mysteries, to ascertain in advance when its many character arcs would need to hit their targets, to predetermine when best to pull the plug, Cuse and Lindelof were insisting on a sit-down with their bosses that would be in everyone's best interest. The creators, the network, the fans—all would benefit. To set limits to one of contemporary television's most amazing creations would make it more likely to be remembered as such. The clearly defined terminus of the Harry Potter books (there will be seven and only seven) was cited as a role model. *The X-Files*' extension beyond its natural life was evoked as a cautionary tale.

After all, the buzz on *Lost* during the Season Three hiatus suggested a growing unhappiness with the ongoing progress of the series. We had been told the "miniseries" that began Season Three—six episodes with a primary focus on the Others' captivity of Jack, Sawyer, and Kate—would end with a cliffhanger that would leave fans hungry for the series' return. The "shocker" turned out to be fairly predictable, however, and not at all the sort of development that, following a half dozen good but not terribly memorable episodes, would whip *Lost's* imaginative, insatiable fandom into a frenzy of speculation during the coming winter doldrums.

Even before the miniseries' end, speculation about *Lost's* decline (demise?) had begun among television critics. Were not ratings (although still quite impressive) continuing to decline? A growing impatience was in the air, a feeling that *Lost* was not providing solutions to its myriad mysteries quickly enough (the Season Two finale, which did reveal the cause of the crash, had been specifically designed to forestall such irritation: it failed to do so). Nor was the introduction of completely new characters welcomed by fans and critics who were convinced that Lindelof, Cuse, and company were not providing sufficient screen time for existing favorites.

So, at the outset of this new edition of *Unlocking the Meaning of* Lost, two and a quarter seasons (fifty-six episodes, or approximately 2,408 minutes or 40 hours) into the series, it seems like a good time to go back to the beginning and to remind ourselves how *Lost* came into existence in the first place.

LOST AND **ABC**

Although originally described by ABC Entertainment President Stephen McPherson as part of a new Fall 2004 line-up that would be "not spectacular, but good," *Lost* has turned out to be a spectacular success by any measure, a key ingredient in the resurgence of a network "that recently seems to have set the world record for airing stinkers."

In 2003–2004 ABC lost viewership for the third straight year in the prized 18–49 age demographic. But shows like *Lost* and its (even bigger) fellow hit *Desperate Housewives* reversed that trend. In its first week (September 22, 2004) *Lost* had the best opening for a drama in nine years. Throughout the season, it would average eighteen million viewers a week and consistently rank among the top ten programs while proving to be a major international hit as well.

McPherson gets much of the credit for ABC's 2004–2005 ratings comeback. But it was his fired predecessors—Susan Lyne, who discovered and supported *Housewives*, and Lloyd Braun, *Lost's* biggest backer and the benefactor who provided the $12 million dollars for making the pilot—who identified and green-lit the properties that would make it possible. In January 2004 Braun brought the basic concept—what Damon Lindelof succinctly calls "Plane Crashes on Island"—to J. J. Abrams, who was already helming *Alias* for the network and was about to begin directing *Mission Impossible 3*. (An earlier script by *Tuck Everlasting* coauthor Jeffrey Lieber had been rejected.)

Already heavily committed to the development of other projects, Abrams was initially unimpressed:

I was like, "Why? What the hell's that show? How would that work?" I just didn't get it. Then I started thinking about ways [of doing it] that, for me at least, would be thrilling. If the island wasn't just an island and if you started to look at where they were as part of the ongoing story, it started to become increasingly clear that this was a big idea.

One of those creative individuals who thrives on multitasking, Abrams would nevertheless sign on and ask for help. And, at that moment, *Lost* truly began.

The chapter that follows examines carefully how *Lost* got made and who made it, how the castaways ended up on that mysterious island, and how its huge international audience ended up there with them.

CHAPTER ONE

THE MAKING OF *LOST*

A successful television series may seem fated, and yet, if the path leading to its eventual triumph had been different, if at any level—writing, directing, casting—the series had chosen differently, the result might well have seemed not so inevitable. If Steve Van Zandt, Bruce Springsteen's guitarist, had been cast as Tony Soprano, a possibility briefly considered, would we still be talking about the Jersey mob around the water cooler on Monday morning? Hundreds of television series were certain they had the right chemistry, the right concept, the right actors and actresses, the right creative team to become hits—only to find themselves cancelled and forgotten.

The success of *Lost*, as we have already seen, was anything but predestined. We are still talking, and writing, about *Lost* because its creative team made the right decisions to make it work, and it is to the central members of that time, J. J. Abrams, Damon Lindelof, and Carlton Cuse, that we now turn our attention.

J. J. ABRAMS

"I lucked into this incredible medium. The hours are brutal, the pressure's tremendous, and the need for material is insatiable. But it's so exciting to work with the same group of people on a long-term basis, and you're writing something you know is going to get shot. That just doesn't exist in features."

—J. J. ABRAMS

Abrams is sometimes spoken of as *Lost's* sole creator. As simplistic and incorrect as that notion may be in the collaborative medium of television, it is understandable. In an era in which it has become more customary to equate prime mover and show—Joss Whedon's *Buffy the Vampire Slayer* and *Angel*, David Chase's *The Sopranos*, David Kelley's *Ally McBeal* and *Boston Legal*, Aaron Sorkin's *West Wing* and *Studio 60 on the Sunset Strip*—the temptation to speak of J. J. Abrams's *Lost* was perhaps irresistible, even if he has directed only one episode (the pilot) and written or coauthored two episodes (the pilot and "A Tale of Two Cities," the first episode of Season Three).

The son of producer Gerald Abrams, Abrams wanted to make films since he was a teenager. A screenplay he wrote while a student at Sarah Lawrence College eventually became *Taking Care of Business* in 1990. Other scripts likewise found their way to the screen: *Regarding Henry* (1991), *Forever Young* (1992), *Gone Fishin'* (1997), and *Armageddon* (1998), none of which made their author a big name in the business. "[A]s someone who was an accredited writer on *Armageddon*," Abrams admits, "my one real question is, is that something you really want to publicize?" Abrams may not be bragging about his first outing as a big budget film director either: *Mission Impossible III*, starring Tom Cruise, barely made back its costs (an estimated $150,000,000), although critics attributed much of its lackluster box office to Tom Cruise's antics in the TomKat era.

Abrams's scripts did lead, however, to development (with Matt Reeves) of a television series for the WB: *Felicity*, which ran from 1998 to 2002. Like his contemporary Whedon, Abrams imagined his future would be in film, not the small screen. But he found himself fascinated by television's possibilities.

Fantasies about expanding the parameters of *Felicity's* narrative universe—by making its college coed heroine a spy—led to the creation of *Alias* (2001–2006). Because *Alias's* creator, in the words of Mark Cotta Vaz, "has memory circuits wired to the mythic mainframe of pop culture," Abrams's new series was a generic amalgam, a mixture (in Stafford and Burnett's taxonomy) of spy drama, comedy, romance, family drama, science fiction, Hong Kong martial arts, *Twilight Zone, thirtysomething, Mission Impossible,* and *Avengers.* "I loved all sorts of movies and television," Abrams told Kevin Dilmore. "I loved Irwin Allen disaster movies, James Bond movies. I was a fan of cheesy ABC shows of the 1970s like *The Six Million Dollar Man* and *The Bionic Woman.* When I was a kid, I loved all that stuff." *American Werewolf in London* is likewise mentioned as a major influence, as are the films of David Cronenberg.

Hybridizing genres was not the only pleasure Abrams found in *Alias.* While making *Felicity,* he had been reminded of "what he always enjoyed about writing: capturing small, private moments that resonate with viewers, then weaving them into a narrative that's compelling to watch." He sought to fill *Alias* with such moments. His acknowledged displeasure with the series' third season (during which his hands-on involvement diminished because of other commitments) stemmed in large part from its neglect of private moments.

Abrams's experiences with *Felicity* and *Alias* taught him important lessons about the kind of imaginative universe he might want to live in: "When you write a pilot, you're building a dream space. . . . You want to populate that area with as many fun props as you can, so that when you're living in it for hopefully years, you're not bored." Abrams built into the *Alias* universe the sci-fi indeterminacy of Rambaldi (the Renaissance scientist and inventor whose discoveries were 500 years before their time), which has enabled fantastic expansion of its storytelling capability as needed in order to prevent his boredom—and ours.

So it should not surprise us that, given the opportunity to colonize the dream space of a South Pacific island, Abrams would need something more than *Gilligan's Island, Cast Away, Lord of the Flies,* or *Survivor.* To Edward Gross's question about why his new creation *Lost* needed a monster and all of the other mysteries of

the island—why it couldn't just be a drama about survival—
Abrams replied:

*It wouldn't work for me. Personally, [the monster is] what interests
me. Someone else I'm sure could do the show with that absent from it
entirely, but it wasn't the version I was interested in. . . . What would
give the show story tent poles that were compelling and mysterious and
bigger than the obvious stuff that you see play out? Increasingly it
became clear that it was about adding an element that was, for me,
hyper-real. . . . It's just my tendency. Whether it's smart or successful
storytelling or not, it's just what interests me.*

In episode commentaries and in mini-documentaries on the
Alias and *Lost* DVDs, Abrams shows himself to be wonderfully
knowledgeable about all aspects of filmmaking, from special
effects to scoring, and he has clearly thought long and hard about
his own creative path and explains it with eloquence: "I'm not
sure how the process works in me . . but I know that when I'm
writing, there'll be moments that will occur to me inspired by a
premise, and then the premise changes inspired by moments."
Abrams calls this process "writing as nanotechnology."

One of the many keys to the mystery offered by *Lost*'s inquisitive and imaginative fans is that the island is overrun by nanotechnology (the now in-development use of molecule-sized
machinery to control the structure of matter, even at atomic levels). Like much Internet speculation, the idea seems ingenious
but unlikely (in podcasts, Lindelof and Cuse repeatedly deny any
nanotechnology on the island). *Lost*'s nanotechnology is behind
the camera, not in front of it, released by Abrams's imagination,
but alive now and endlessly evolving in the series' narrative drive.

With his higher name recognition, J. J. Abrams has been given
perhaps too much credit for *Lost*'s genesis. In the inherently collaborative medium of television, others deserve recognition as well.

THE REST OF THE TEAM

In various media interviews during *Lost*'s first season, both cast and creators made the analogy between the survivors of Oceanic 815 and the group of actors and actresses who came together in Hawaii to perform as a synergistic ensemble. Each major character's complex and often unexpected pre-island backstory has been revealed in *Lost*'s richly textured flashback sequences; and the actors' pasts have been investigated—not in flashbacks, but in places such as *Entertainment Weekly* or *People*.

But the creators of *Lost* have rich stories, too. How did they end up on the island?

"The deal on *Lost*," Abrams told Edward Gross, "was always that I was going to help mount the show, but not run it day to day." That assignment would fall to two relative unknowns who have now become *Lost*'s showrunners and spokesmen.

DAMON LINDELOF

"You'll have to ask J. J. why he needs me (hell—I'm still asking myself that), but as to why I need him? Come on."

—DAMON LINDELOF

Television creativity, with its recombining of widely different sensibilities on divergent projects, can often energize new potential in writers, directors, and producers. The TV past of Damon Lindelof—as a writer on *Nash Bridges* (1996) and writer-producer on *Crossing Jordan* (2001–2003)—would not seem to foreshadow the imaginative achievement of *Lost*.

But Lindelof, a graduate of NYU's film school, had a personal list of influential TV series that Abrams would certainly find likeminded: "*Twilight Zone, Incredible Hulk, Six Million Dollar Man, Hill Street Blues, Police Squad* (six glorious episodes!), *Twin Peaks, Misfits of Science, X-Files, Profit, Quantum Leap, Buffy, South Park, The Tick* (cartoon version), *Mr. Show, Dexter's Lab*, and the greatest show ever—*The Simpsons*."

Even while working on *Crossing Jordan*, Lindelof aspired to do more. He confessed to Ain't It Cool News: "I'd been an *Alias* addict for almost three years . . . and had been pushing my agents (and anyone who'd listen) just to get a meeting with J. J. [Abrams]. Ultimately, it was Heather Kadin (an incredibly bright woman who defines the term 'network executive') who pitched me as the person to sit down with J. J. on this concept."

Hence Lindelof found himself, in Spring 2004, perfectly positioned to become the chief collaborator with Abrams on *Lost*. Immediately recognizing their simpatico imaginations, Lindelof and Abrams, with some assistance from Jesse Alexander and Jeff Pinkner, *Alias* staff writers, hammered out a full outline of the pilot that would eventually be filmed. Four days after the idea had first been proposed, at the end of the development season for the network, the series was green-lit by ABC. Eleven weeks later, the pilot (the most expensive to date in the history of television) was in the can.

The benefits of his collaboration with Lindelof were not lost on Abrams either. In August 2004 he told *Television Week*: "Damon showed up and I couldn't stand that we had never worked together. . . . He was incredibly smart. He had a point of view and seemed to have a take on what this show could be. He pitched, in the room, this idea for how he had to open the show, which is literally shot for shot what's there."

In addition to his central role in transforming the series from dream into reality, Lindelof has become, with Carlton Cuse, *Lost*'s co-showrunner and has penned, with Abrams, the two-part pilot. On his own, or in collaboration with Cuse, Lindelof has written twenty episodes, including the following:

- "Tabula Rasa" (1.3), in which we learn that Kate is a fugitive, captured in Australia by a U.S. marshal who was retuning her for trial in the United States when 815 went down
- "Confidence Man" (1.8), exploring Sawyer's criminal past

- "Homecoming" (1.15), a Charlie-centric episode concerning his post-DriveShaft struggles with heroin addiction

Collaborating with Jennifer Johnson, Lindelof also scripted "Whatever the Case May Be" (1.12), in which Kate acquires, in a bank robbery, that toy airplane that means so much to her.

With Cuse, he coauthored:

- "Deus Ex Machina" (1.19), with its Locke flashbacks in which the island's mystery man is flimflammed out of a kidney by his biological father and Boone is seriously injured doing Locke's bidding
- The three-hour finale, "Exodus" (1.23 and 1.24), in which (among other things), the Black Rock is revealed, the black smoke rises, Rousseau steals a child, the Hatch is opened, the raft is launched, and Walt is taken captive
- "Man of Science, Man of Faith" (2.1 and 2.2), in which we meet Desmond for the first time and learn how Jack and his wife met
- "The Other 48 Days" (2.7), telling the entire story of the Tailies' survival of the crash and their time on the island
- "The 23rd Psalm" (2.10), which gives us Mr. Eko's backstory
- "One of Them" (2.14), in which we meet Henry Gale/Ben Linus, a leader of the Others
- "?" (2.21), in which Eko and Locke discover the Pearl Hatch and Locke loses his faith
- "Live Together, Die Alone" (2.23 and 2.24), in which we learn what caused Oceanic 815 to crash and what happens when the button isn't pushed, and Jack, Sawyer, and Kate are taken captive by the Others
- "A Tale of Two Cities" (3.1 and 3.2), in which we witness the crash from the Others' point of view and see their world for the first time

- "I Do" (3.6), Kate's backstory about her brief marriage—the final episode of Season Three's miniseries

When members of the cast and crew of *Lost* came to the stage to accept their 2006 Golden Globe award in January 2006, it was Lindelof, fittingly, who held the statuette and delivered the acceptance speech. J. J. Abrams remained in the background, silent.

CARLTON CUSE

"We're on a first name basis with all our viewers."
— Carlton Cuse on *The Adventures of Brisco County, Jr.*

Carlton Cuse was no stranger to a mixed-genre television series when, long after the series had built a full head of steam, he joined *Lost* as Lindelof's co-showrunner in October 2004. (Cuse and Lindelof had collaborated before on *Nash Bridges*.)

One of Cuse's early (1993–1994) ventures in television as an executive producer was with *The Adventures of Brisco County, Jr.*, a Fox series scheduled in the Friday night slot preceding *The X-Files* and later relegated by TNT to Saturday morning reruns. However, Brisco was far from a typical Western or a children's show. Part comedy, part science fiction, part drama, and part buddy series, its snappy dialogue defied the "Thank you, ma'am" and "This town ain't big enough for the both of us" school of Western dialogue. Double entendres and comments on nineties' culture (that's 1990s, not 1890s) permeated the episodes. For example, an Elvis impersonator became a recurring character and a slab of beef placed on a bun was eternally saved from being known as a "cow patty" by Lord Bowler's timely comment.

Cuse, who created *Brisco* with Jeffrey Boam, also wrote the teleplay or story for seven episodes of *Lost*, spanning different genres and playing with popular culture icons. "The Orb

Scholar," the second episode in the series, begins the mythology of the mysterious orbs. Episode 20, also written by Cuse, completes the orbs' story with a time-traveler denouement.

A few *Brisco* plot elements foreshadow ideas later found in *Lost*. In the series' final two episodes, Brisco and Lord Bowler fake their deaths before a firing squad. In *Lost's* first season, Shannon and Charlie seem to die, only to be spared that fate. The concept of killing off main characters—or teasing viewers with that idea—is nothing new to *Lost*.

Plays on words also grace both series. *Brisco* features a lawyer named Socrates; *Lost's* characters include John Locke and Rousseau. *Brisco's* chapter or segment titles include "The Blast Supper" and "Spur of the Moment" (from the pilot); an episode about Dixie Cousins is entitled "Deep in the Heart of Dixie." *Lost's* episode titles often refer to song titles or lyrics, such as "Born to Run" (1.22) or play with the theme of the episode, such as "Whatever the Case May Be" (1.12), about the marshal's briefcase.

Brisco County, Jr. isn't a prototype for Jack Shephard (Matthew Fox), but the two share common traits. Brisco fails to gain his father's approval and support while his father is alive. He is shy of commitment around Mae West-esque good "bad girl" Dixie, but he is genuinely fond of her and looks after her.

Similarly, *Lost's* Jack is a good man who sometimes keeps secrets or strays from the moral high ground. Like Brisco's father, Jack's dad dies before father and son work out their differences. Jack, too, sees his father's ghost (or hallucinates the visions) and gains insights from seeing the apparition. He shies away from greater involvement with bad girl Kate, but his attraction to her is obvious.

Cuse demonstrates an attraction for a "buddy" theme in *Brisco* later echoed in *Nash Bridges*. (On that series, Cuse worked with Daniel Roebuck, who was brought into *Lost* as short-lived science teacher Leslie Arzt.)

As in all of the series in which Cuse is involved, a wide variety of often quirky characters come together to pool their disparate knowledge and skills for the greater good in plots that are occasionally otherworldly. Although Cuse doesn't blatantly steal from his previous work, the themes of friendship, father and son relationships, and supernatural or mystical elements operating in an otherwise logical world frequently turn up in a Cuse series.

A latecomer to the island, Carlton Cuse has become one of its most influential inhabitants. In addition to his many duties as executive producer, Cuse has also collaborated on no fewer than thirteen scripts, one with Javier Grillo-Marxuach ("Hearts and Minds," 1.13) and a dozen with Damon Lindelof, including "Deux Ex Machina" (1.19), "Exodus," "The Other 48 Days," "The 23rd Psalm," "One of Them," "?," "Live Together, Die Alone," and "I Do."

In *Entertainment Weekly*'s "Best of 2005" issue, we learn that the "Jewish and empirically minded" Lindelof and the "Catholic and willing to leap beyond logic" Cuse are a kind of Scully and Mulder, whose very different conceptions of reality are in many ways reflected in *Lost*'s ongoing clash between "man of science" Jack and "man of faith" Locke. The clash has proved effective, despite others' doubts. In fact, the Powers That Be at the FBI originally felt that Scully's medically trained skepticism and Mulder's open-to-conspiracy-thinking faith that the "truth is out there" did not seem a promising collaboration on *The X-Files*. *X-Files* creator Chris Carter knew better: the collaboration of opposites may produce a generative, expansive, ongoing creative friction.

When Lindelof invited Cuse to become one of the "*Lost* boys," he demonstrated the same wisdom. The collaboration of Abrams and Lindelof resulted in a strong foundation for the series; the partnership of Lindelof and Cuse, in turn, has energized its ongoing evolution as a serial narrative. On *Lost* podcasts, the pair have even become an entertaining, playful comic duo as they answer fan questions and hint at ("prehash") developments to come.

THE OTHERS

Although clearly the prime figures in *Lost*'s inception and continual unfolding, Abrams, Lindelof, and Cuse are hardly the only creative individuals. A more systematic investigation into the making of *Lost* would certainly need to examine carefully the contributions of its most important directors Jack Bender and Stephen Williams (the study of television to date has had virtually nothing to say about directors), executive producer Bryan Burk, and writers such as Javier Grillo-Marxuach and David Fury (no longer with the show), Drew Goddard, Leonard Dick, Edward Kitsis, Adam Horowitz, and Stephen Maeda. Award-winning composer Michael Giacchino also should be commended for his original orchestrations that help set the mood created by the writers, directors, and editors. *Lost*'s strong creative team has nevertheless faced, and will continue to face, a myriad of challenges: propagating the mysteries that have made the show famous without frustrating viewers anxious for answers; maintaining interest in its many (too many?) characters; keeping its actors happy; and continuing to inspire its energized fandom.

LOST IN A GOOD STORY: THE PROBLEM OF SERIAL CREATIVITY

"[C]ontinuous serials must of necessity build and sustain a cult status to stay on the air . . . viewers supposedly cannot bear to miss an episode. To stimulate and maintain that level of interest, you need to draw viewers into watching the show and then keep them hooked."
—MARC DOLAN, "THE PEAKS AND VALLEYS OF SERIAL
CREATIVITY: WHAT HAPPENED TO/ON *Twin Peaks*"

In a column in *Entertainment Weekly* entitled "*Lost*'s Soul," Stephen King offers some fascinating speculations on what lies ahead for a series he has touted as the best on the small screen. "There's never been anything like it on TV for capturing the imagination," he insists, "except The *Twilight Zone* and *The X-Files*."

And yet he fears *Lost* might succumb to the same serial narrative fate as the latter, a great series that ended badly because it violated the Nietzschean dictum to "die at the right time," remaining faithful instead to what King deems "the Prime Network Directive: Thou Shalt Not Kill the Cash Cow." "I could have throttled the executives at Fox for doing that, and Chris Carter for letting it happen," King rants, and he has no desire to experience déjà vu.

As *Lost* became both a mainstream top-ten show and an international cult phenomenon, the extraordinary tests faced by the *Lost* castaways have turned out to pale by comparison to those faced by Abrams, Lindelof, Cuse, and company. An episodic television story hasn't encountered greater narrative challenges since *Twin Peaks*, another rule-breaking, genre-defying ABC series that started strong but flamed out in its mystifying second season, and *The X-Files*, a *Lost* ancestor with a complex and perplexing mythology that perpetually promised but seldom delivered solutions to the innumerable puzzles that it raised (alienating its fans in the end).

How can *Lost* sustain its suspense while retaining the good faith and credibility of a deeply inquisitive viewership determined to puzzle out its mysteries? Can it become a "long-haul show" (Sarah Vowell's term) while maintaining immediate watercooler buzz? How can *Lost*'s creative team out-imagine its obsessed, ingenious fan base? ("People who post online—they're infinitely smarter than anyone working on the show," Abrams effused on *Jimmy Kimmel Live*.) Must *Lost*, of necessity, eventually disappoint?

Challenges to *Lost*'s ongoing development came from above as well as below, from network doubts as well as fan demands. Both before and during *Lost*'s first season, ABC made its concerns about the show's course well known. *Daily Variety* reported in July 2004 that the network had expressed alarm over the series' fear factor, evidently worried that too much of the scary might drive away viewers, especially in *Lost*'s early evening timeslot. In mid-season, David Fury, who had been a major contributor as both writer and director for both *Buffy the Vampire Slayer* and *Angel*, reported in an interview in *Dreamwatch* that network interference had intensified.

Fury had written or cowritten several pivotal *Lost* episodes, including "Walkabout" (1.4), in which we learn that survivalist Locke had been confined to a wheelchair when he boarded Oceanic 815; "Special" (1.14), which focuses on Michael, his mysterious, possibly telepathic son Walt, and the reappearance of a geographically anomalous polar bear; and the marvelous (and very funny) "Numbers" (1.18), which reveals that Hurley is a multimillionaire after winning the lottery with numbers to be found on the mysterious Hatch that Locke and Boone discover in "All the Best Cowboys Have Daddy Issues" (1.11).

Because each of these episodes introduces elements of the fantastic, it shouldn't surprise us that *Lost*'s deviations from standard television realism, a given in Fury's tenure on *Buffy* and *Angel*, were on the mind of both interviewer and writer when he sat down to talk with Tara DiLullo: "We didn't run into any network interference," Fury admits, "until roughly around episodes 9 ["Solitary," written by Fury] and 10 ["Raised by Another," written by Lynne E. Litt]." The network, he suggests, became "terrified" at the creative team's decision to "goose things and take it a bit further" and asked that the "hard-to-explain things" be avoided.

Why would a network that once had the audacity to broadcast *Twin Peaks*, one of the most bizarre series ever to air on the small screen, be terrified by the plans of Abrams, Lindelof, Cuse, and Fury? Had not the central mystery of *Twin Peaks*, "Who killed Laura Palmer?" been satisfactorily answered? Yes, *Twin Peaks* ratings had, of course, plummeted, as it finally began to disclose its answers in its second season, such as the identity of BOB. But that was so last century. Surely ABC couldn't be worried that its new Goose That Laid the Golden Nielsens could be destroyed by the "goosing" that Lindelof wanted to undertake? Weren't the fans anxious to be goosed? Fury, who has since left the show (for *24*), admitted to "a frustration for me as a viewer, in that I'd like some clearer answers [to *Lost*'s mysteries], but those answers were resting in the area of sci-fi and that's where we had to draw the line."

At this point, Fury's efforts to say what he isn't allowed to say become completely enigmatic—as enigmatic as *Lost* itself:

We were holding back, but it's not like we want to burst forth and admit we are a sci-fi show in the closet coming out. . . . It's more about trying to find the elements of the island that become the metaphors for character stories that we are trying to tell. It's about trying to find those mystical elements and yet give them an element of being possibly mystical, or not, by perception.

Using a metaphor drawn from one of *Lost*'s ancestors, Fury even manages to find a way to make this triangulation sound like a good thing:

We are respecting the network's desire to not make the show too "out there" too fast. . . . We were trying to approach the show from the Scully perspective and always try to have a reasonable explanation for everything, despite anything that seems out of the ordinary. That was our self-imposed mandate because the networks are scared of genre television. But it wasn't a constraining element. It was more of a way of looking at the show in a way that helped keep things more subtle and grounded and that's a good thing.

Fury observes with disarming cogency that while the Powers That Be at the network "are content with the mysteries, they are not content with the answers."

Hyperconscious of the classic "surprise or acceptability problem" that Marc Dolan identified (see the epigraph), Fury knew very well that such a situation had inherent risks: "There is the challenge of how long an audience will be invested in the show and in these characters without getting enough concrete answers." If "we answer some of these questions, and if we do it in the most reality based way, I think people will feel cheated." On the other hand, supplying answers to *Lost*'s enigmas "in the most interesting sci-fi way" could well result in "alienat[ing]"— a telling word choice—"the core audience of the series." Did we mention that Fury, now working on *24*, is no longer with the show?

LOST SO FAR

At the beginning of Season Two, *Lost* had become the most imitated show on television. All of the networks, seemingly no longer concerned that sci-fi or fantastic story lines might drive viewers away, decided to experiment with science fiction and the fantastic in their fall schedules. *Threshold* on CBS, *Night Stalker* on ABC, *Supernatural* on the WB, *Surface* on NBC, and *Invasion*—*Lost*'s partnered follow-up show on ABC—came and went (mostly went). In Season Three, *Lost* was again flattered by imitation. New series such as ABC's *The Nine*, *Day Break* (which took over *Lost*'s programming slot during its winter hiatus), and *Six Degrees* (executive produced by J. J. Abrams), NBC's *Heroes*, and Fox's *Vanished* all owed something to either *Lost*'s nonlinear narrative structure or to its bringing together of seemingly disparate characters with astonishing backstory connections (only *Heroes* has proven to be a breakout hit).

Lost nevertheless remains firmly perched on the horns of its indigenous creative dilemma. Some, it seems, have begun to fear that the shark (perhaps the one with the Dharma logo that menaces Sawyer in "Adrift" [2.2]) might be ready for jumping.[1] Lindelof and Cuse are well aware of the shark threat. On a July 31, 2006 *Lost* podcast, in fact, Lindelof suggests that the moment the show's creators don't risk jumping the shark will be the moment that they take the leap and *Lost* becomes a bore. *Lost* is all about taking narrative risks.

Serial storytelling can be an attention-getter and keeper, but also a quagmire. One reviewer used currently favored political terms to suggest that ABC and *Lost's* creators needed to plan an "exit strategy" for getting out of the series' plot dilemmas.[2] But is the battle lost after only two and a quarter seasons?

Lost still benefits from a serial approach to storytelling by being able to layer the plot and cover longer-range arcs and story developments that take much more than approximately forty minutes to resolve. *Lost* could make a series of smaller, single-episode points about the nature of good and evil, the power of or possibility for redemption, and the difficulty of following its mantra "live together or die alone." However, by revealing these themes through small examples within an episode (frequently via a backstory) and creating a longer arc through which we can see long-term changes, character development becomes richer and more true to life.

Two characters, Locke and Eko, who often are compared because of their spiritual quests on the island, illustrate the benefits of long-term character development revealed through bits and pieces of the serialized story.

During the first season, Locke becomes less mysterious—but possibly more frightening—when his connection to the island as a spiritual force is understood. Locke's nature—and how far he'll take looking for signs to determine what to do next—is revealed in small ways. By the end of Season One, we've learned that Locke was once wheelchair-bound, has had troubling relationships with his biological parents, and often feels stifled by authority figures who tell him what to do. By then, Locke's belief in the island and in himself as a tool for divine change makes more sense. Locke is neither a madman nor a cruel manipulator who ends up getting Boone killed. He's a devout follower who, because of his profound belief in his destiny, may be even scarier than if he were mad. Jack, for one, doesn't know how to deal with, or possibly stop, this kind of leader, who poses a direct threat to his authority. By slowly revealing Locke's past and showing his growing interest in the island across twenty-four hours, Locke's character gains depth and plausibility. We take the journey to unlock Locke, just as he's revealing, layer by layer, the entrance to the Hatch.

Season Two takes Locke in a drastically new direction, but that change is made plausible by his belief in the island's guidance and the season's theme for Locke: man of science, man of faith. Locke slowly becomes a man of science, as he and Mr. Eko analyze the meaning of button pushing and uncover *Lost*'s mythology: a murky mix of the Others, multiple hatches, broken films, and hidden maps. Locke attacks the new information more as a scientist than as the man of faith he proclaims himself to be; he looks for data to support his theory. This progression needs to be taken slowly—Locke wouldn't believably give up his faith in one or two episodes of revelations. By the end of Season Two, we see just how much Locke has changed and how far away from his destiny he's traveled. It takes the big implosion and explosion at the end of Season Two to jolt Locke back to his faith, which begins his return to Locke the Hunter in Season Three.

Locke's backstory in Season Three, "Further Instructions" (3.3), shows why Locke is more likely to look for a sign from the island than from any other source; seeking guidance in a sweat lodge is a logical plan for Locke as a man of faith. This gradual return to the real Locke in Season Three also paves the way for a new type of leadership among the castaways; Locke proclaims a more participatory form of government. He tells Hurley that, unlike Jack, he intends to bring everybody in on scouting expeditions and decision making.

Fans complained about Locke's detour as a man of science during Season Two. Even Terry O'Quinn expressed displeasure with this version of Locke. However, with that digression, we, and Locke, have a clearer motivation for his return to faith in the island, no matter how many sacrifices the island seems to require. Locke's character has a greater depth because of this change, which is plausible because it takes place during a whole season instead of during just one "very special episode."

The opposite problem occurred with Mr. Eko. For many reasons, Adewale Akinnuoye-Agbaje thought that he could wrap up the character in one season, especially with such a well-done episode as "The 23rd Psalm" (2.10) providing his backstory.[3] Mr. Eko became a new breakout character during Season Two; he successfully evolved from a warlord into a priest. Like Locke, his faith is tested by the Hatch. Whereas Locke unfortunately reaffirms his faith just as the Hatch implodes, Eko loses his spiritual path in the aftermath of the implosion. The breaking of the Jesus stick and the loss of the cross around his neck signify Eko's new, less spiritual direction. In "The Cost of Living," Eko again faces the Monster, but this time his warlord persona is unable to overcome his foe. Eko dies, to the shock and outright anger of many fans.

Eko's story arc is well written; it not only provides an interesting end to this character's island story and life, but it emphasizes one of *Lost*'s recurring themes: redemption. As Lindelof and Cuse have said in interviews, life might end at any time. Former *Lost* writer Javier Grillo-Marxuach noted that "at some point if [characters] don't change [their] circumstance there is this . . . deadline bearing down on [them]."[4] A character may not have forever in which to take that second chance for a new life or to be redeemed. Eko's story illustrates that point.

Fans who found Locke's character development too slow then shouted their displeasure with the too rapid development and ending of Eko's story. Some fans felt cheated because they invested time and emotion in this character, who then became the next casualty. Yet death has to remain a part of the plot on *Lost*; island life is dangerous on so many levels. Main characters, as well as background space fillers, need to die to give the story emotional weight. Eko's death is more than a rating stunt; it becomes an interesting development in the story arc. It provides us with more information about the Monster and makes us think again about redemption and the cost of living. However, it also is a risky direction for the story to take if ratings are the ultimate goal of effective TV storytelling.

Lost's creators often face a damned-if-they-do and damned-if-they-don't situation: they have to make some unpopular changes to character and plot in order to tell the story they wish to tell. They must keep adding twists to every character's life and to the collective group's actions. This is a very big story, both in scope and depth. That's one reason for *Lost*'s continuing popularity, but it's also what might lead to its untimely demise.

During *Lost*'s immensely popular first season, it excelled in character development. Serial storytelling can focus on character development and, as in real life, emphasize that development in small moments across several episodes, as well as during more monumental, life-changing events. Most stand-alone episodes of other TV series may include a shocking development in a character's life or an expository speech revealing something about the character's past. However, the emphasis is on action—getting a story told in less than an hour. The plot involves a single event (e.g., a murder, a criminal investigation, a first date, an office promotion). The situation might be the source of drama or humor, but the characters, no matter how well drawn, are more likely to serve the plot than the other way around.

A serial allows plots to be developed slowly, which allows the writers to emphasize characters. Much of any single hour of *Lost* is devoted to a character's backstory, which may or may not be directly related to the island plot. Some critics and fans don't like a backstory that can't be tied to the current action, even if we learn more about the character in general that can be applied to more than the current episode's plot.

Revealing tiny pieces of a much larger story also helps with mythology development. Season Two suffered a ratings decrease in part because *Lost*'s creators stuffed lots of mythology into one season:

- Henry Gale and the Others
- Walt's abduction and testing by the Others
- The arrival of the Tailies and the "flip side" to the crash-survival story
- The opening of the Hatch, which provided entry into a deeper understanding of the island's history
- The inclusion of the outside world in the island-based story (not to mention the four-toed statue that can take the island's backstories to historic proportions).

The many facets of the mythology often seem unrelated and require a lot of story building and linking; only by looking at individual trees for more than twenty weeks can we finally get an idea of how big the forest might be. One reason why *Lost* may not have garnered the major Emmy nominations after Season Two is that each episode is difficult to fathom outside of the context of the larger story and the growing mythology.

Season Three promises more character development, but, with an increasingly large cast, even split into separate groups, it's becoming more difficult to give each group air time in each episode. During the first six episodes, the story reveals new Others and explores this group's dynamic. Although the environment isn't ideal for romance, Sawyer and Kate finally get together in every sense of the word. Jack the Manipulator becomes a more fearsome type of leader—if he can ever get back to the beached castaways—and he shows a surprisingly well-developed self-interest. Although *Lost* fans, specifically Sawyer and Kate (Skate) fans, received a payoff—some prison loving for the pair—fans of other characters felt left out because the first six episodes showcase Jack, Kate, and Sawyer and take the time to introduce Juliet as a new key player.

Lindelof and Cuse were correct in building a mythology for *Lost*; the series needs more than a string of character-based backstories to keep us watching. However, too much mythology and too little character building turns off some fans. Splitting characters into groups—on a sailboat, in cages, on the beach, in the Hatch or in the jungle after the implosion—splits our attention. As some fans complain, if we watch primarily because we love a few characters and those characters don't make it on the screen for weeks at a time, our interest is going to wane. Poor Claire fans—Claire only gets to tell Charlie to ask Locke what happened after the implosion; there's no character development there. Her next opportunity to speak is months away, if she even is featured in the next episodes. Fan-favorite Hurley has a memorable, possibly prophetic line when he questions whether Desmond might "Hulk out" and gives Desmond the shirt off his back, but then he's relegated to chopping papaya in the background.

What is a blessing can also be a curse with such a large cast. Lindelof and Cuse say that it's more fun to play with "new toys," new characters with whole new realms of backstories to explore.[5] But if we love our old toys and want to see how their characters continue to evolve, we may not want to play with the newer models. Of course, with a storyline involving several locations, apparently on two islands and the outside world, the entire cast can't sit around the campfire together anymore. The plot must expand; fans also want the plot to keep moving forward to answer questions or provide new clues to solve mysteries, and only so many characters can be featured each week. However, focusing on one group for a long time is bound to cause some fans to leave—possibly to tune in later when their favorite characters are going to be featured.

Lost reinvents itself each season, with new characters and new plot directions. Lindelof and Cuse gleefully announce when new bombs will be dropped to take the story in even newer directions. A character bomb and a plot bomb helped launch Season Three episodes in February 2007 after *Lost*'s thirteen-week break from U.S. television.[6] Changes and reworkings should keep fans interested and wanting to see what happens next; however, they also point out another problem with serial stories—attracting new viewers.

People who have heard about *Lost* and want to drop in to view an episode or two may literally be lost; Season Three makes more sense with an understanding of what happened in Season Two, which was a radical departure from Season One. Of course, people who want to catch up can "get *Lost*" in a number of ways—through DVD sets, books such as this one, and millions of fan and official websites with episode summaries. But how many new fans want to commit this much time to a series that prides itself on continual changes?

If fans become hooked on a serial, they're likely to return week after week. They won't skip an episode; they make the program appointment viewing. *Lost*'s fans do just that, and they hate hiatuses—no matter how many games or teasers are provided during the break. They want to know what happens next, and this keeps them coming back week after week. Approximately fourteen to sixteen million fans in the United States, still a hefty number, watched each episode in Fall 2006, and millions more download episodes to watch whenever they like. The serial format is working for *Lost*, but it may be playing a game of diminishing returns. The benefits of serialized storytelling—involved plots requiring multiple episodes, greater mythology building, in-depth character development—also point out some flaws with this form of television storytelling.

Whether or not fans want to wait for the payoff in an age when instant gratification is the expectation is a major problem. How long fans will care about a mystery or unanswered question is hard to determine. After grousing about so few answers by the end of Season One, fans received a few answers at the end of Season Two: We now might be able to blame Desmond for bringing down Oceanic 815. However, in true *Lost* fashion, that's likely to be only one possible answer, or a partial answer, or the wrong answer. Maybe Desmond just likes to feel guilty and completely misread the data. We don't know who the Others are or what the Dharma Initiative is today; we have only cryptic comments, such as Juliet's remark that who they were is very different from who they are. Fans who didn't play the Lost Experience in mid-2006 may not have the same conspiracy theories about who's behind the island's activities as those who faithfully watch only the episodes.

Lost can be as frustrating as it is rewarding. There's nothing else like it on television today, for better or worse. It offers an intriguing but complicated mythology, an ever-changing direction and type of story, and dozens of wonderful characters. Each scene can usually be interpreted in more than one way; *Lost* deals with important themes that make us want to think about what we see on screen and apply it to our lives and to the world around us. That's not always an easy or pretty task.

Lost requires us to think and to be patient, two traits that most TV programs don't require. In fact, the need for pure (or maybe prurient) entertainment may be one reason why CBS's *Criminal Minds* recently won the U.S. ratings race against *Lost*. As reviewer Lisa de Moraes noted, "Turns out, three cute blond soccer-playing chicks stuck in a hole by a bad man who promises to keep them there until two of them kill one of them and he doesn't care which trumps some lame 'Lost' whacking."[7] *Lost* offers a different level of storytelling, which may or may not continue to attract new viewers. When will 16.1 million people watching an episode (such as "The Cost of Living") not be enough when the competition has 17 million viewers (as occurred with this episode of *Criminal Minds*)?

The dangers that *Lost*'s creative team faces are very real and have proved fatal, either in the short or long term, to all previous episodic television. But then, the *Lost* boys are not governed by a traditional paradigm. As both creative consultant Jeff Pinkner (in an interview on the Season One DVD set) and Lindelof have acknowledged, *Lost*'s ongoing narrative drive is modeled, in what may be a television first, on the storyworld of video games. As in a video game, in which players acquire new weapons and capabilities within its digital geography and learn more about how to play from the collective knowledge of gamers online, *Lost*'s characters and its audience are both sequentially acquiring the tools they need to play. In an interview for The *Lost* Chronicles, Lindelof recalls a moment very near the show's inception when Abrams had insisted that "whatever we wanted to do in *Lost* we had to build all that stuff into the pilot, we had to stock this world with all the elements and hints and clues." *Lost* is clearly well stocked, both by the creative team and the fans.

"With most shows, the 'watercooler' moments are what you see on screen," Lindelof told *Entertainment Weekly*. "With *Lost*, what gets people talking is what they think they saw. A Dharma Initiative logo on a shark. Sayid on a TV in Kate's flashback. . . .The greatest thing about *Lost* is that people can own it. They can plug in, engage, interact, and imagine." "The mantra at [ABC] these days," *Newsweek* reported at the time of *Lost*'s inception, "handed down by [former Disney CEO Michael] Eisner, is 'It's a marathon, not a sprint.'" From the outset, Abrams and company have insisted that the story they want to tell is complex enough to take years. We may be *Lost*— playing *Lost*—for at least a few more seasons.

NOTES TO CHAPTER ONE, "THE MAKING OF *LOST*"

1. The idea of "jumping the shark"—the name refers to a preposterous moment in the 1970s comedy *Happy Days* when "the Fonz" did in fact perform such a leap—originated with a website (http://www.jumptheshark.com/) that seeks to catalog the precise point in a series when it begins its downward turn—when the good goes bad.

2. Michael Hewitt, "'Lost' Must Find an Exit Strategy." Retrieved November 15, 2006, from http://www.ocregister.com/ocregister/entertainment/columns/article_1354062.php

3. Adewale Akinnuoye-Agbaje said he felt, after "The 23rd Psalm," "the character was complete . . . I know I would be able to sew him up in a season." Armstrong, "The Tailie's End," p. 44.

4. St. Cloud, "*Lost* Again," p. 64.

5. William Keck, "All Is Not *Lost* for First Gang." Retrieved October 17, 2006, from http://www.usatoday.com/life/television/news/2006-10-17-lost-main_x.htm?csp=34

6. Neil Wilkes, "'Lost' Creators Discuss Show Return." *Digital Spy.* November 13, 2006. Retrieved February 15, 2007, from http://www.digitalspy.co.uk/cult/a39391/lost-creators-discuss-show-return.html.

7. Lisa de Moraes, "Viewers Rebel as 'Lost' Whacks Another Character." *The Washington Post*, November 3, 2006: C7. Retrieved November 3, 2006, from http://www.washingtonpost.com/wp-dyn/content/article/2006/11/02/AR2006110201831_pf.html.

PART TWO:

THE MANY MEANINGS
OF *LOST*

Done well, a title can encapsulate not only a work's basic theme, but its vision, purpose, and scope.

Consider the title "*Lost.*" It captures the basic premise of the show: the survivors of Oceanic flight 815 are at least one thousand miles off course when their plane crashes, and no one has come to save them. To the outside world, it seems that the group is, indeed, lost and as time passes, much less likely ever to be found. But the title does more than indicate the show's high concept.

The title "*Lost*" takes on many meanings in this series, just as in life. As time passes, the number of ways in which the castaways become lost—as well as the possible ways they might find themselves—increases. But the fourteen original main characters aren't the only ones who have lost their way. During Seasons Two and Three, new and recurring characters add further depth to the story; like the original castaways, these characters also have plenty of problems. Even "the Others," who may know exactly where they are geographically, can be lost in numerous other ways.

In this chapter, we look at what it means to be "lost"—in the world, on the island, from and within society, among friends or family. We also consider how we can find meaning in *Lost* by interpreting what we see on screen, how the castaways view each other, and why symbols may help us find even deeper meanings in the characters as well as insights into the series' mysteries.

CHAPTER TWO

LOST WITHIN AND WITHOUT

The title "*Lost*" takes on many meanings, evident in the series' first season. What makes *Lost* always intriguing—as well as continuingly successful—is that the characters often become lost in even more ways as the episodes progress.

Most serial series solve enough mysteries to find the characters or resolve at least one crisis before a season ends (e.g., *Buffy the Vampire Slayer, 24, Desperate Housewives, Prison Break*). Titles often indicate the nature of the series: *Vanished* solves the puzzle of a senator's wife who vanishes from a fundraiser; *Kidnapped* covers the abduction of a boy from his parents. Even *24* provides an easily understood framework for events transpiring with the twenty-four hours of one day and one night. *Lost*, however, provides some interlocking puzzle pieces but then reveals an even bigger picture, with lots more pieces to be connected. If *Lost* only dealt with one tragic event (the plane crash) and its aftermath, it might not have been so successful after even a single year's worth of episodes. The characters' lives continue to illustrate ways in which we all become lost in our lives from within and from the outside world. The title "*Lost*," as series creators delight in showing us, can have many different meanings.

During Seasons Two and Three, new characters and events reveal even more layers to the plot and characterizations. *Lost* provides new perspectives on what it means to be lost: geographically, emotionally, psychologically, and spiritually. As new societies establish themselves, interact, and re-form with new members, the castaways are more than lost on an island; they may feel at odds with themselves, their friends, and families (families created through marriage, biological relationships, or less formal extensions), as well as the larger world of the island and everything beyond it. However, for all of the many old and new ways that these castaways can get lost, the chance that they can redeem themselves and act differently than they have in the past remains ever-present. Ultimately, *Lost* is a story of redemption, and how the castaways find themselves is as varied as the missteps that make them lose their way.

LOST FROM THE WORLD

We might not realize at first how unlikely it is to be geographically lost. Tracking and communication devices abound in our world, and the modern concern is more about how to escape (in search, say, of downtime) than wanting others to track us down. After Oceanic 815 crashes, the survivors don't know where they are, and, as the days wear on, it seems obvious that their rescuers are looking in the wrong place, if indeed anyone is trying to find them. (In the final moment of Season Two, of course, that someone is Penelope Widmore, in search of her lost love Desmond.) The survivors are lost in the geographical world; they don't know their location, although they try to signal aircraft or anyone listening electronically. Even after nearly two months of being stranded, Bernard becomes obsessed with building an S.O.S. with rocks on the beach, in case a plane flies over ("S.O.S.," 2.19).

Something seems to hide the island from the rest of the world. The island, itself a character, is part of the mystery of *Lost*. In fact, the pun can be made that this island truly is paradise *Lost*, much like a Garden of Eden in Christian mythology. It's beautiful, with everything humans need to survive: food, water, warmth, shelter, and even companionship; this bountiful land is theirs to explore and cherish. But this island has a catch; paradise isn't as glorious as we might imagine.

After the castaways quite literally fall, the far-from-innocent survivors discover that the island is as full of secrets and perils as the technological world they left behind. A seemingly huge, menacing Monster suddenly snatches survivors. Anomalous animals, such as polar bears, attack without warning. The castaways are imperiled by cliffs from which to fall, rip currents in which to drown, and rising tides threatening their makeshift dwellings.

During Season One the island seems to be the opposite of the modern world from which the castaways have come. Although the crash survivors quickly realize that they must learn a whole new set of skills just to live, much less live well, in this new world, they do recognize the beauty of the island. In spite of their struggle, several castaways still see the island's natural magnificence, exquisitely framed through the series' cinematography. Locke lives in awe of the island; Rose sees beauty all around her; even Kate and Sawyer take time to strip down for a dip in a waterfall-fed pool.

Out of necessity, they first explore the jungle and caves, but Sayid takes exploration several steps further when he feels the need to leave the group because of his mistreatment of Sawyer ("Solitary," 1.9). Sayid decides to map the island, a logical step that inadvertently leads him to a much greater discovery— Rousseau. The island is inhabited by many Other people. The island is home to more than the castaways first thought, but that revelation isn't comforting.

When Sawyer, Michael, Jin, and Walt set sail on the raft, ostensibly to go for help because no one comes to rescue them ("Exodus," 1.23–24), they learn another important fact about their island world—it's huge! Sawyer asks an important question: If the island is so large, much larger than we would have ever thought, then how come no one else can see it? Surely a mountainous landscape this big must be on somebody's map.

During Season Two it becomes obvious that other people do know about the island, but they either don't want anyone else to know, or perhaps, even, they can come and go as they please but what pleases them is keeping Oceanic 815's survivors on the island. Someone sends food drops to the island, apparently targeting the Swan Hatch ("Dave," 2.18). Henry Gale/Ben Linus first gives Michael a boat and the coordinates to travel away from the island ("Live Together, Die Alone," 2.24) and later offers Jack a way off the island if he agrees to perform surgery ("The Cost of Living," 3.5). The Others seem to know much more than they want to reveal about the nature of the island, and they apparently have a not-yet-revealed agenda. The castaways, however, lack this vital information and remain as geographically lost as ever.

The Others capture the Tailies children shortly after the crash, but what disturbs Ana Lucia Cortez, the de facto leader of this band of survivors stuck on the opposite side of "our" castaways' island, is that the Others make a list ("The Other 48 Days," 2.7) on which are the names of people to be abducted. How could another group that has been stranded on the same island—apparently for much longer than those from the Oceanic 815 crash—know who was on the flight? When the Tailies merge with Jack Shephard's society of survivors ("Collision," 2.8), they compare notes and determine that the Others, although too dangerous to confront, obviously have more information about what's happening on the island.

Locke's discovery and exploration of the Hatch further disturbs the castaways. Hatch-dweller Desmond tells strange tales of Kelvin, who dragged him into the Hatch and made him push a button every 108 minutes to keep the world safe ("Man of Science, Man of Faith," 2.1). Whether the "world" is the entire world or just the island is unclear, and Jack doubts the button's presumed significance. Season Two's encounters with more people on the island expand the scope of the castaways' world and open some intriguing possibilities about it.

The location of this world also may be outside the castaways' frame of reference. Desmond, a good sailor who successfully navigated a boat halfway around the world before he, too, became trapped on the island ("Live Together, Die Alone," 2.23), reports sailing away from the island only to be brought back every time. However, Other leader Henry Gale (aka Ben Linus) gives Michael coordinates to chug toward home on the same dilapidated motor boat the Others used to kidnap Walt ("Live Together, Die Alone," 2.24). Either Gale misleads Michael—a highly likely possibility—or Michael really can find a way out of the maze that seems to prevent everyone else from escaping. With Michael's recent activities shortly before he leaves (e.g., murder, betrayal), perhaps he'll never want to tell anyone where he's been, if he can find the way back.

Early in Season Three, Gale/Ben makes a deal with Jack so that they can equitably trade information ("The Glass Ballerina," 3.2). If Jack does what Ben later asks (but doesn't yet tell him just what that will be), then he will send him home. To show that he indeed can make good on that promise, Ben tells Jack that he has outsider information: the Boston Red Sox have won the World Series. Of course, Jack doesn't believe such an outrageous fact—until Ben rolls in a television so that Jack can see the final play. At least one person on the island knows how to leave, but native islander Ben says he prefers to stay right where he is. Later information about his spinal tumor ("Every Man for Himself," 3.4) makes us wonder if Ben is telling the truth about wanting to stay on the island when, theoretically, he could head to a more advanced medical facility somewhere else.

Despite what Ben says, the island still could be in another space that makes escaping from it or finding it impossible—unless someone is specifically brought there for a purpose. Fans speculated that the island is in another dimension or an alternate universe, citing theories from physics to support their speculation. Literature and film, after all, have given us many disappearing realms: Avalon in the Arthurian legend, *Lost Horizon*'s hidden valley of Shangri-La, and *Brigadoon*. Henry Gale, a character *Lost* shares with *The Wizard of Oz*, could be another possible indication of a mysterious realm, Oz, to which, as the wizard tells his subjects and Dorothy, he can never return once he leaves. When he sails away in a hot air balloon, he won't be coming back. However much the castaways might want to return to Oz (or Australia), they may not be able to go where they please, at least not without help from someone like Ben Linus.

Although Desmond does not use science or the arts to support his theory, he seriously questions if the rest of the world still exists (and many fans wonder the same thing). Gale also alludes to the strange nature of the island as a place even God can't find ("The Whole Truth," 2.16). Being lost geographically, even in a highly technological world, may be easier than we thought at first. Science, as well as myth, suggests that the world around us may be complex, and being found requires more than global positioning satellite coordinates.

But some people who are not living on the island know about it, even if they don't want to help. "Manna from heaven" is dropped near the Swan Hatch, which plausibly explains Desmond's Dharma Initiative-labeled supplies. The unexpected (at least to the castaways) gift of junk food as well as staples seems like divine intervention to people weary of island fare. At least every few months, a plane drops a shipment that parachutes close to the Hatch—so someone knows about the Hatch and the people within. Charlie asks a logical question: "Did anyone hear the plane?" The castaways conclude that it must have flown high enough to be out of the range of sound as well as sight. Whoever sends the food, and those who complete the task, don't come back to rescue the castaways and apparently haven't alerted anyone else to do so.

What is more troubling is that the blast doors inside the Hatch are activated before the food drop, so that anyone inside the Hatch can't go outside, much less see or hear how the shipment arrives ("Dave," 2.18). The castaways' new world looks more and more like an experiment being controlled by outside entities—a terrifying technological world instead of the beautiful natural world they first encountered.

Even the sets and locations indicate a shift in the castaways' attitude toward the island. More scenes take place within the Hatch, and even more hatches are uncovered during Season Two, a shift away from purely natural settings. More and more preoccupied with their relationships with each other and with growing threats from other people, the castaways seem less and less aware of the beauty of their surroundings.

There may still be hope for rescue or escape, however, because Desmond's former love, Penelope Widmore, continues the search. Her wealth might be able to buy enough searchers and the proper equipment to find Desmond and, thus, the other castaways. As Penny reminds Desmond after she tracks him to Los Angeles a few years earlier, "With enough money and persistence, anyone can be found" ("Live Together, Die Alone," 2.24). For currently unknown reasons, Penny's team in the Antarctic looks for electromagnetic anomalies that may point to Desmond's location. At the end of Season Two, such an electromagnetic flux helps them get a better idea of where he might be ("Live Together, Die Alone," 2.24). This much, at least, is clear: Penelope, a character bearing the name of the long-suffering wife of Homer's Odysseus (who waited for two decades for her husband to return from the Trojan War), somehow knows that to find the location of such electromagnetism is to find where her Odysseus, Desmond, disappeared.

Penny may have more altruistic, if personal, reasons for wanting to retrieve Desmond. She seems to love him and want him back, but so far her efforts have been thwarted. Unknown other entities—perhaps someone from the Hanso Foundation, Widmore Industries, or Dharma Initiative—know exactly where the island is located and may be keeping its location hidden from the sight of the rest of the world. Given the sophistication of global positioning satellites and constant surveillance by the agencies of various governments, the ability of these independent corporations to keep an island hidden from the rest of the outside world is a frightening thought.

THE PERILS OF THE MODERN JUNGLE

Even on a fairly simple level, *Lost* raises questions about the very nature of the modern world. What seems during Season One to be a story about plane crash survivors stuck on a tropical paradise quickly turns into *Paradise Lost* with a touch of *Lord of the Flies.* But even that twist might only seem interesting at the story level, but less personal to members of the viewing audience. To ratchet up the paranoia factor for the castaways and the fans, *Lost* adds the possibility that every aspect of their lives may be manipulated by people with more money and power. Characters like Jack, Shannon, and Boone—who have enough money and social status to get what they want most of the time—are used to being the ones in charge. Locke doesn't do well when people, such as his rich but remote and equally manipulative father, tell him what he can and can't do. Sayid, possibly more than anyone else, knows from his military experience how futile a single person's wishes may be when faced with a limited number of equally difficult and damning choices. If these characters we know and with whom we identify can be unwittingly drawn into such a deception and their every act manipulated as easily as if they were laboratory rats instead of humans, how sure are we, here in the outside world, that we too aren't being similarly controlled? How much power do we have over our own lives? How far can or would corporations, governments, or philanthropies go in the name of the so-called greater good?

Lost's second-season finale also presents a troubling parallel with the recent ineffectiveness of governments and philanthropic agencies to be able to help even those they want to help.

International media cover tragedies arising from war, terrorist attacks, tsunamis, hurricanes, and earthquakes, among other disasters recently in the news, but assistance for the people caught in these tragedies is often slow to arrive, if it ever does. Individuals have to rely more on themselves for survival; they often can't afford to wait for rescue or aid, even from those willing to provide it. If Jack and company are going to leave the island to return to the world that they presumably still want to rejoin, they may have to rescue themselves and deal with far greater challenges than just finding out where they are on the map.

Season Two's emphasis on the hatches and the less natural elements of the island also signals a modern concern about the future of such theoretically idyllic paradises; Season Three's emphasis on the Others continues this theme. Even people with the best intentions about preserving the world often end up going astray from their original purpose, often to the detriment of the natural environment. Ben's and Juliet's comments seem to indicate that the current Others are connected to the original Dharma Initiative; however, we can't be sure of that connection. They use the Dharma Initiative's former testing facilities and seem to know their original purposes. Although the Dharma Initiative may have had altruistic aims at first and may have been involved in a conspiracy to save the world—quite literally—from destruction,[1] the ends still may not have justified the means. The island, although beautiful, also harbors monsters and is mined with many types of traps. Experiments have disturbed the natural ecosystems; storms arrive and dissipate irregularly, and animals live outside their natural habitats. An incident creates energy fluxes that must be discharged before they build to critical mass, and concrete poured over everything is a temporary measure against contamination. The natural world of the island has become highly unnatural. Even if the current Others aren't part of the Dharma Initiative but are instead a later, completely separate group, they seem to be little interested in undoing the effects of the work begun on the island and they instead focus on gathering "good" people. Their methods, however, are often less than friendly toward people or toward the environment.

People who joined the Dharma Initiative may have thought they were doing something good with their lives. Kelvin thinks that this career move is a positive direction for his life, especially after his ruthless past in the military. He joins the Dharma Initiative, a supposedly easier job that would let him redeem himself. However, the job is less than desirable. Kelvin misleads Desmond about contamination in the world above the Hatch; he witnesses his former colleague's suicide; he plans to escape and leave Desmond to save the world on his own ("Live Together, Die Alone," 2.24). Even Juliet, who seems to side with the current society's aims (but, after all, she lives in comfort on the suburban side of the island), acknowledges that the Dharma Initiative isn't what it once was. "Who we were doesn't matter," she tells Jack during one of their first meetings. "What matters is who we are" ("A Tale of Two Cities," 3.1). In an eerie repetition of Jack's rather noble sentiment to Kate soon after the crash, Juliet's statement indicates how much the Dharma Initiative has changed over the years. The group's initial mission, complete with experiments that no longer seem to be the focus of island activity, isn't imperative to the current residents. The Dharma Initiative isn't all it was supposed to be—as the Others also can attest—yet it may be the best group to protect the world from complete destruction. Perhaps this is Henry Gale's/Ben Linus's ultimate justification for the Others's actions.

But the island world, as only one example, is far from saved. People, as well as animals, are brought to the island and tested against their will. Technology interferes with nature. There is no balance in nature—everything on the island is manipulated in some way. Henry Gale/Ben Linus enjoys controlling the flow of information and playing the castaways against each other. He alone seems to decide who is good enough to join the Others, and he likely determines the punishment for those who don't follow their rules. Just as the island faces an imbalance in nature, Gale/Linus instills an imbalance in power among the people on the island. The Others are the "haves"; the castaways are decidedly the "have nots," at least as far as tangible goods, level of technology, and control over their freedom. Acting as a judge of human character, Gale/Linus sets up situations that test not only the physical limits of characters (e.g., Kate, Sawyer), but the limits of their morality (e.g., Michael, Jack). *Lost* raises questions of how far characters (or we) would go to gain or keep their freedom and whom they would betray to improve their status in life.

Is that the fate of our world? Is every living creature at the mercy of one large corporation or another to manipulate the world's resources? Does the world require such intervention to survive? Even if that's the case, what is lost in the name of progress, or even of survival? As a society, and as individuals, we have to decide what kind of world we'll have. The members of the Dharma Initiative decide to act proactively instead of waiting for destruction, but is their method of saving the world possibly even worse than the annihilation of the planet? Does the power given to a small group of people, or one man such as Ben Linus, justify the subjugation of many more people? *Lost* raises questions about the quality of modern life versus the possibility of no life at all. Like the stranded castaways, we may have no escape to a better world and we may be left to deal with interlocking webs of problems and solutions that do not guarantee an ideal answer.

LOST FROM ONESELF

As the series progresses, it emphasizes ways that the people can become lost, not just geographically but psychologically and socially. The title "*Lost*" also captures the flagging spirit of the fourteen characters who were most prominent in the first season and the characters already on the island that our original survivors meet during the second and third seasons or, roughly, during the first three months on the island. (Season Three begins sixty-seven days after the plane crash.) At the time of the crash, each character is lost in his or her life. The survivors are disillusioned, addicted, imprisoned, and crippled in many ways. The irony of *Lost* is that, as the survivors' probability of being rescued decreases each day, their likelihood of finding themselves and starting a new life increases. Jack explains to Kate in "Tabula Rasa" (1.3), "It doesn't matter . . . who we were—what we did before this . . . Three days ago we all died." What does matter is who these people become on the island. But being lost isn't the sole province of the new arrivals.

Everyone arriving on the island has issues from the past. Desmond's shipwreck is only a metaphor for the rest of his life— estrangement from former love Penny, dishonorable discharge from the military, imprisonment. He is clearly smart; he was once interested in medicine and tells Jack that he almost became a doctor. However, he is trapped socially and financially, and, on the island, he is imprisoned in the Hatch and stuck in a dead-end job ("Man of Science, Man of Faith," 2.1; "Live Together, Die Alone," 2.23–24). His eventual freedom from the constraints of the Hatch still does not free him from the island or from his relationship woes. Only love can set Desmond free, as he realizes after reading a letter from Penny. Even if he remains geographically lost, Desmond is highly likely to find himself because of Penny's devotion.

Rousseau, also a shipwreck survivor, may have had a pleasant pre-island life, but her on-island life is traumatic, and, unlike Desmond, she hasn't had a redemptive epiphany. She loses a child to kidnappers and then kills her crew—by necessity, according to her— including her husband ("Solitary," 1.9; "Exodus," 1.23-24; "Maternity Leave," 2.15). Rousseau is lost without her family, especially her child, and everything she does on the island revolves around her daughter's kidnapping.

Henry Gale/Ben Linus seems in charge of a lot of what the Others do, but he likely also reports to someone else. His past may include some disappointment or disillusionment, because he acts fervently on the belief that what the Others do is right. His repeated statements about the Others being good indicates that he has knowledge of the "bad guys." As the pasts of yet other Others are revealed in Season Three, they too have troublesome backgrounds.

THE ADOLESCENTS' DILEMMA: FINDING ONE'S PLACE IN SOCIETY

Children who are born on the island, for whom it is their birthplace and home, may never feel lost from a civilization they've never known; they may never feel geographic displacement. Still, as they grow up, they can't escape from potential conflicts with family and friends or possible traumas inflicted by people or nature. Ben Linus says that the island is his home; if he indeed grew up there, his example may not be the shining one for teens to emulate, no matter how successful he seems in island society.

Alex, Rousseau's now-teenaged daughter reared by the Others, may not always agree with her adoptive family; she helps Claire escape from Ethan in the medical hatch ("Maternity Leave," 2.15). Later, Alex acts more like a typical teenaged girl when she asks a captured Michael about Claire ("The Hunting Party," 2. 11; "Three Minutes," 2.22). She eagerly inquires about the baby in a way that suggests fondness for Claire, herself an older teen, rather than a need to gather information about the whereabouts of a potential child to abduct. Alex shows no eagerness to hurt others, to the point of only grudgingly following orders from Other leaders, her surrogate family. She apologizes to Michael before she knocks him out with the butt of her rifle ("Three Minutes," 2.22). During Season Three, her concern for Karl, earlier seen caged near Sawyer, prompts her to infiltrate the compound in anger and frustration in an attempt to find him. She futilely throws rocks at Other family members before they take her home ("I Do," 3.6).

Alex recognizes that she is often powerless to control what happens to her or her friends. Like teens in most families, she doesn't make the big decisions; those are the responsibility of her "parents." In the Others's communal society, however, Alex doesn't even own something as simple as a dress. Sneaking in a quick conversation as Kate works on the chain gang breaking rocks, Alex wonders how Kate came by her pretty dress; it turns out that the dress belonged to Alex ("The Glass Ballerina," 3.2). Her personality invites her to challenge the rules set by her surrogate family, but she doesn't go so far in her defiance to invite punishment, which seems to be quite severe for rule-breakers. She even tries to play one adult against another to get her way. Certain elements in "I Do" (3.6) indicate that Alex may have a strong bond with Ben; she asks to talk with him when her rock-throwing efforts fail. Ben later asks if Alex inquired about him before his quickly scheduled surgery, only to learn that she has been returned home. Although her family seems strict, Alex reacts like a typical teen in many ways.

It will be interesting to see Claire's son Aaron and Sun's child grow up on the island (if the series runs that long). Will they turn out to be typical children who face the usual questions of adolescents as they establish their place within society and an identity for themselves? Like their parents, both have the potential to become disillusioned with familial relationships, whether they live on the island or in the outer world.

FINDING OUR WAY IN THE WORLD

The title "*Lost*" as a descriptor also can apply to all of us. In a precarious world fraught with unexpected dangers, many of us find the old rules no longer applicable, global politics increasingly important but volatile, and the expectation to do more with fewer resources a new given. Security is a misnomer; no one feels completely safe or secure. Dichotomies are deepening, dividing one religion, one political party, one country, and one worldview against another.

In real life, we may feel as lost in our lives as the characters we watch on *Lost*. The dilemmas faced by the castaways—whom to trust, how much of oneself to reveal to others, and how to bridge seemingly insurmountable differences in order to coexist with others—are the predicaments of modern life, not just of this television fiction. Michael promises Walt, "We're going home now. It'll be OK" ("Live Together, Die Alone," 2.24). Perhaps, after all that Michael goes through to retrieve Walt and, as he promises even before he builds the raft, to get Walt off the island, he truly believes that being geographically lost is the only difficulty. Maybe he knows how to deal with city life more than island life. But it's doubtful if his or Walt's life will magically be wonderful when they get back home.

How people deal with life's ups and downs, large or small, ultimately determines whether they stay lost in their lives. Rose loves Bernard and she is one of the most even-tempered castaways, although she still becomes annoyed with her husband when he forgets her birthday ("S.O.S.," 2.19). Hurley agonizes over approaching Libby for a date ("Two for the Road," 2.20). Claire worries that more than roseola is the cause of her baby's rash ("Maternity Leave," 2.15). Locke and Jack argue over who knows the combination to the arsenal ("The Hunting Party," 2.11). Mundane anxieties as well as life-changing events are part of island life as much as they are part of real life. The illusion of an idyllic life on a tropical island may be as difficult for *Lost* characters to grasp as it is for *Lost* viewers.

If *Lost* teaches us anything, it's that no place—even a remote island, wherever it may be—is completely safe or worry free. However, that doesn't necessarily mean that the castaways—or we—should give up in despair. Even in a world full of potential terrors, on the island or off, people can still lead joyful, meaningful, productive lives. They don't have to remain lost from themselves or their society. In Seasons Two and Three, several castaways begin to accept that idea.

Being lost entails a separation from something—a person, a place, or even aspects of oneself. In their ongoing search for what they think they need in order to become reunited, the castaways seek not to be lost. Because the characters are lost on the island, they provide us with both dramatic and comedic possibilities for learning to live in a new environment. However, because this international group's carry-on baggage includes contemporary anxieties about relationships, world events, and personal traumas, their significance goes beyond the archetypes they represent. The characters reveal universal human fears and frailties, as well as heroism and triumphs, as they realize what they have lost and move toward finding what they need not only to survive, but to have a meaningful life.

DEFINED BY OCCUPATION

What we do for a living often defines us in modern society and is a common frame of reference for establishing who we are and where we fit in the larger world. But what happens when that frame of reference no longer applies? The type of work necessary for island survival is far different from the former employment of most of the castaways, and even the concept of a job changes from salaried tasks to the necessary activities of gathering food and maintaining shelter.

Most Westerners greeting someone at a social event ask "What do you do?" as an icebreaker. Occupation often defines us, and self-identification with a job or title is a large part of our sense of self. After the crash and its immediate aftermath, occupation still remains a defining factor when the survivors begin to learn more about each other.

During the first season, Jack is identified immediately as a doctor and, largely because of his occupation, becomes the group's leader ("White Rabbit," 1.5). Charlie expects others to think of him as special because of his previous fame as the bass player in a one-hit rock band, and he is often disappointed when women fail to recognize him as a celebrity. Once Michael is defined as a construction expert, he gains status among the survivors, not only as the leader of rescue efforts when Jack and

Charlie are trapped in a cave-in, but later to determine that the caves are safe for habitation ("The Moth," 1.7). The expectation that Michael, if anyone, can build a raft seaworthy enough to escape from the island seems only logical.

However, what happens if there are no architectural marvels to construct (and the castaways can build rudimentary shelters on their own), surgery is (fortunately) infrequent, and rock concerts are nonexistent? Characters must redefine themselves in other ways. Jack's medical knowledge and skills are still highly valued in the castaways' new society, but Jack doesn't need to spend long days in surgery or patient consultations any more. Although he keeps the high social status of his profession—without the money, of course—he has lots of time on his hands when he doesn't have to play doctor. His medical experience is broadened to less exotic treatments, such as evaluating diaper rash and stitching a split cheek. Instead, Jack's take-charge, analytical personality promotes him to leader and chief decision maker for the group, a role he initially doesn't want but later doesn't want to relinquish.

There's no need for Charlie to worry about the next gig or fighting off groupies, but music can still be an important part of his life, albeit without the possibility of fame or fortune. Perhaps, as he asserts many times ("The Moth," 1.7; "Fire + Water," 2.12), his life really is "all about the music." On the island, he often composes songs, even if baby Aaron is his only audience, and plays guitar on the beach. Even as his hopes for a new album or a world tour fade, so far he still seems interested in his music.

Michael's career as an artist and his avocation as a construction worker seem completely at odds with his island life. After the raft fails to transport him and his son to a rescue boat, much less to the outer world, Michael's sole purpose (i.e., obsession) is to free Walt from the Others. Nothing else seems to matter.

Whereas Locke, during Season Two, gleefully returns to his former work habits as a manager by scheduling shifts in the Hatch, overseeing workers, pushing buttons, and entering code, Hurley is noticeably less enthusiastic. "At least we have jobs again, right?" perky Kate tells him as she prods him toward his shift. "Yay. Jobs," Hurley despondently replies ("Everybody Hates Hugo," 2.4). Hurley sees the nine-to-five work day as a burden rather than a blessing. Even before he became a millionaire, he often questioned whether going to work was worth it. For him, a job isn't who he is; it's something he does in order to survive. For Locke, Jack, and Charlie, their jobs define who they are, not only to themselves, but to the world at large; their careers form their self-identity.

Being identified by occupation isn't limited to the living. Jack eulogizes Ana Lucia as a police officer. Hurley does the same for Libby, although he's not quite sure if she was a psychologist or a psychiatrist. He finally humanizes her by calling her his friend ("Live Together, Die Alone," 2.23). Whereas Hurley first might feel obligated to connect Libby with a formal profession, as Jack does with Ana Lucia, what is most important to Hurley is that Libby befriended and helped him. Hurley doesn't need to equate personal value with occupation. What someone does for a living has less lasting importance—at least to him—than the personal impact of one life. Friendship far outweighs degree or job status.

In a Season Three TV promo airing on U.S. television in late summer 2006, the castaways state their occupation: Jack, doctor; Michael, artist; Charlie, rock star; Sayid, soldier; Hurley, millionaire. Then they question who they should become. Without this common identifier of occupation, many characters may question their very identity.

These characters grow when they realize that they are valuable, not just for the work that they do or the money they accrue, but for who they are. They can't buy others' affection but have to earn it through selfless actions. They can't rely on celebrity and media attention to signal that they're important. In short, they have to know who they are as people first and not as workers, a concept foreign to most people in a consumer- and media-oriented world. When the castaways are able to value people for who they are and not only for what they can do, they have found themselves.

DEFINED BY SELF-DOUBT

Sometimes characters' self-alienation or personal doubts and weaknesses become obvious to Other people. During the opener for Season Three, "A Tale of Two Cities" (3.1), the Others imprison Jack, Kate, and Sawyer in unique ways, each according to the Others's perceptions and knowledge of the castaways. Jack is sequestered in a glass box where he can interact with others; Kate finds herself on the beach having a last meal before her sentence begins; Sawyer wakes up in the zoo. Each choice of prison indicates something about the castaway's former life in particular, but the past keeps spilling into their current life as, the longer they're on the island, the more the castaways gradually reveal their personality traits.

Jack "under glass" resembles a specimen in an observation jar or even under a microscope. Throughout his life, his behavior has been carefully scrutinized, especially by his father. Everything he does is watched because he's such a promising surgeon; he seems marked for medical greatness. But his particular prison also brings to mind the familiar warning about the people who live in glass houses. Although Jack's behavior often seems above reproach, he nevertheless turns in his father for drinking on the job. Workaholic Chief of Surgery Christian Shephard ended up as an alcoholic loner. In his previous life, Jack certainly shares that workaholic tendency (a reason for the destruction of his marriage), and, in the airport bar, on the plane, and a few times on the beach, Jack enjoys a drink. Is (or was) he likely to wind up like his father?

The room where Jack is held once was a tank for sharks and dolphins—perhaps not both at the same time. When Jack attempts an escape and floods the chamber, he quite literally swims with sharks—Juliet and Henry Gale/Ben Linus. Swimming with sharks may be an apt metaphor for Jack's earlier life as a prominent surgeon in a competitive environment; in that world, Jack knew how to succeed and make difficult decisions. He knows, but may choose not to participate, in the shark-like environment created by the Others.

Kate ends up in the same type of animal cell that holds Sawyer, but the situation surrounding her incarceration is different. Whereas Sawyer is simply thrown into a cage, Kate receives a last meal in a beautiful setting, a reminder of the outside world, before her jail sentence begins. Kate is handcuffed, and the cuffs chafe enough to rub her wrists raw before she is led away to her cell. Kate soon begins her sentence: working on a chain gang of sorts to break rocks. A beautiful woman wearing a lovely dress who hefts a sledgehammer to smash boulders—this incongruous image befits the complex Kate ("The Glass Ballerina," 3.2).

Sawyer's sometimes crude behavior and inability to learn from his experiences turn him into a zoo animal. When he wakes up in an outdoor cage in Season Three, Sawyer first explores the enclosure, testing the levers and buttons marked with red hand symbols. He hits the food lever once and hears a mechanical voice drone, "Warning." No food appears in the chute, but there's also no apparent sanction for hitting the level. So Sawyer does it a second time. Another prisoner in an adjoining cage dully says that he wouldn't do that. No doubt, this man knows from experience or observation what happens when the warning isn't heeded. Sawyer smarts him off and hits the lever a third time. This time he flies across the cage, landing painfully in the dirt ("A Tale of Two Cities," 3.1). Although the Others's behavioral conditioning is heavy handed, perhaps Sawyer needs this type of education or conditioning in order to learn what's best for him. In his past as a con man, he trusted his partner more than once and was burned more than once—the ill-fated "Tampa job" ("Confidence Man," 1.8) and the tip-off about the man Sawyer wanted to murder ("Outlaws," 1.16). Arrested more than once, even serving a lengthy prison term ("Every Man for Himself," 3.4), he still returns to illegal activities.

Although a cage seems a drastic choice of prison for Sawyer, it symbolizes effectively much of his past behavior and a possible way for him finally to learn from his experiences.

LOST FROM FAMILY

Even before the episode called "All the Best Cowboys Have Daddy Issues," *Lost* revealed that most, if not all, of the characters had problems with one or both parents.

Jin rejects his father because he's a lowly fisherman, not the role Jin envisions for himself as a prosperous businessman. Sun's family is affluent, but her parents want to marry her off before she becomes any older; when she does marry Jin, her father controls the marriage by controlling her husband, who is an employee in the shadier aspects of the family business.

Jack's father dies after losing his career as a prominent surgeon; the only scene between Jack and his mother shows her berating him for driving her husband to his downfall and demanding that Jack travel to Australia to track down his father and bring him home. But Jack's father doesn't stop interfering in his son's life even after death. Jack sees his father on the island, although he doesn't know what to make of the apparently dead man ("White Rabbit," 1.5). Although Jack turned out to be an excellent surgeon, he still reacts to life based on the pressure of living up to the standards his father set for him.

Locke, reared in foster homes, is finally found by his possibly crazy and often institutionalized biological mother. She leads Locke to his biological father, who not only cons Locke into donating a kidney ("Deus Ex Machina," 1.19), but later pops into his life again to ask for help getting money from a safe deposit box. Whatever Locke's wealthy father becomes involved with has a dark undercurrent, and Locke not only risks his life, but his romantic relationship with Helen in order to help him. The last time Locke sees his father, the man is headed out of the country, money in hand ("Lockdown," 2.17), and Locke is again left without a father—now without the support of the woman he wants to marry. Another backstory, most likely from a time before Helen, revolves around Locke's experiences at a commune. Again, Locke seems to be too trusting for his own good; he's betrayed not only by his family of like-minded, back-to-nature enthusiasts but his new friend, Eddie, who turns out to be an undercover police officer ("Further Instructions," 3.3). No matter where Locke establishes a family, the family members abandon him, either when he fails to live up to their expectations or when they finally get what they want from him.

Sawyer's parents don't live long enough to watch him grow up, but their final moments seal his future. The boy's father kills his wife and then himself while their child listens in hiding ("Confidence Man," 1.8). Although Sawyer seems self-educated in popular culture and spends as much time reading as conning others on the island, he still can't seem to get over the trauma of his childhood. As an adult, Sawyer lies, cheats, and kills in the name of getting even with society until he can find the person he feels is responsible for ruining his family.

Sawyer's lack of positive role models may be one reason why he decides not to acknowledge baby daughter Clementine publicly ("Every Man for Himself," 3.4). Of course, Cassidy, the baby's mother, may have invented the child as one way of getting back at Sawyer for conning her out of her money. After all, she reported Sawyer to the authorities, who later caught and imprisoned him. Sawyer tells Cassidy that he wants nothing to do with her or the baby, but he later leaves a fortune in a bank account for little Clementine. Perhaps Sawyer feels that money is the best way to provide for his child; his lifestyle and attitude, even more than his sordid past, make him a less-than-ideal daddy.

Claire doesn't know her father (it may turn out to be Christian Shephard, Jack's father, as we learn in "Two for the Road," 2.20), but she has problems dealing with her mother. Claire doesn't return home when she's left pregnant and without her baby's father ("Raised by Another," 1.10). In fact, a second generation of fatherless children may also have daddy issues: Aaron is abandoned by his biological father, and his self-appointed surrogate father Charlie sometimes suffers mood swings that bring him in and out of Claire's life.

Charlie's problem with his father stems from a lack of support for his music. Although as a young man he sincerely wanted to devote himself to music, his working-class father required him to go into a responsible trade. Pulling Charlie in the opposite direction was his mother, who believed Charlie could improve his family's fortunes through a musical career. Add to the mix older, taller, more conventionally handsome brother Liam, who eventually abandons Charlie and his dream of a successful band in favor of reconciling with his wife and baby daughter ("Fire + Water," 2.12).

Kate's parental problems may be the most severe. Until she is grown, she believes that her father is Sam Austen, a respected military officer, whom she adores. However, her biological father is really the man who later becomes her stepfather and who is an abusive alcoholic. After Kate disposes of him, blowing up the house in which he lies in a drunken stupor, she visits her real parents. Her mother reports Kate's actions to the authorities, and Austen later discloses that she's visited him, resulting in her capture by a federal marshal. After subsequent escapes, a few years later, Kate visits her dying mother, who again alerts authorities of her daughter's whereabouts. Not only does Kate have to deal with failing her parents; she also believes that she is forever condemned by being the biological daughter of such a terrible man ("What Kate Did," 2.9).

Adults who don't outgrow parental troubles aren't the only ones with daddy issues on *Lost*. Ten-year-old Walt first resents the reappearance of his biological father, Michael, in his life. He also grieves for his mother, who dies just before he heads for the United States with Michael ("Special," 1.14). On the island, Walt faces losing his remaining parent; no matter how often they've quarreled, Walt still wants his dad. But how will Walt come to grips with all that his father does to get him back? The boy sees that the Others's society misleads visitors; the outward rough appearance of their dress and homes masks who they really are. Walt is happily reunited with his father, but, as soon as they hug hello, father and son motor off, presumably back to the real world ("Live Together, Die Alone," 2.24). Even if Walt doesn't ever learn that Michael has killed two people (both accidentally and deliberately) who would stand in the way of his plans, the boy still realizes that four of their friends remain gagged and bound on the dock while he leaves the island. No matter how close their relationship or how wonderful their lives when (if) they return to the United States, Walt's love and respect for his father may be forever clouded by this memory.

Lost's castaways illustrate almost every possible combination of dysfunctional family relationships. As with other aspects of behavioral and spiritual development, *Lost* asks some important questions about families: Does nature or nurture take precedence in child development? Are these characters doomed to be lost because of their formative relationships with parents and siblings? Do the same issues and problems between parent and child have to be played out in the next generation?

As the series enters its third season, closer relationships blossom among the castaways. Sun and Jin savor her pregnancy and plan for their child, who will have a fisherman father now that Jin's role is more one of successful fisherman than businessman. Will Jin's child also resent his or her father's so-called lowly profession? Will Jin (and the child) someday learn that another man quite possibly is the biological father ("The Glass Ballerina," 3.2)?

At the end of Season Two, Claire and Charlie share a first, brief, romantic kiss. What kind of family might they form if, indeed, they succeed in working out their relationship? Lindelof and Cuse hinted that, although they like the Claire and Charlie dynamic, another love triangle might be formed.[2] How might that affect baby Aaron's childhood?

The Jack-Kate-Sawyer triangle is popular among fans, who wanted to see Kate choose between her potential suitors. During the fall finale 2006, "I Do" (3.6), Kate and Sawyer "did it," but many fans were left unsatisfied. Many viewers felt that Kate deserved better than furtive sex in an animal cage where anyone could see her rendezvous. [3] The scene was hot, as in sweaty, but it lacked the romance that Kate deserved. If anything, the scene added weight to the Sawyer-animal comparison, leaving fans as shocked as Jack when he inadvertently sees the couple's postcoital cuddling on the Others's ever-present TV monitor. How will Kate's choice affect each member of the triangle? Is the Sawyer-Kate romance as doomed as it seems to be?

The Others also boast that they are a family. Ethan tells Claire that her baby will be loved by his new family, although she can't be a part of it. According to Ethan, the limited supply of vaccine means that only the baby can survive the island-inducing illness, as long as he continues to be injected with the medicine ("Maternity Leave," 2.15). The Others may adopt their children through abduction; so far, no biological children born within their camp have been seen on screen. Although to us, the Others act as a cult, a family in the sense of Jim Jones cult or even Charles Manson's followers, they fervently believe that the adults act as better parents for the abducted children than even their biological parents could. They want to protect these children by keeping them among the good people, and the adults train children in their ways. Teenage Alex obviously knows what's going on and participates in the Others's patrols. Families on *Lost* may not consist of biological parents and children; they may be extended families or adoptive ones. Nevertheless, they undoubtedly shape the next generation of island dwellers. How lost will these parents and children remain, not only in the present, but through their influence on future generations?

LOST WITHIN SOCIETY

As island societies collide or combine, not everyone feels as though he or she is a part of the group. Few societies, newly formed or long established, create a cohesive blend of all ideas and personalities. For a long time now, U.S. society has been dubbed a "salad bowl" more than a "melting pot," but even that description is inaccurate. Sometimes the disparate cultures within the country fail to work together to make a unified salad; perhaps the new millennium in the United States is more of a buffet. The United States isn't alone in its changing composition; many Western countries question how or if apparently disparate cultures—based on ethnicity, national origin, shared language, geographic region, political ideals, religion, or socioeconomic status—can work together toward a unified society.

The complexity of *Lost*'s characters also means that some people may feel outside the mainstream; they may become lost or estranged temporarily or permanently from the larger society. They experience *otherness*: individual isolation—sometimes by choice but often in more socially stigmatizing ways—from other people. Anything deemed outside a society's norm can form the basis of *otherness*.

On *Lost*, *otherness* is a blatant issue. The original group of castaways first has to band together to, in Jack's words, "work together or surely die alone" ("White Rabbit," 1.5), a theme echoed by Jack's repeated line to Michael, "Live together, die alone, man" from the similarly titled episode ("Live Together, Die Alone," 2.24). This "we're all in this together" attitude prevails during much of the first season, or the first forty days on the island, as the castaways begin to overcome the trauma related to the crash and face instead the terrors on the island that threaten to destroy them. One of the most important first-season instances of *otherness* occurs when Sayid ostracizes himself from the larger group because he tortures Sawyer for information and then can't live with himself ("Solitary," 1.9). On his journey to explore the island and rediscover himself, he finds Danielle Rousseau, also an isolationist. She has killed her infected crewmates from a doomed scientific expedition and now hides from the Others. Although, as Locke notes in a later episode, "pretty much everyone is 'Other'" to Rousseau ("One of Them," 2.14), even labeling another society as the Others illustrates how easy it is not only to label, but to demonize people whose behavior seems outside our society's definition of what's acceptable.

What is shown about the Others illustrates how different they seem from the castaways. Mr. Friendly draws a line in the sand—literally—and dares Jack to step over it ("The Hunting Party," 2.11). The Others infiltrate the castaways' groups and kidnap the "good" people to join their family. They claim that the island is theirs and that all latecomers are only allowed to live there with the Others's permission—or by their grace. They revel in being *other*, which, to the Oceanic 815 survivors, seems to stand for deceit, dominance, and cruelty. Yet, at the beginning of Season Three, we learn that the Others are not so alien after all; they live a kind of suburban lifestyle in an idyllic small village made up of picturesque cottages. They even have a book club where they discuss Stephen King and eat home-baked muffins ("A Tale of Two Cities," 3.1).

As is typical of groups identified as being *other*, a myth has grown around the Others. They walk silently through the jungle and leave no footprints ("The Other 48 Days," 2.7). They kidnap children ("Exodus," 1.23–24; "The Other 48 Days," 2.7). They signal with a mysterious black smoke ("Exodus," 1.23–24). These myths are based on facts that we and the castaways have seen played out. But is our, and their, interpretation of events completely unbiased? Are the Others as bad as they seem? Should the castaways attempt to understand them or avoid them? Or, as Jack suggests, fight a war against them?

The Others's reputation grows throughout Season Two with the capture of Henry Gale (beginning with "One of Them," 2.14),

Claire's island-based backstory of what occurred when Ethan abducted her ("Maternity Leave," 2.15), and the capture of Kate, Jack, Hurley, and Sawyer ("Live Together, Die Alone," 2.24).

The common image created from these bits of information is that the Others sound like terrorists—that's the image fostered through the castaways' limited interactions with individuals from this group. Ethan Rom kidnaps Claire and Charlie ("All the Best Cowboys Have Daddy Issues," 1.11), leaving Charlie hanging from a tree ("Whatever the Case May Be," 1.12). In "Maternity Leave" (2.15), Ethan is shown as a doctor caring for the pregnant Claire, but his friendly care includes sedating her and encouraging her to give up her baby to a good family—the Others. It seems as though the Others run the facility; they may plan to harvest Claire's baby and then kill the mother. Claire is helped to escape by another Other, the teenaged Alex, and, when Ethan later comes for Claire, Charlie shoots him dead ("Homecoming," 1.15). So begin the confrontations between the Others and the castaways. One group's limited information about another and the violence when the two intersect fuel more suspense, as well as the need, in Jack's mind anyway, for an army to protect his group ("The Hunting Party," 2.11).

"Them" and the Others are prominently named in several episodes. Charlie refers to Ana Lucia as one of "Them," in other words, the Tailies ("What Kate Did," 2.9). Before the Tailies learn that the Others are the group terrorizing Jack's band of survivors, the dwindling group from the back of the plane refers to the Others as "Them" ("The Other 48 Days," 2.7). Separating people into groups based on length of stay on the island, anticipated political or social agendas, or even location of seats on the airliner is a common practice, but it reaches new heights of fear, protectionism, and, increasingly, isolationism and defensiveness during the second season of *Lost.*.

The current global political climate seems to encourage an *us* and *them* mentality. As a society, we might pay lip service to diversity issues, but the rising concern about protecting our borders and making sure that democracy prevails over other governmental systems seems to suggest that diversity may not always be a socially accepted or even wise idea. In addition, polarization along racial as well as political lines (most evident in the United States after Hurricane Katrina) indicates that differentiating between *us* and *them* is very much part of the modern American mindset. *Them* seems worse than *Others* as a label; *Them* is in complete opposition to *Us*. This type of categorization indicates two-dimensional, black-and-white thinking, in which the *Lost* narrative temporarily engages, only to subvert it with other perspectives in later episodes. As we and the castaways learn more about the Others, individuals in the group seem more complex and no longer just the "bad guys." Some Others are friendlier and more helpful to the castaways; some Others seem intent on manipulating or confusing them. Henry Gale definitely seems Other compared to Jack as a leader, but even his machinations become more understandable as the story unfolds.

On *Lost*, Rousseau calls Henry Gale one of Them and, instead of avoiding him, captures Gale and turns him over to Sayid for questioning. Rousseau suggests that Sayid could learn a lot from Gale but that he most likely will lie for a long time before telling the truth. Perhaps Rousseau knows that Gale is different from the rest of the Others and can provide information that Sayid's group should know. This episode is even entitled "One of Them" (2.14).

With the arrival of Henry Gale, Sayid strangely reverts to the person (in Season One) who he swears to have left behind forever. Rousseau makes sure that Sayid is the one who finds Gale in her trap. She suggests that Sayid will know how to get the truth from the lying Gale. From their first encounter ("Solitary," 1.9), Rousseau recognizes in Sayid not only grudging respect along with wariness, but also the kinship of being a torturer. Rousseau and Sayid recognize that this special talent unites them in otherness from their comrades. No matter how well they subdue this part of their past, they know that their ability to interrogate enemies may come in handy. Both Rousseau and Sayid maintain a love and hate relationship with this part of their lives—and with themselves.

While Gale is being held in a makeshift jail in the Hatch, Sayid encourages Charlie's current brand of otherness, which is taking the form of ostracism from the main group of survivors. Sayid attempts to turn Charlie against Gale by using the same tactics that U.S. soldiers used with Sayid. He tells Charlie that Henry Gale is one of Them, those people who kidnapped Claire and hanged Charlie. "Do you remember, Charlie?" Sayid smoothly asks. "Jack and Locke don't seem to remember what they did. Do you?" ("One of Them," 2.14).

This military (as well as a common bully's) tactic of getting someone to strike out emotionally against those who are different is a malevolent form of otherness. Sayid reminds Charlie of past injuries and tragedies in order to fuel further dissent and to increase the split between *us* and *them*. At this point in the story, Gale hasn't admitted being one of the Others. For all that Sayid and Charlie know, he might be an innocent survivor who crashed on the island. Although he might be one of Them, some of Them could be good. However, if Sayid can convince Charlie that Gale is guilty by association of crimes committed against him, Charlie can rationalize whatever happens to Gale.

During "The Whole Truth" (2.16), Sayid agrees to help Ana Lucia look for Gale's balloon, but only so he can give Gale what's coming to him when the balloon isn't found. Sayid no longer even blames Ana Lucia for killing his lover, Shannon. He acknowledges that Ana Lucia was just trying to protect her people. The real murderers are Them—the ones behind everything bad on the island. Sayid would have no remorse over killing Gale as a representative of Them.

Guilt by association often seems to be a social theme in modern society, especially when we become concerned about protecting ourselves from every possible threat. Sayid's method of dealing with someone labeled as other is not uncommon; people tend to fear what (and whom) they don't understand, and when people have power over someone labeled other, they often abuse that power (e.g., bullying children at school; humiliating and torturing military prisoners of war). When the castaways let their fear control their actions, they are in danger of forgetting that they may become the monsters they want to protect themselves against.

Otherness also refers to how the survivors of Oceanic 815 choose to separate themselves from the rest of the group. Locke, although a part of the group, is considered other for his early identification with the island and his spiritual certainty that they all are destined to be there. His knowledge about the island and how to survive in nature adds to the initial perception that he is other. Jack is separated from the rest of the survivors because of his medical knowledge and his role as a doctor; however, he also further separates himself by taking on the role of leader, which makes him a second type of other. Knowledge and power are two ways by which the castaways are divided into "us"—average people—and "other"—those with more knowledge or sociopolitical power.

Socially unacceptable actions in the past also create otherness. Kate believes that she is genetically flawed because of her worthless, abusive biological father; even her beloved stepfather, who she long considered her real dad, thinks that Kate has "murder in her heart" ("What Kate Did," 2.9). When Kate sees a black horse in the jungle—not just any black horse, but one from her past—she believes that she is going crazy and is convinced that it is payback for the outlaw life she's led. She can't be as inherently good as Jack and accepts that she is too other to be in his league. Her past actions, including robbery, assault, and murder, mark her as other in her own mind.

Sawyer often revels in being other, so much so that even Kate reminds him that he needs to participate in island society a bit more ("Solitary," 1.9). Sawyer, however, lives by the axiom, "Leopard don't change his spots" ("The Long Con," 2.13), and his conning of Kate as well as other castaways keeps him as an outsider from the island's mainstream society. When Charlie wants to lash out against the way his friends treat him, he joins forces with Sawyer. Perhaps Sawyer is so used to maintaining an edge to be an effective con man that he doesn't know how to live within regular society; he may actually feel more comfortable as an outsider looking (and breaking) in.

Sawyer wants to achieve a high-status level of otherness by having economic and thus political power over everyone else. He takes back more than the goods that were his before the raft sailed; he steals the Hatch's arsenal, medicines, and statues, which are filled with heroin. As long as Sawyer has the unique and highly valued commodities needed to protect the castaways, he is the most important man in the group. Everyone must visit Sawyer for guns or medicine.

Sometimes otherness is conferred by the fledgling society to make people conform to the group's norms or else risk being identified as other and ostracized. Charlie learns the hard way how this works when he commits acts, such as taking Claire's baby, that may be crazy, may be misunderstood as far as his motives are concerned, or may be sinister—which is the way the group perceives his actions ("Fire + Water," 2.12). So Charlie is ostracized to what one reviewer from the Television without Pity website called "Pariah Beach."[4] Once there, however, Charlie briefly joins forces with Sawyer and commits acts that even he finds terrible and doesn't want the castaways to know about. He attempts to kidnap Sun as a diversion in Sawyer's elaborate con to get control of the group's weapons. Charlie only wants to get back at Locke by making him look stupid, but Sun is accidentally hurt as part of this plan ("One of Them," 2.14). The actions that Charlie puts into motion, even unwittingly, separate him further from the majority of the castaways.

Finally, otherness may be conferred on some characters by those who know them well and see in them a special talent. Walt,

Locke, and Charlie are all labeled as special by at least one parent and are treated differently because of this attribute. Walt is turned over to Michael because the boy's stepfather finds his special gift unnerving. Locke recognizes that Walt is special and teaches him how to visualize acting and then successfully doing what he visualizes ("Special," 1.14). Even the Others identify Walt as a "very special boy" because of his possible psychic abilities ("Exodus," 1.24). Gale makes a deal with Michael, allowing his departure from the island, because Walt has given the Others "more than what we bargained for" ("Live Together, Die Alone," 2.24); perhaps the tests Walt mentions ("Three Minutes," 2.22) indicate Walt's teleportation or telekinetic abilities; whatever the boy's special talents are, they make Gale smile.

Locke's mother calls him special, but then she's a frequently committed schizophrenic ("Walkabout," 1.4). Still, Locke seems to believe that, despite frequent setbacks, he has a special calling in life. The island allows him to fulfill what he perceives as his special destiny.

Charlie's mother labels her son special because of his musical talent, but she encourages him to "save the family" by using this talent ("Fire + Water," 2.12). Charlie grows up believing that he is special and should be treated as such, but few people beyond his mum seem to recognize his uniqueness as positive.

Being identified as other or special by a parent, themselves, or the larger society doesn't seem to help these characters so far in their lives. It does, however, teach them to view themselves as different from the mainstream and to have to meet different expectations for success. Otherness, instead of making characters feel valued as unique or special, often makes them feel lost from the others or even from aspects of themselves.

Diversity, also perceived as otherness, is a positive force during *Lost*'s first season and became a selling point for the series. The diverse cast and characters continue to illustrate differing viewpoints and perspectives. Everything from slang to customs to worldviews differs among these people from around the world. As the cast changes, more cultures are represented.

During Season One, Charlie's early attempts to befriend Claire often hinge on the otherness of a shared British culture amid a large group of American castaways; the two share common Commonwealth links. Charlie, for example, invites Claire to join him for a cup of afternoon tea ("Tabula Rasa," 1.3), a custom that separates them from the uncivilized castaways. When Charlie later asks Claire about her favorite foods, she laughs that she's probably the only Australian who'd miss peanut butter. Charlie confides that he misses a British dessert, banoffee pie ("Confidence Man," 1.8).

Otherness on *Lost* is not always portrayed as a force for good or even a source of positive examples of interesting cultural differences. It seems to be merely an acknowledgement of a diverse and vibrant talent pool, in which everyone has some helpful skill or trait and that distinguishes one character from another. Otherness is increasingly part of a divisive *us or them* mentality, leading viewers to wonder if the survivors are more lost now than they were prior to the crash.

The castaways' formation of a fledgling society prompts questions about our own society. How much otherness is acceptable in a politically correct culture? Is diversity resulting from ethnicity, gender, or race all right, but diversity with origins in different political or religious philosophies dangerous to the group's survival? Are people so used to creating *us* or *them* categories that this process has become automatic? Although *Lost* as a series, with its multinational, multiracial cast and characters, goes a long way in promoting diversity, the storylines often show that otherness is a fragile concept that can be as divisive and controversial on the island as it is in the outside world.

Lost Without Technology

Technology offers us many conveniences, and we're loathe to give them up. During the first season, *Lost*'s castaways are alternatively annoyed by the inconvenience of being stuck on a remote island and overwhelmed by their lack of survival skills without the aid of modern technology. Communication and medical technologies, in particular, become the focus for their initial anxieties about life in a primitive world.

LOST WITHOUT MODERN COMMUNICATION

We take communication for granted: Speed dial a cell phone, text a friend, check e-mail, leave voicemail. Part of being lost from the rest of the world is trying to find one's way without much technology. That a plane crashes and no one finds it seems odd in an age of global positioning satellites and international intelligence. That a place might be so out of the way that no passing aircraft, search plane or commercial airliner, spots wreckage or locates a large group of people living on an island seems incongruous with our concept of the world's smallness. The sheer number of people in the world and the immediacy of global communication mean that someone somewhere knows what's going on at any time. It's difficult to be an anonymous citizen, much less to disappear without a trace.

In our society, a normal response to crisis involves counting on the global networks of satellites, the Internet, telephone and radio communications, and other broadcast technologies. Immediately after the crash, and continuing throughout the later episodes of the first season of *Lost*, technology and modern communication devices seem to be the best way for the survivors to be rescued. Technology is often perceived as a savior, especially in emergencies. The survivors of Oceanic 815 use several typical strategies to help others find them.

One of Boone's first acts after the crash is to open his cell phone and try to make a call. We hear a fast beep, indicating a lack of signal. Boone tries again but still has no luck ("Pilot," 1.1). Boone seems perplexed: Where in the world could he be that a signal can't be generated if the phone is still working? After all, even during a flight, several thousand feet above the earth, passengers can make calls. How remote is this island if a signal can't be received? Boone reacts as most of us would; he reaches for his cell phone when he needs help and seems unsure what to do next when the phone fails to work. What does someone do if there's no way to call for help?

At first, Shannon patiently waits for the rescue boat to arrive. When Boone offers her a candy bar, she sneers at his offer and then watches while he spitefully munches the snack. What is Shannon's reason for refusing the candy? She will eat on the boat and not resort to candy bars when real food is headed her way. As she reminds Boone, the plane had a black box, and rescue is only a short time away. A pedicure and tanning on the beach ("Pilot," 1.1) are more important pastimes to Shannon than salvaging goods from the plane or establishing a temporary home on the island; she assumes that technology will find her and the other castaways soon.

Jack knows that if he can locate the plane's cockpit, he might find a transponder and be able to use it to signal rescue planes. Surprisingly, in the wreckage of the cockpit and part of the first-class section, the pilot is found injured but alive. He confides to Jack that the flight was far off course when turbulence eventually broke up the plane. The instruments, it seems, failed to work properly even earlier in the flight, and so the pilot turned toward Fiji for a possible landing. However, the airliner did not make it that far. With no accurate instrumentation and flying well off the flight plan, Oceanic 815, the pilot explains, will be difficult to find; a search grid would most likely not cover as wide an area as necessary to find the debris field. The one bright spot is that the transponder, which is still functioning, is also in the cockpit.

Every moment of clarity on *Lost*, however, seems to be accompanied by a deepening of mystery. The Monster suddenly rattles the cockpit and savagely pulls the pilot from the plane. In the frenzy to get out of the wreckage and run as far away as fast as possible, Jack nonetheless has the presence of mind to grab the transponder ("Pilot," 1.1). Even in the face of danger, technology still seems the most likely way to get off the island.

During the first few days after the crash, Sayid manages to get the transponder working and to take it to higher ground where a signal can be sent. But once again, technology backfires on the survivors. Instead of being able to send a message, the transponder picks up a distress call on the frequency that Sayid plans to use for his signal. The message further shocks the survivors: Not only is the message in French, from a woman stranded on the island, but the distress call has been on a loop being broadcast for sixteen years ("Pilot," 1.1).

So even if technology functions on the island, it seems to be ineffective. If a distress message broadcasting for sixteen years has not yet garnered a response, what is the likelihood that this group of survivors will ever be found? As the castaways later learn, the Frenchwoman, Danielle Rousseau, still lives on the island; technology has been unable to save her.

Late in the first season, however, communication technology once more seems a possible savior. Locke and Boone discover a drug-runner's Beechcraft, its pilot long dead. The plane balances perilously over the edge of a cliff, hanging from the canopy of tall trees. Boone, manipulated into climbing up to the plane by an injured Locke, finds that its radio still works, and he desperately sends a distress call. Miraculously, he receives an answer to his Mayday. But another mystery is revealed. The person on the other end of the transmission incredulously reports, "We're the survivors of Oceanic 815!" The communication abruptly ends as the plane falls from the cliff, crushing Boone ("Do No Harm," 1.20).

In an interesting view of this broadcast from the recipients' perspective, the second-season "catch up" episode about the Tailies' experiences reveals more about the broadcast. Bernard finds a radio in an abandoned bunker and tests the it for a few minutes at a time to conserve its battery. During one check, he hears a Mayday and responds to it. However, group leader Ana Lucia squelches further use of the radio, believing that the Others are trying to locate the castaways. Ironically, the message from Boone, if interpreted correctly by Ana Lucia, could have saved his sister's life. If one group of Oceanic 815 survivors had known about the other group, the merger likely would have been bloodless ("The Other 48 Days," 2.7).

Lost teases us with the idea that more advanced technology is available on the island. Claire remembers Dr. Ethan Rom running prenatal tests in a medical hatch; masked surgeons prepare an operating room for the approaching birth of her baby ("Maternity Leave," 2.15). However, when Claire remembers enough to return to that hatch, it seems to be long deserted. Cobwebs cover the empty rooms. Nevertheless, the Others, as we learn in Season Three, have additional access to medical and communication equipment. With the discovery of the Pearl hatch ("?", 2.21), plus Walt's warning to Michael that the Others's camp isn't as primitive as it seems ("Three Minutes," 2.22), we first suspect that the Others have a lot more modern technology, which, so far, they aren't willing to share with the castaways.

Season Three reveals the Others's surgical unit, complete with modern equipment such as x-ray machines. Yet even the Others don't have everything they need; Juliet explains that some equipment is broken, and Jack lacks the precise tools needed to keep Colleen alive during surgery ("Further Instructions," 3.3). After the electromagnetic fluctuation on the island, the communication system goes on the fritz, and Mr. Friendly can't seem to fix it. Although the Others have more of the advanced technology that approximates a normal urban community, they may not have the latest technology or even everything they need or want, and, as with technology everywhere, sometimes it just doesn't work.

What is certain is that some communication technology works, but it's unavailable or unreliable for connecting the castaways with the outside world. Ben may have the results of the

World Series, but he's not sharing his television with the castaways on the beach. So far, Jack knows the most about the
Others's technology, but the castaways left on the beach may be
able to figure out more than the Others suspect. During Season
One, Sayid follows a cable from the ocean into the jungle
("Solitary," 1.9). Obviously someone uses or used the cable, but
for what? power? communication? Against all likelihood, Michael
exchanges messages with Walt via the Hatch's computer. It does-
n't seem to work that way for anyone else, and it doesn't provide
Internet access, but the computer allows Michael to communicate with his son, although he doesn't know where Walt is. Or
does it? Michael has no way of knowing whether the person who
keys in, "Dad?" onto the screen is really his son. [Several episodes
feature Michael typing or attempting to send a message, including "The Hunting Party" (2.11) and "Three Minutes" (2.22).]
The Pearl hatch also provides visual communication technology—live closed-circuit television—but the broadcast is only one-
way and doesn't allow the observers to interact with the observed
("?" 2.21). During a second trip to the Pearl hatch ("The Cost of
Living," 3.5), Locke, Sayid, and new characters Paolo and Nikki
manage to turn on more monitors, showing activity in other, previously unseen hatches. In one, a one-eyed man (perhaps the
owner of the glass eye found in an abandoned hatch during
Season Two) knows that he's being observed and covers the camera lens. Locke immediately suggests that the castaways pay him
a visit. Communication technology may be found on the island,
but it isn't yet useful for the castaways' rescue or even for con-
versing with everyone on the island. Face-to-face encounters
remain the only way to get to know the neighbors.

Which is more frustrating—living without technology
because it's not an option or living without technology as a "have
not" group on an island of "haves"? With the implosion of
Locke's Hatch, which provides more technology to the castaways
during Season Two, the castaways' return to a technology-free

world seems likely at the beginning of Season Three. If they want access to effective communication technology, they may have to work with the Others, who aren't likely to let them talk with the outside world.

LOST WITHOUT MODERN MEDICAL TECHNOLOGY

An even more pressing need than communication, both immediately after the crash and in the following weeks, was medical technology. We—and the castaways—have grown accustomed to having medicine fix anything. It isn't surprising that Jack's (soon to be) ex-wife Sarah tells Jack that his need to fix people or situations is too great ("The Hunting Party," 2.11); his obsession helps destroy their marriage. As a doctor, and later as leader of the survivors, Jack the doctor fixes people physically and emotionally, but he also has the desire to control and fix dangerous situations. He seems to think that every problem has a solution; he just needs to find it. Similarly, we often believe that medicine (and doctors) can perform miracles all of the time; life-saving or life-prolonging treatments and medications are commonplace in the modern world. When the survivors, especially Jack, carry that attitude onto the island, they realize just how lost they are without modern medicine and the latest high-tech equipment.

Fortunately for the number of people saved or stitched up in the first season, Jack survives the crash. He prescribes treatments for hives and rashes ("Solitary," 1.9), poor eyesight ("Deus Ex Machina," 1.19), and heroin withdrawal ("Hearts and Minds," 1.13). He sews up Sayid's leg ("Raised by Another," 1.10) and keeps Sawyer from bleeding to death ("Confidence Man," 1.8). He brings Rose ("Pilot," 1.1) and Charlie ("Whatever the Case May Be," 1.12) back to life through CPR. Jack is often a miracle worker, living up to his name as a "good shepherd" for his flock of survivors.

On ABC's *The View* in May 2005, Matthew Fox, who plays the good doctor, noted that Jack has to "reinvent himself as a doctor."[5] Because Jack is comfortable with medical technology, one of his first acts as a leader is to look for antibiotics in the salvaged luggage. Later, as supplies diminish, he rations aspirin and stronger medication as part of his treatments for Sawyer and Charlie and demands the last of Sawyer's alcohol as a disinfectant before Boone's surgery. Yet even though Jack is a talented surgeon with a compelling desire to save people, he is limited by his reliance on technology.

When Shannon suffers asthma attacks and no inhalers can be found, Jack expends his energy to coerce (and encourage Sayid to torture) Sawyer into giving up the inhalers. To Jack's chagrin, Sawyer does not have the medication; only Sawyer's belligerent pride, not his protection of the salvaged goods, makes the former confidence man defy Jack ("Confidence Man," 1.8). In his quest for a technical or medical solution to the problem, Jack ignores the basic Hippocratic principle: first do no harm. During Season Three, Jack is tempted again to ignore his oath in order to gain his, and possibly Kate's, freedom. He considers Juliet's proposal to agree to undertake Ben's surgery—but to kill him during the procedure. Juliet promises to protect Jack from repercussions; she only wants Ben out of the way so that new management of the Others can take over ("Every Man for Himself," 3.4). Jack relies on technology to help solve problems, but the real problem may be ethical dilemmas about when and how to use life-saving technology.

Many first-season medical problems are actually solved by Sun, who uses natural remedies instead of high-tech solutions. She finds eucalyptus and makes a balm that helps Shannon breathe during an asthma attack ("Confidence Man," 1.8) and even procures sea urchin spines from which to make a fine enough needle for Boone's blood transfusion ("Do No Harm," 1.20). This young woman, who was reared in prosperity and revealed in flashbacks as more concerned with parties and romance than public service, begins to find in herself the qualities of a healer. However, her approach to healing, and to life, differs from Jack's. Sun uses what is at hand and works with the natural world, a place where she frequently seems to find herself.

An episode late in the first-season highlights not only Jack's and Sun's different approaches to healing, but their acceptance of technology, or the lack of it, in their treatments. In "Do No Harm" (1.20), Boone lies dying, his injuries too great for Jack's expertise, probably even without Locke's incorrect information about their cause. Jack diligently works to save the young man, to the point of transfusing his own blood into his patient. However, Boone's condition only gets worse, and Jack determines that the only possible way to save Boone's life is to amputate his crushed leg using part of the fuselage, with a heavy sliding door, to sever it.

This final effort seems horrific, not only for us, but for the castaways. Sun begs Jack to reconsider, and Boone becomes lucid long enough to persuade Jack to just let him go. Boone knows that he is too badly damaged to survive the amputation and that Jack has tried every method at his disposal to save him. Jack still contemplates the amputation for a moment, believing even yet that Boone might be saved. Sun's approach seems the more rational in this sad story; she agrees with Boone that sometimes people can't be saved and heroic measures do more harm than good. Boone dies, but part of his heroism, as Sayid later tells a grieving Shannon ("The Greater Good," 1.21), is that Boone wanted the few remaining antibiotics used, not on a lost cause, but to help others in the future.

Even in the most modern hospitals, much less in the jungle, technology and gifted surgeons cannot save all patients. Jack's realization that he cannot always be a savior, with or without technology, is devastating. As one who relies on medical technology and the latest information to perform miracles, he has become accustomed to defeating death. However, as Sun and Boone understand, life is cyclical. Although it is sad to lose a friend—or one's own life—the grace and dignity of death should supersede the ability to prolong life. Sun's natural approach to healing seems to be in opposition to Jack's technological approach. Whether the two come to a point of balance in later episodes or if the distance between the two will widen remains to be seen. Especially now that Sun has killed an Other ("The Glass Ballerina," 3.2), she may need to stay on the beach with the castaways, where natural remedies and simpler medical techniques remain the norm. By choice or coercion, Jack may stay with the more technologically advanced Others, who challenge him ethically while providing him with a level of technology that is more within his comfort zone.

Coming to grips with a lack of medical technology is crucial for any group of survivors. During the first forty days after the crash, on the other side of the island, Ana Lucia's band of survivors faced a similar dilemma. Libby, who claims that she completed a year of medical school before dropping out, sets a man's broken leg. When she later expresses concern that the man is near death because of an infection, Ana Lucia replies, "What do you want me to do about it?" ("The Other 48 Days," 2.7). She knows that they have no medical supplies or way to treat this, or any other, crash victim.

When Sawyer is forced to hike with the Tailies through the jungle, his infected shoulder wound also draws Libby's concern. However, with her limited medical skills and no technology to help, she can do little more than treat the injury superficially and try to provide emotional comfort ("Abandoned," 2.6). Although both groups of plane crash survivors benefit from the aid of trained medical personnel, technology is often the deciding factor in who lives and who dies.

During Season Two, Jack becomes a bit more cynical about what he can do to help save people. Although he plays poker with Sawyer and confidently wins back the (legal) medicines ("Lockdown," 2.17), he knows they aren't enough. Paralleling events late in the first season, a fatal accident again forces Jack to realize that he can't save his patient. However, this time Jack accepts that he can't save Libby; her gunshot wound is too severe. Whereas a few months earlier he might have insisted on surgery in a vain attempt to repair the damage, this time Jack merely injects Libby with heroin to ease her suffering ("?" 2.21). This cynicism continues in Season Three, when Jack uses his surgical skills as a way to barter for something he wants; he seems far less interested in trying to save a critically wounded Other than in turning the situation to his advantage ("Further Instructions," 3.3).

Jack's stash of medical supplies is replenished in the Hatch, but even that source is limited, and, with the destruction of the Hatch, few if any medicines may be available to the castaways left on the beach. The first six episodes of Season Three remove Sun and Jack from their friends, who may find life increasingly difficult without modern medicine or doctors.

The castaways' need for medical technology only increases over time, no matter how many herbal remedies they develop or how carefully they hoard the remaining pharmaceuticals. Will they be able to accept the greater likelihood of death as they rely more on a natural lifestyle than on medical intervention to solve their health problems? Or will the castaways barter with the Others for medical expertise, supplies, and advanced technology? At some point, the castaways have to determine just how much medical technology is necessary and how much is desirable, as well as the price they are willing to pay for it. They may never be returned to a society with highly refined medical tools and a reliance on medicine to fix nearly any physical problem or flaw, but they likely won't want to rely on plants and folk remedies alone to sustain them. A more interesting dilemma is how far they may be willing to work with the Others, not just to gain life-saving technology, but to regain their sense of security by having access to machines that can assess their level of health.

Lost with Technology

When the castaways are first forced to live with very little technology, they seem unsure of what to do to survive. They value the scraps of technology still available to them, such as the broken transmitter or the metal from the fuselage. As they learn to live a simpler life without electronics, they find that they can survive and don't, in fact, require as much technology as they thought. The castaways are less lost without technology; they find alternatives, make what they need, or do without.

Technology in the second season takes an ominous turn. The Hatch leads to an underground research base, complete with a computer (however old), clothes dryer, stereo and turntable, film projector, and shower, among other luxuries. However, being chained once more to technology is another way to lose one's way. For much of the castaways' recent past, someone needed to enter a code (4, 8, 15, 16, 23, 42) and then push the Execute button every 108 minutes ("Orientation," 2.3).

Locke eagerly keeps the system going and settles into the first shift, a job he relishes for much of Season Two. However, other castaways are reluctant. Hurley, after all, associates the code with the cursed numbers that seem to have plagued him since winning the lottery. Charlie alone is lured into this mundane work with the promise of good or fun technology: Locke tells him he can play records in the Hatch ("Everybody Hates Hugo," 2.4). Rose stays away from the Hatch and prefers doing laundry outdoors; the creepy factor is enough to turn her away from the Hatch's dryer ("Abandoned," 2.6).

The Tailies at first may not associate the Hatch with anything sinister because it has already been opened by the time they arrive. Libby gladly hauls her laundry to the Hatch ("Fire + Water," 2.12), and her presence even lures love-smitten Hurley to accompany her. As time goes on, Hurley seems to overcome his initial reluctance to have anything to do with the Hatch. He and Charlie listen to music as they debate what women really want; their "guys' night in" keeps them happily in the Hatch ("The Hunting Party." 2.11).

Among the castaways, we see the gamut of responses to technology, from love it to leave it. Many survivors still lack a comfort zone in dealing with the perils of technology. During the first forty days before the Hatch is opened. most castaways survive and even begin to think of the island as their new home. If, like Rose, they can live that long without technology, they likely can continue to do just fine without it. Objects seem to matter less to Rose than relationships, especially with husband Bernard. Hurley fears that the discovery of a well-stocked pantry—and Jack's decision to let Hurley decide what happens to it—will turn him into a social outcast; after all, winning the lottery and suddenly having more money than his friends once cost him his best friend and a relatively uneventful life ("Everybody Hates Hugo," 2.4). After Hurley makes his new friends happy with his distribution of the Hatch's food, he has a better feeling about the Hatch and is shown visiting it more frequently. Charlie steers clear of the Hatch (and mundane office work) as long as he has somewhere else to go, usually with Claire and the baby. When Claire kicks him out of the house, Charlie turns to music for solace, and the Hatch's stereo provides a welcome diversion ("The Hunting Party," 2.11). Technology, even on the island, can lead people to question what they value in life and to what extent they are willing to become slaves to technology in order to enjoy its benefits.

The castaways' individual responses to the Hatch depend on the value that they place on technology. Locke believes for a long time that the Numbers must be keyed and the Execute button pushed or something very bad—like the end of their world—will take place. His response is the ultimate reliance on technology for life or death. At the opposite extreme is Rose, who seems content to stay far away from the Hatch unless she is given a specific job to do there, such as help Hurley take inventory of the pantry. The rest of the time, we get the feeling that Rose would much rather stay on the beach, especially now that Bernard has returned from the back of the plane. Their responses mirror modern society, in which some people love the latest gadgets for status as well as convenience and others prefer a simpler life not revolving around a modern technological gadget that most likely will break down or otherwise fail them at some point.

With the destruction of the Swan Hatch, technology remains primarily in the hands of the Others. How far will the castaways on the beach go to regain some necessities or comforts? Will they be satisfied with the primitive lifestyle they led before the Hatch was discovered? If the Others have ready access to higher levels of technology, why do they pretend to live without modern conveniences? Why do they themselves hide behind a primitive lifestyle?

The Technology of Destruction

One of the few types of technology that survived the crash was weaponry. Locke's suitcase of knives definitely comes in handy, used mostly to kill boar and to serve as everyday tools (e.g., for cleaning the carcasses and cutting plants). Although they could be deadly weapons used against humans, they often have more benign purposes.

Firearms are another matter altogether. The suitcase of the marshal who held Kate in custody on the plane contains several handguns and lots of ammunition. Sawyer also takes a gun from the marshal's body, with which he shoots the first polar bear that the survivors encounter ("Pilot," 1.1). At the time, of course, it seems like a good idea for Sawyer to confront the charging bear and shoot it point blank—one of the few times so far that a gun actually saves someone's life on the island.

Jack tries to regulate the use of firearms by locking the gun case and keeping the key on a string around his neck. When a situation warrants the possible use of guns, Jack issues them to those who know how to handle firearms, usually Sayid, Sawyer, Locke, and Kate ("Whatever the Case May Be," 1.12). Guns have a way of getting into other hands, however, usually with tragic results.

In "Homecoming" (1.15), the hunting party of Jack, Sawyer, Kate, Locke, and Sayid surrounds the pregnant Claire, who is being used as bait to capture the supposedly evil Ethan. The group only plans to snare him and try to learn why Claire was kidnapped and how he came to be on the island. (His name is not on the flight manifest for Oceanic 815, but he clearly lives on the island and seems very familiar with life there.) Information from Ethan will be valuable not only to solve the immediately interesting riddle of the kidnapping, but also to help the castaways learn more about the mysteries of the island.

Unfortunately, Charlie also gets his hands on one of the guns and figures out how to use the weapon. Without warning, he blasts several shots into Ethan ("Homecoming," 1.15). Charlie believes he is saving Claire from her kidnapper; most likely he also wants to exact revenge because Ethan hanged him and left him for dead. Shooting Ethan haunts Charlie, however, even as he believes Ethan's death was justifiable in order for Claire and her baby to be safe. The ready availability of the technology for killing no doubt makes Charlie's emotional choice easier (Would he confront his enemy as readily in a hand-to-hand battle?).

In a similar way, in "The Greater Good" (1.21), Shannon feels betrayed that Sayid refuses to murder Locke, because she wants revenge for her brother's death. Both Shannon and Jack blame Locke for Boone's demise. Locke not only put Boone in danger, but he lied about the way that Boone had been injured. Getting a gun from the locked case, Shannon tracks Locke and angrily confronts him in front of Sayid, Kate, and Jack. As she fires the gun, Sayid knocks away her hand, so that the bullet only grazes Locke's head. Shannon feels remorse only in that she hasn't achieved vengeance.

When guns, or other destructive technologies, are available, they often wreak havoc. Rousseau, the Frenchwoman, also has a weapon and knows how to use it. She is cut off from the other survivors in part because she chooses to shoot first and ask questions later. She lives defensively and doesn't hesitate to use a gun. Whether her paranoia is the result of her island experiences or simply a manifestation of being isolated for so long, Rousseau trusts only herself.

The second season shows that life on the other side of the island often involves a near reverence for the gun that Ana Lucia takes from Sawyer ("Orientation," 2.3). The weapon gives her a sense of power over the Others, even as she realizes that having only a few bullets is not protection against a group of attackers. Unfortunately, Ana Lucia thinks she is defending her group against the Others when she shoots Shannon ("Abandoned," 2.6). Shannon's death at the hand of another Oceanic 815 survivor likely would not have occurred if a weapon other than a gun had been in Ana Lucia's hand ("The Other 48 Days," 2.7).

Reliance on firepower only escalates during the remainder of the third season. When Claire decides to retrace her escape from the Others, Kate goes with her, but first she goes to Sawyer to get a gun ("Maternity Leave," 2.15). Sawyer's theft of the arsenal gives him the most power among the castaways; anyone who needs a firearm or ammunition has to see him. If he doesn't approve the request, either someone has to tackle a problem without a gun or try to find another way to convince Sawyer that a gun is necessary. When Kate asks for a weapon, Sawyer doesn't comply until he knows why. He teasingly calls Kate "Thelma," because of her "girls only" outing. Mention of the film *Thelma and Louise* evokes images of two women off on an adventure or even of Kate's outlaw nature, but the reference also takes on a darker undertone: Thelma and Louise end up killing men and choosing to drive off a cliff rather than face (male) justice. Although Sawyer eventually hands over the gun, he also knows Kate's potential for violence.

Kate doesn't hesitate to shoot first when she feels threatened. For all of her pleas that she's innocent of crimes on the mainland, she shows a rather damning ability for cold, calculated killing. Bending down to fix her boot on the jungle trek to free Walt, Kate murmurs to Sawyer that they are being followed, presumably by a couple of Others. Kate calmly says that, when she stands up, she's going to shoot and asks Sawyer if he'll join her. He does, and the two former outlaws prove just how deadly they can be when armed ("Live Together, Die Alone," 2.24).

Kate isn't the only one disposed to deadly violence. Michael asks Locke's guidance in learning how to shoot a rifle ("The Hunting Party," 2.11), presumably to help him get Walt back. When Michael later decides to steal a gun before he slips into the jungle, he first knocks out Locke and then locks Jack in the armory with the unconscious man. When Michael eventually returns to the Hatch without Walt, he depends on firearms as a main ingredient in his next plan. The result is that Michael shoots himself in the shoulder to avert any suspicion that might be directed toward him after Ana Lucia and Libby are found shot to death ("Two for the Road," 2.20).

These murders prompt Jack to seek revenge. However, his power is limited by lack of firepower, as Sawyer reminds him. Because of Jack's ill-fated hunting trip a few weeks earlier, the Others now have most of the castaways' guns ("The Hunting Party," 2.11).

When Jack hands out the remaining guns to those who will go after the Others in order to retrieve Walt and seek revenge, Hurley refuses to take a weapon. If he takes one, he realizes that he'll kill somebody. "Isn't that the point?" snarls Sawyer. Hurley contends that the point is to get Walt ("Live Together, Die Alone," 2.24). Hurley, the voice of reason, knows that armed people are likely to shoot and may lose sight of their original priorities.

Early in Season Three, even Sun threatens and then shoots the Other who tries to kidnap her aboard Desmond's sailboat. Sun badly wounds Colleen but then becomes a target herself when Others on the boat shoot at her as she escapes ("The Glass Ballerina," 3.2). When Colleen is carried past the cages on her way to surgery, Sawyer cheers, knowing that one of his friends shot her ("Further Instructions," 3.3). This action prompts another round of revenge when Colleen's widower comes after Sawyer ("I Do," 3.6).

On *Lost*, guns become a common metaphor for a serious situation. As Desmond and Locke debate the importance of button pushing, Desmond asks, "Do you need to look down a barrel of a gun to find out what you believe?" ("Live Together, Die Alone," 2.24). Instead of simply asking Locke how long he might wait before entering the code, Desmond relies on the effective analogy of being held at gunpoint to make a life-or-death decision.

Suicide by gunshot may be the choice of people stuck in the Hatch too long. Kelvin points to a spot on the ceiling and claims that his former associate Rozinski killed himself with a shotgun. Desmond chooses a handgun when he plans suicide, but he becomes distracted before he can kill himself ("Live Together, Die Alone," 2.23–24). In many ways, guns become the most common and most destructive technology in the castaways' lives.

A lack of weaponry does not eliminate people's ability to kill others or exact vengeance, but the ready availability of weapons allowing longer range killing seems to determine the castaways' choice of whether to fight or flee, kill or confront their enemies in other ways. The castaways have to decide for themselves when and how to use weapons. They operate in a little society with no formal laws or ways to enforce them. They rely on their own judgment, and, if they feel lost in their lives, they most often base their actions on momentary emotions, rather than on rational deliberation. The one type of technology that becomes easily available to many survivors at one point or another during the first season is firearms. Choosing to use a gun to solve a problem may make characters feel more lost in their lives, more separated from who they want to be or even from the other survivors.

As with other aspects of being lost, the use of technology for killing raises several questions. When is the use of deadly force reasonable, or even desirable? Is destructive technology necessary for survival? What strategies for mediating disputes or confronting enemies can be successful if destructive technologies aren't available? Does easy access to, say, firearms also make it easier for good people to lose their way when they search for solutions to problems? Does the use of deadly force make someone bad or good? With the castaways divided into at least two and possibly three groups, will they feel forced to use firearms against each other at some point? Does survival depend on the society with the greatest firepower or the most willingness to use it? Many questions about the place of technology in everyday life reveal parallels between the survivors' experiences on the island and our own.

Technology offers a society many benefits, whether the society is island-bound or metropolitan. However, technology's virtues often come with a high price. Like us, the castaways must struggle with the issue of how much technology is necessary for a higher quality of life versus how much personal freedom and interpersonal connectedness is likely sacrificed in reliance on technology. Although the castaways are often lost without the level of technology to which they've grown accustomed, they may find themselves equally lost within the Dharma Initiative's technoscientific world.

LOST IN LIFE-OR-DEATH SITUATIONS

Monsters often lurk in unexpected places and defy easy solutions, and life seems more precarious than ever. *Lost* again mirrors our concerns about the fragility of life and possibility of unexpected death.

At the end of the first season, the creators of *Lost* said that new characters are to be introduced in subsequent seasons, a promise they've kept in Seasons Two and Three. Some characters die; others live but become less important over time; new characters gain prominence in the story. As in other aspects of real life, *Lost* mirrors the increasing uncertainties of modern life. Even though characters are loved by millions, they too can face untimely and unexpected ends.

As Season One drew to a close, the cast did not know which characters would be eliminated. The anxiety leading to this revelation affected not only the cast, but us as well. No one wants his or her favorite character (or the character he or she portrays) to die. A similar situation occurred when Maggie Grace's character Shannon died early in the second season. When Michelle Rodriguez's and Cynthia Watros's characters were shot during the May 2006 period of (U.S.) sweeps ratings, questions arose over whether these murders were random. Did the actors' arrests (for drunk driving) in Hawaii have anything to do with the characters' shocking demise? According to Damon Lindelof and Carlton Cuse, and the actors themselves, the answer is no. As Lindelof laughingly noted, *"Lost* isn't about to become only a warning about drinking and driving."[6] They promised that future character deaths wouldn't be motivated by keeping cast members in line.

At the cliffhanger ending Season Two, several characters' lives hang in the balance, most notably Locke's, Mr. Eko's, and Desmond's. These three remain in the Hatch during its fateful destruction, and they don't turn up by the closing credits. In Season Three this type of cliffhanger and the shock deaths continue.

Cuse and Lindelof announced at San Diego's Comic Con in July 2006 that a bombshell would be dropped just when *Lost* fans face a long hiatus before new episodes air in February 2007.[7] For many fans, the shock occurred in the fifth episode, "The Cost of Living," when Mr. Eko quite literally dies by the hand of the Monster. Was Eko, played by recently arrested Adewale Akinnuoye-Agbaje, killed because of the actor's indiscretion? Akinnuoye-Agbaje, a devout Buddhist who doesn't drink, didn't have a valid driver's license at the time he was stopped by police, but the problem was soon cleared up. In fact, both the actor and the producers claim that Eko's death had been planned several months before the arrest. [8]

As is typical before a hiatus, in late 2006 Cuse and Lindelof announced new bombs to be dropped during the next batch of episodes. *Entertainment Weekly* critic Jeff Jensen hypothesized that Juliet might be Ethan's sister, providing her with motive to go after Ethan's killer, Charlie.[9] Still other rumors suggest that Jack may die, perhaps because of his double-dealing ways with the Others (and Matthew Fox's potential movie career).[10] An interview with Elizabeth Mitchell in early November 2006 stated that Juliet was about to shoot someone in the next scene to be filmed for an early February 2007 episode.[11] On hearing these rumors, fans immediately began speculating who might be killed or whose life threatened. Playing *Lost* roulette invites such theorizing and jumping from one reported cause to lots of possible effects. No character is safe.

However, as the creators reiterated in several interviews, that's life. Does that make deceased characters any less memorable or important? If we knew at the beginning of the series that Boone would die before the end of the season, would we still have loved him or cared about his backstory? Do we feel that we wasted our time learning about this character when he ended up being killed off? More important, would we feel that way about a friend or family member who fails to survive to a ripe old age, or who has a life-threatening condition?

Part of understanding what it means to be found is to know that loss occurs and how to handle that loss. Mr. Eko most likely knows that his brother is dead; Yemi is shot and roughly loaded on the Beechcraft just before it takes off. Yet Eko cries and asks forgiveness when he finds his brother's body on the island ("The 23rd Psalm," 2.10). Despite their disagreements and different lifestyles, the brothers loved each other, and the loss truly moves Eko to become a priest, not only in name but in practice. Sayid faces a more shocking and sudden awareness of Shannon's death ("Collision," 2.8); he cradles her body as she dies only moments after he has sworn his undying love. Much of Sayid's initial bitter and violent behavior is a result of mourning Shannon's death and seeking retribution.

Are we, or the survivors, ultimately going to be lost without a certain person? Is part of being found the ability to love others fully, even though they might not be around tomorrow, either by choice or fate or some divine plan? These questions affect not only the characters on the island, who do not know their future or likely longevity, but also the viewers (and *Lost*'s actors), who do not know which characters will live or die or disappear in the next few weeks. Dealing with loss is just another way of surviving being lost—for cast, characters, and viewers alike.

Most people want their lives to have significance. They may want their fifteen minutes of fame, but they also want to leave an enduring (and preferably positive) legacy to future generations. They need to know that they counted or mattered. What is the legacy of a character (or a family member, friend, or colleague) who dies unexpectedly or is killed? In island terms, what mark did Boone and Shannon make on the world, or even on the survivors who knew them for about a month? Does Ana Lucia's redemption count if only her murderer hears about her change of heart? Will Hurley continue to love Libby even though their relationship was just beginning, or will she be forgotten as he moves on with his life? Does Eko's death really have a purpose, as Locke claims? Living life on an isolated island brings up these questions, just as viewers may also feel isolated in the private islands of their life— the small communities, mundane jobs, and insular homes.

Lost brings up many issues about the meaning of life, what it means to be lost, and how to be found. These themes are important to viewers internationally. Our interaction with the series shows how much we tend to search for meaning and answers. Although some viewers are content to find meaning at the surface level of each episode, the fans who have made *Lost* into a cult series only begin at this level of deriving meaning. Hardcore fans not only watch an episode multiple times, but they freeze images and post their findings on the web. They work harder than most characters to decode the island's meaning (and the writers' cryptic messages). They play dialogue backward, enlarge images, and do research. They analyze code to determine the origins and authenticity of websites; they find layer on layer of hidden meanings in their search for answers.

This type of audience also demands answers. When not enough information was presented in "Exodus," fans protested at conventions, on discussion boards, and through e-mail. The series' creators acknowledge that this outcry for more answers prompted them to include more information in the Season Two finale, "Live Together, Die Alone" (2.23–24), although they also introduced even more question-provoking scenes. Many viewers like to know in advance what will happen, perhaps to have a head start on interacting with *Lost*'s subtext and decoding messages. In this way they derive more meaning from the series than can be gained through casual viewing. *Lost* offers hardcore fans the ability to create meaning for themselves, in a sense, to find themselves not only as audience members, but as equal castaways on the island.

Lost is based on the fundamental understanding that everyone faces personal monsters or loses his or her way at some point in life. Everyone, at one time or another, longs to make a fresh start. With *Lost*, the characters and audiences are all survivors of the chaos in modern life, who still seek answers to fundamental questions and hope to find meaning in their dilemmas. They often try to find themselves, even as they face ever more numerous ways to become lost.

NOTES TO CHAPTER TWO, "THE MANY MEANINGS OF *LOST*"

1. The Lost Experience reveals that the Valenzetti Equation—Hurley's Numbers—can lead to the destruction of the world. The Hanso Foundation used the Dharma Initiative to avert this crisis. Other corporations might not be as altruistic and choose instead to threaten the world for their own gain. An interesting history of the game, accompanied by fan commentary, is archived at www.thelostexperience.com.

2. Official ABC *Lost* Podcast, October 17, 2006, with Damon Lindelof and Carlton Cuse. This teaser was also summarized in "*Lost* Podcast Spoilers" at http://spoilerslost.blogspot.com/search/label/podcasts.

3. Heather Havrilesky, "I Like to Watch." *Salon.com.* November 19, 2006. Retrieved November 20, 2006, from http://www.salon.com/ent/iltw/2006/11/19/winners_losers/print.html

4. *Television Without Pity*. Retrieved February 24, 2006, from http://www.televisionwithoutpity.com/articles/content/a907/.

5. Interview with Matthew Fox. *The View*. ABC. May 5, 2005.

6. Gina Serpe, "'Lost' Loses Two More?" *E! News*. Retrieved February 15, 2007, from http://www.eonline.com/news/article/index.jsp?uuid=e5f186c9-414b-43f4-8fca-17f5b54555b1.

7. Scott Chitwood, "*Lost* Season 3 Scoops from Comic Con!" July 22, 2006. Retrieved August 1, 2006, from http://www.comingsoon.net/news/tvnews.php?id=15614.

8. Armstrong, "The Tailie's End."

9. Jeff Jensen, "Gone (for Now) . . . but Not Forgotten!" *Entertainment Weekly*. November 14, 2006. Retrieved November 14, 2006, from http://www.ew.com/ew/article/commentary/0,6115,1559558_3_0,00.html.

10. "All May Be 'Lost' for Dr. Jack," *New York Post*. Retrieved November 21, 2006, from http://www.nypost.com/seven/11202006/tv/all_may_be_lost_for_dr_jack_tv_.htm

11. Snierson, "Spotlight: Elizabeth Mitchell."

CHAPTER THREE

FINDING *LOST* MEANINGS

"Find yourself *Lost*"—the Season Three marketing phrase in U.S. print promotions—is both a promise and a curse. Many fans find themselves each season looking forward to the many twists and shockers certain to be a part of upcoming episodes. Much of their time is spent decoding the clues not only found within episodes but through events such as The *Lost* Experience, an international intrigue too complicated to be called merely a game. Visits to a myriad of real and misleading websites add layers of meaning to *Lost's* basic premise. (Some fans even create bogus sites so realistic that they confuse other fans as to whether they are official.)

Some viewers who prefer to spend an hour each week watching their favorite characters don't want to be any more lost in the plot developments and connections among characters than they already are. But other fans love the series' mythology and look for multiple meanings and hidden information, even where there may not be anything to find. *Lost's* creators and writers tightrope walk an increasingly thin line between providing a hardcore, largely Internet-based global fandom with more ways to "get *Lost*" and keeping fans who prefer to watch only the television episodes with their weekly "fix" of entertaining drama.

Whether you're more of a couch potato who hides the remote so that no one can change the channel during *Lost* or an electronic globetrotter uploading and downloading clues, you can make meaning from *Lost* in many of the same ways that the characters themselves do.

A first layer of meaning can be derived by what we observe—characters' actions, body language, inflection during dialogue, and the dialogue itself. What's happening within a scene—what happens, where it happens, when it happens—also provides meaning. This basic level of information provides us with a starting point, although these first impressions may mislead us.

Second, we can compare what we've observed with what we know about the world. Again, preconceptions might lead us astray from *Lost*'s truth, but the backstories, for example, help us compare what's taking place in current time with what seems to work in the real world and what the characters have done before. Repeated scenes and dialogue and connections among characters help us with this step.

Next we can move to a deeper search for meaning by looking at the many symbols within *Lost*. Symbols are trickier because we might interpret them differently than the writers intended, or a symbol might be specific to an episode rather than universal. However, symbols are important to us as viewers because they help us derive our own meaning from *Lost*, making what happens important to us.

Finally, we draw conclusions based on all the information we've gathered from observation and analysis. This quasi-scientific method allows us to keep adding to the core of information we've learned or interpreted from earlier episodes and expanding our understanding of the *Lost* world.

A unique marketing approach to the Season Two Complete DVD Set encourages such a scientific approach to watching *Lost*. On Disk 7,[1] the mysterious lab-coated Dr. Candle [or at least that's his name during the first orientation video ("Orientation," 2.3), but not the one that Locke and Eko find in the Pearl hatch ("?" 2.21)] explains our job in watching the DVD extras. In turn, he explains what we should do during three phases and how important it is for us to be careful in our observations and documentation.

Hardcore *Lost* fans do indeed look for clues under such a microscope; for them, making meaning from every conceivable bit of information about *Lost* is possibly as rigorous and definitely as time consuming as their regular employment. Not every television series could get away with such scrutiny or suggest that fans should participate at this level. However, *Lost* fans expect to make meaning in many ways and at many levels to enhance their fan experience as well as their viewing experience. They want to be drawn into the *Lost* world, and the Season Two DVD set encourages this behavior. Through the format of Disk 7, as well as other marketing tools, *Lost* blurs the line between the real world and the fictitious *Lost* world. It is another example of marketing ploys to "bring reality" to television fiction. (See Chapter Seven for more details about the blurring of reality and fiction.)

A good example of peeling back multiple layers following this methodical, analytical approach can be found in the episode "Fire + Water" (2.12) and the DVD breakdown of filming that episode. Fans who watch only the episode see a dream sequence in which Charlie plays a piano in his parents' home in Manchester, England. His mother encourages him to use his music to "save the family," but as Charlie begins to play, he sees his father hard at work in his butcher shop. Mr. Pace encourages Charlie to give up his music and find a real job, such as being a butcher. While he speaks, he slams a cleaver through red meat. But as Charlie watches, the scene changes, and his father next hacks apart baby dolls.

How can we make meaning from this surreal scene? Here are some initial conclusions based on what we observe:

1. The scene doesn't represent real situations on the island and must take place outside island reality.
2. Charlie is at home, wearing pajamas, and his parents are with

him. Charlie's parents haven't been seen on the island before, which further indicates some alternate reality, yet this doesn't look the same as a typical backstory flashback sequence.

The most likely conclusions are

1. Charlie is having a dream. The scene isn't real, and no plastic dolls have been harmed in the making of this episode.
2. Charlie's dream is more significant because of this imagery. Probably Charlie has some serious family issues to deal with.

We also might question what caused the dream. It may be drug-induced (Charlie may be back on heroin). The dream might be stress induced, because Charlie appoints himself as Aaron's father figure. The dream may be divinely inspired. The Others may have a way to implant dreams in Charlie's mind. Any of these individually, or in combination, may lead (and have led) to fan theory development and further understanding about how the island operates.

At the symbolic level, the doll might represent baby Aaron. Charlie may be worried about baby Aaron because in the past he himself wasn't as nurtured as he should have been. Or Charlie may be worried about the baby because a real danger (although probably not cleaver-toting butchers) might harm him. Perhaps Charlie even equates himself, as a baby who wasn't saved from a stern father, with Aaron, who has become Charlie's surrogate son. Charlie wants to save Aaron, but he may not be sure from what.

The piano, too, prominent in several flashbacks and dream sequences, has more than literal meaning for Charlie. It's a (rather work-related) Christmas present. Charlie as a child is expected to make good as a musician, but his older brother receives several toys and encouraged to have fun. The piano might also represent Charlie's commitment to his family and his way of becoming special to them. The piano becomes so closely associated with Charlie's family life that when Liam sells it without telling him, and then leaves for Sydney to reconcile with his wife and child (i.e., real family), Charlie feels as though he has lost everything. The piano, like his family, is beyond his reach, and he has nothing with which to buy them back.

Perhaps that's as far as we can go from only watching this scene. The DVD, however, provides even more information about why this particular dream sequence was written this way. The baby-hacking is an homage to the Beatles' *Yesterday and Today*; the band wanted to chop up dolls for an album photo shoot, but Capitol Records must have been rather horrified by this artistic concept and nixed it. Except for die-hard Beatles fans, most *Lost* fans may never connect the dream image from "Fire + Water" with a failed album cover design, unless they look to the DVD for more information.

With this information, more intense *Lost* fans get a clearer artistic interpretation of the scene and a more specific connection between one-hit-wonder DriveShaft and eternally popular Beatles. Charlie has always been blind to the band's limitations; he sees DriveShaft as a band with the potential to be as great as the Beatles. Both bands, after all, rise from humble origins in northern English cities, and to Charlie's way of thinking, both achieve international fame.

In Charlie's dream, the Beatles' reference might be interpreted as his father's opinion of DriveShaft, or at least Charlie's likelihood of succeeding as a musician. Charlie may feel a kinship with the Fab Four because of their working-class origins and the need to prove that, like them, he is indeed more special than other children who grow up to follow their fathers in (to Charlie's mind) dead-end jobs. Mr. Pace seems determined to hack away at Charlie's cherished dream and insist on a trade, unlike Mrs. Pace, who sees Charlie's talent as a ticket to a more affluent life. Even if his father was never violent toward his son, Charlie clearly remembers his father's vehement opposition; perhaps this is one reason why adult Charlie tries so hard to gain others' approval. During Season One in particular, Charlie often looks to surrogate father figures such as Locke and even Jack for support.

Dominic Monaghan's fans might even attribute more significance to this choice of artistic inspiration. In numerous interviews, Monaghan, who plays Charlie, expresses his interest in the Beatles and his devotion to John Lennon in particular. He, and thus Charlie, sports a tattoo: "Living is easy with eyes closed." That choice, too, can be analyzed in multiple ways as to why Monaghan or Charlie would choose that particular lyric from the Beatles' "Strawberry Fields Forever."

Not every *Lost* fan wants or needs to look for so much meaning within every single scene of every single episode, but many do. *Lost* allows fans to lose themselves in lots of facts and interpretations about every facet of the series. But the creators and writers are also careful to make sure that casual viewers can make sense of the episodes each week without becoming too lost. So far, both extremes of fandom have been satisfied—most of the time.

MAKING MEANING FROM WHAT WE SEE

We can make meaning in more ways than the characters can. So far they haven't been seen watching DVDs of themselves or becoming privy to each person's secrets, revealed to us through backstories. *Lost* is rich in the ancient storytelling technique known as *dramatic irony*, in which the audience knows much more than the characters themselves realize about their situation. The way that characters figure out who they—and each other—are differs each season, reflecting differences in the length of time they are on the island, get to know each other, and reevaluate themselves after the pivotal event in their lives—the crash of Oceanic 815 on an apparently uncharted, unreachable tropical island.

During the first season, physical appearances, postcrash actions, and small talk provide the first impressions, but as a new society begins to form in Season Two and more people show up to interact with our original characters, the discovery process changes. New situations require characters to take on different roles and show new aspects of their personality. They also have plenty of time to decide if they actively want to change their lives or be forced by circumstances into changing. By the third season, their society has evolved, developing leaders and a "group philosophy" challenged by interactions with other societies on the island. Love interests, friends, and enemies become better established. The castaways act more like relocated refugees than crash survivors awaiting rescue.

SEASON ONE: SURVIVORS OF OCEANIC 815

At first, many characters try to put forth a different personality than they really have. Perhaps they want to impress others, or mislead them, or maybe they just don't want anyone else to know their business. During much of the first season, the characters are still living like Oceanic 815 travelers facing an unexpectedly long flight delay. They don't see the need to know each other on a deeper personal level, because they expect to be rescued soon.

However, as the days wear on and no rescue appears on the horizon, just living in such close proximity makes the castaways gradually reveal more of who they really are. They also have to face their own strengths and weaknesses as they live on their own in the wilderness. Once the initial shock of the crash wears off, however, the castaways realize just what it might mean to become island dwellers. Even if they cannot achieve closure with people from their past who have wronged them or whom they have wronged, they can at least relate differently to those stranded with them. If they can indeed start a new life, they can, at least theoretically, become whoever they truly want to be.

So who are these people? At first, the group of fourteen castaways featured prominently in the first season's episodes seem to represent basic types. In fact, the opening narration to the catch-up or summary episode aired April 27, 2005 (in the United

States), appropriately entitled "*Lost*: The Journey," simplistically classifies several characters. For example, Jack, Kate, and Charlie are reduced to basic types: doctor, prisoner, and addict.

People have a tendency to label themselves and each other. It's an easy, if superficial way to identify possible allies and to stereotype possible foes. At first, we and the characters construct labels based on sight: race, gender, ethnicity, age, and attractiveness. The next way to label comes from bits and pieces of information gleaned from what someone says and does. Based on the castaways' words and actions immediately after the crash and limited knowledge of each person's past, we jump to conclusions about the characters; the survivors, too, determine someone's "worth" or "likability factor" based on appearances and actions.

First visual impressions include the following:

- Beautiful women abound: Kate, Shannon, and Sun. Claire is pretty, too, but she is more likely categorized as "pregnant." As she tells Charlie a few days after the crash, the others often fail to look her in the eye, as if they think of her as a "time bomb of responsibility" ("White Rabbit," 1.5).
- The men are good looking, too, especially Jack, Sawyer, and Jin; there's eye candy to suit every taste.
- Some characters may be defined by their skin color or racial traits: Sun, Jin, Walt, Michael, Sayid, and Rose may be defined by their culture, country, or race.
- Hurley is overweight.
- Age may be yet another method of classifying castaways: Locke is noticeably older than many of the other men; Rose, a secondary character in the first season, is an older married woman. Walt is only ten years old (but resents being treated like a child).
- Family relationships further characterize the group. Shannon and Boone are siblings—eventually amended to stepsister/stepbrother and one-time lovers ("Hearts and

Minds," 1.13). Rose misses her husband, who she feels is still alive in another location, and later she is proved right ("Collision," 2.8). Walt and Michael are son and father. Claire eventually gives birth to a son and takes on the role of mother ("Do No Harm," 1.20).

Characters' early actions and responses to the crisis add a bit more depth to these first visual impressions:

- Jack, an American spinal surgeon, attempts to alleviate Rose's anxiety about the in-flight turbulence, and he later saves her life on the beach. He is a responsible leader who tries to save everyone, literally running from crisis to crisis to help others in the moments after the crash.
- Kate agrees, despite her fears, to help Jack; she is a budding leader who later volunteers for treks into the jungle.
- Sawyer, an American Southerner, seems bent on starting fights and scavenging whatever he can from the wreckage; he acts like someone who is only out for himself.
- Sun and Jin are a traditional Asian couple, who speak no English and prefer to remain separate from the others; Jin is a conservative, repressive husband; Sun, a subservient wife.
- Shannon, a spoiled, blonde, rich girl, is more interested in how the crash affects her than anyone else; she gives herself a pedicure instead of helping others.
- Boone, also spoiled, shows a penchant for nagging his sister; he helps out but often is ineffective and needs guidance.
- Claire, a pregnant Australian, fears going into labor immediately after the crash and worries about her unborn child.
- British Charlie is a heroin addict more concerned with his drugs than anything or anyone else.
- Devoted American father Michael's first concern is to find his son, Walt, and provide him with shelter, food, and water.
- Locke, another American man, runs to help when Jack

first calls him to assist in moving an injured man from under the fuselage. He is strangely separate from the others, as he sits in the sudden rainstorm in apparent bliss, arms outstretched.

- Sayid, a Middle Eastern man, is stereotyped by Sawyer because of his ethnicity; Sayid tells Hurley that he's a former member of the elite Iraqi Republican Guard.
- Hurley pitches in but sometimes has trouble with what he's asked to do (e.g., he passes out when assisting Jack in makeshift surgery).

Characters' multiple layers are revealed through their backstories, disclosed in a series of flashback scenes recalling significant moments in their past, revealing to us the reason behind their current reactions to situations or people. Although the survivors have the chance to start fresh on the island, their current actions often are based on past experiences and relationships.

By the end of the first season, we (but not necessarily the castaways) know a great deal about all characters before their departure on Oceanic 815 from Sydney, Australia:

- Happy-go-lucky Hurley seems neither happy nor lucky on his trip to the outback. Although he has won millions in a lottery, the money does not bring him happiness. His "luck" instead may be a curse.
- Although Claire is the only one of the original 14 main characters whose home is in Australia, she is leaving for her baby's new home in California. She leaves Sydney so her baby will be adopted by loving parents (the baby's father has abandoned them). To complicate issues further, Claire is hounded by a psychic who insists only she must raise her baby.
- Jack's father is found dead in a Sydney alley, the result of a massive heart attack induced by alcohol. Estranged from his father, Jack feels guilty about his part in his downward slide.

He argues with the airline representative and finally is allowed to take his father's body back to Los Angeles for burial.

- Kate is a prisoner of a federal marshal and is being brought back to the States, most likely to face sentencing for her crimes. Her capture is worth a $23,000 reward.

- In Australia, Sawyer murders a man who he thought once seduced his mother and stole from his father, acts which apparently enraged Sawyer's father so much he killed his wife and himself. However, the death that Sawyer anticipates for so many years fails to bring him either satisfaction or revenge, for he kills the wrong man after being set up by a former partner.

- Locke tries to go on a walkabout in Australia, a spiritual quest he had long planned. The excursion, however, requires him to walk about, and Locke is wheelchair bound.

- Charlie hopes for brother Liam's agreement once again to front their band DriveShaft so that the group can tour as an opening act. Since the band's demise two years earlier, Charlie survives by charming women and then stealing from them. His dreams of a return to fame are dashed when Liam refuses to return to the band. Charlie also disappoints Liam, who, himself a former addict, recognizes that his brother still uses heroin.

- Sayid stays in Sydney one day beyond his scheduled flight in order to claim the body of his college roommate, the man chosen to be a martyr for a terrorist cell. Coerced by American and Australian intelligence agents to infiltrate the cell (they promise he will be led to Nadia, an Iraqi insurgent and childhood friend he once helped to escape), Sayid succeeds and delivers the group's explosives. Although he tells his former roommate to flee when he reveals he is a double agent, the man takes his life in front of Sayid. To give his former friend a proper Muslim burial, Sayid refuses to leave Australia until he claims the body.

- Shannon and Boone sit together on the plane, but they are far from together in any other sense of the word. Boone flies to Sydney to rescue Shannon from an abusive boyfriend, only to discover that Shannon has set him up in order to get money. Once Boone pays off the boyfriend, Shannon and her friend plan to split the money, but Shannon herself is scammed this time and left with neither boyfriend nor cash. Inebriated and rejected, Shannon seduces her stepbrother and then tells him that they will never let anyone know.
- Sun and Jin are in Sydney because Jin needs to complete business for his employer, Sun's powerful father. Although Jin hates his job and plans to start a new life in the United States after this business is completed, he has not, of course, revealed his plans to Sun, who dislikes the man her husband has become. Sun secretly speaks English and crafts a way to disappear. When the moment comes for her to leave her husband, however, she does not go through with her plan.
- Michael flies to Sydney to retrieve his son Walt. With the recent death of Walt's mother and his stepfather's desire to be rid of the boy, Michael finally gains the opportunity to be a real father to his son. Walt, however, doesn't remember the father of his babyhood, and a belligerent ten-year-old boards the flight. Neither father nor son knows each other, and both must be anxious about their future relationship.

This pattern of labeling and then adding new labels or amending old ones is established every time, in every season, that new characters make an appearance. Perhaps we, as well as the original characters, learn from experience that we only become more lost by limiting ourselves to superficial information. Getting to know each other and ourselves requires a big time commitment and an open mind.

SEASON TWO: MORE SURVIVORS AND COLLIDING SOCIETIES

The second season continues the trend of troubling backstories
("Collision," 2.8) as new regular characters join the original
group of survivors. Ana Lucia Cortez is a police officer who, like
Jack, goes into the family business; her mother is also an officer
and her captain. While on patrol, Ana Lucia and her partner are
called to a robbery. A young man runs out the front door that
Ana Lucia is covering. He exclaims that he is a student, but when
he reaches for his ID, he pulls out a gun instead. Ana Lucia is
shot point blank, an act that not only injures her but kills her
unborn child. Back on the job, Ana Lucia becomes a gun-happy
officer who seems to mistrust most men. After quitting the
police force, Ana Lucia works as a baggage screener, but she
soon agrees to leave this job for a temporary trip to Australia,
serving as a kind of bodyguard/companion for Christian
Shephard ("Two for the Road," 2.20).

Mr. Eko is a former Nigerian drug lord, with all that implies
about his shady past. However, he gradually returns to the
Catholic Church of his youth. After the crash of the tail section
("The Other 48 Days," 2.7), he immediately sets about helping
other crash survivors, especially children. Although he is a large,
strong man, he defers to Ana Lucia as leader. Eko at first seems
to be a gentle, most likely religious man, even before his backstory reveals his troubled past and fluctuating spirituality that lead
him to become a priest ("The 23rd Psalm," 2.10).

Libby acts like a professional with some medical training, setting broken bones and offering advice. She says she's a clinical psychologist, but pieces of her former life told in other characters'
backstories reveal that she is a widow ("Live Together, Die Alone,"
2.24) who has spent time in a mental institution ("Dave," 2.18).

What we learn about Desmond, Rousseau, Henry Gale, and
even other bodies buried around the island (e.g., the "real"
Henry Gale) indicate that everyone is lost beyond the geographical definition.

Backstories and characters' comments about life before the island are not happy stories. Each character brings a great number of personal problems that must be resolved, and each seeks something to improve his or her life or to return to the true path from which he or she strayed. "Lost" is the one all-encompassing word to fit each of these characters. (An often-repeated joke among fans and commentators speculates that some future episode of *Lost* might tell the backstory of one of the other anonymous survivors, only to reveal, in an unprecedented plot twist, that his or her life was boring, untroubled, and uneventful.)

The *Lost* world is definitely not "what you see is what you get." Characters who seem nice have shady pasts; Season Two takes a darker turn. Authority figures, such as police officers, may become weapon happy. The Republican Guard soldier tenderly loves an upper-class American but becomes more sinister after her death. The dedicated doctor decides to make war.

But sometimes the expected bad turns good. The former junkie becomes a caring surrogate father. Kate displays a gentler bedside manner (with Sawyer) than Jack does. Rousseau helps Claire, one mother to another.

On the island, no one is who he or she originally seems to be or what we might have expected. As Hurley so aptly tells Jack about African-American Rose's reunion with Caucasian Bernard, "Didn't see that coming" ("Collision," 2.8). Watching *Lost*, we probably think that dozens of times.

Season Two also finds the castaways less prone to racial, ethnic, or national stereotyping. Just when we recognize that "good Iraqis" are possible on U.S. television programs, Sayid returns to being the tortured torturer, a soldier who once again uses past skills he vows (in Season One) to keep in the past. Maybe Sayid shouldn't be considered in terms of being an Iraqi at all, either to be demonized as an interrogator or Republican Guard soldier or to be idolized as a positive representative of his country. Sayid is somewhere in between, both a caring lover who wants no part of the skills he learned in the military [from U.S. soldiers who coerce him into torturing/interrogating his commanding officer, in a nicely nasty twist during "One of Them" (2.14)] and a highly skilled interrogator/torturer who knows exactly how to get a confession from Henry Gale/Ben Linus.

More positively, Jin finds life as a fisherman to be rewarding instead of humiliating—his skills allow him to catch food where others flounder ("Abandoned," 2.6) and to sail Desmond's boat around the island ("Live Together, Die Alone," 2.24). Whereas these skills are vilified in Jin's quest to become a successful businessman and gain a higher social status, they elevate his standing as a provider on the island. What made Jin lost from his family and heritage for many years now finds him able to provide for his wife and friends and gain more status in the new society.

Superficial differences such as skin color or accent matter less to the castaways and audience as time goes by. Instead, as we and the castaways learn more about Oceanic 815's survivors, the unique personalities become most important. The castaways and we in the audience are less likely to think of character changes in terms of what's happening to the Iraqi or that Korean couple. For better or worse, Sayid, Sun, and Jin are the focus of interest or concern; we know them as individuals instead of stereotypes.

Changes during Season Two reflect more knowledge of a character's past but, just as important, more awareness of his or her more recent behavior and ideas:

- Jack's and Locke's differing ideas about the purpose of the Hatch bring them to more violent disagreements, and they each want to lead the castaways. They often don't consult each other but act independently to do what they think is best for the group.
- The Jack–Kate–Sawyer triangle becomes more complex.
- Locke dramatically shifts allegiances from island follower to Hatch dweller.

- Mr. Eko and Charlie find spiritual enlightenment that guides them to what others perceive as strange acts, with far-reaching consequences.
- Hurley loves and loses his love, fellow former mental patient Libby. He seems mentally shaky at times and harbors anger that has yet to explode.
- Claire becomes more independent and relies on herself to determine what's best for her and her child.
- Jin and Sun rediscover their love for each other, but Sun's unexpected pregnancy may still cause problems between the couple.

What keeps these developments from turning *Lost* into another nighttime soap opera is the depth of character development, high-quality acting, and superb storytelling. Although the island's mysteries may lead to convoluted plot threads, we watch not only to solve the mysteries but because we care about these people. "The *Lost* Survival Guide,"[2] airing in September 2006, emphasizes that viewers don't have to—and often don't—follow *Lost* for its mythologies. Character developments bring many viewers back, week after week, especially when we (and the characters themselves) see how often first impressions or stereotypes can be misleading as we all make meaning from what we learn about others' lives.

SEASON THREE: THE OTHERS AND THE EMERGENCE OF NEW RELATIONSHIPS

The first six episodes of Season Three emphasize the Others and introduce Juliet, a muffin-baking, gun-toting fertility doctor who seems to sincerely like Jack one moment and then manipulate him for political gain in the next. The Juliet–Jack dynamic, as captor and captive, is only one interesting new development; Juliet may also have a troubled past relationship with Ben Linus. Whatever the link between them, they now seem locked in an escalating struggle for leadership of the rest of the group.

Still more Others populate what Ben surprisingly reveals to Sawyer as a second island ("Every Man for Himself," 3.4). Tom (aka Mr. Friendly) may be the island's first gay character; he tells Kate not to worry about dressing in front of him because she's not his type ("A Tale of Two Cities," 3.1). Fans speculate that he may be the now-dead Goodwin's partner, one of the unsubstantiated but more interesting rumors on the Internet.[3] A more volatile personality is Danny Pickett, whose love, Colleen, is killed by Sun during a raid on Desmond's sailboat ("The Glass Ballerina," 3.2). Pickett, who didn't really need an excuse to dislike Sawyer, now wants to kill him. These and additional background characters add depth to our and Jack's, Sawyer's, and Kate's understanding of the Others. The dark tone of Season Three shows that the Others, despite their more comfortable suburban lifestyle, are just as dysfunctional and unhappy as the castaways. Material wealth and greater security don't guarantee happiness.

Back on the beach, new characters Paulo and Nikki are awkwardly introduced in "Further Instructions" (3.3). Although Locke's conversation with them in this and the next episode indicate that these two beautiful castaways have been lounging in the background since the crash, they have received little character development thus far. Paulo seems self-centered and little interested in Locke's excursion to the Pearl hatch; he only goes along to appease/impress Nikki. At least she seems interested in learning more about the hatch and getting involved with the scouting party; Nikki even suggests that they try to operate the many monitors in the Pearl hatch, leading to the discovery of another manned hatch.

These new characters suggest more possible pairings: Jack and Juliet, Nikki and Paulo, even Desmond and Claire. Late in Season Two, Desmond shows some interest in Claire and her baby ("Live Together, Die Alone," 2.24), and he saves her from being struck by lightning ("Every Man for Himself," 3.4). Kate chooses Sawyer to become her lover ("I Do," 3.6). As Season Three progresses, mix-ups and match-ups likely will further integrate the Others and the castaways and create surprising alliances.

STRAYING FROM STEREOTYPES

What we (or the characters) see isn't the best way to interpret character changes on *Lost*. In fact, racial and cultural differences are more likely to be analyzed by TV critics and reporters than by characters. Late in the first season, interviewer Elizabeth Vargas teased Daniel Dae Kim (Jin) about his new sex symbol status on the Internet. Although he laughed good naturedly at the comment, he also noted that Asian men were seldom seen on television "as heroes, as leading men." Commenting on a tender love scene between Jin and Sun, before Jin turned to the dark side as an employee of Sun's father, Kim added that he had "worked in this business for twelve years, and this show has given me my first on-screen kiss."[4] Kim reiterated this theme on a *20/20* segment hosted by John Stossel in early September 2006.[5] The segment discussed stereotyping on television, and *Lost* (also airing on ABC, *Lost*'s network) was cited as a series that goes against stereotype. Although *Lost* may help shatter stereotypes by creating stories that provide moments such as Sun and Jin's romantic kisses, Kim shines not because he's Korean, nor in spite of his roots, but because he's a fine actor and a good-looking one to boot. In November 2005, *People* magazine included Kim as one of the sexiest men alive.[6]

The cast as a whole represents what interviewer Vargas called "a mini U.N." Naveen Andrews (Sayid) explained that the characters' relationships and dealings with each other are a "microcosm . . . of society at the moment."[7] Part of the appeal of *Lost* is that it mirrors what is going on in the world, and how we and the characters harbor preconceptions of what an Iraqi, or a Korean, Aussie, Canadian, American, or Brit is likely to say or do. Latina Ana Lucia, Nigerian Mr. Eko, and blonde American Libby enhance the mix during Season Two, and the addition of two Americans and a Brazilian (Rodrigo Santoro as Paulo) further the

"U.N." for Season Three. Recurring (American) Henry Gale/Ben Linus and (Scottish) Desmond also become regular characters at the start of Season Three. International characters, who at first can be labeled by country of origin, race, or ethnicity, soon break any stereotypes we or the characters may have in mind.

* * *

Throughout each season of *Lost*, easy categorizations are shown to be only one small part of each complex character's makeup. The characters are all lost in their lives when their plane or boat crashes, or they otherwise make their way to the island, but for different reasons than we may initially suspect. This layering of characterizations not only makes characters more human as they face universal problems, but it also plays with our concepts of good and evil, friend and foe.

Anything but one-dimensional beings, they are complex, real people, neither completely good nor completely evil, who bravely set out to change aspects of their lives and then face setbacks, men and women as biased, altruistic, annoying, lovable, strong, broken, mundane, and inspirational as anyone else we know. They go beyond lost souls to become just like us: people who are doing (sometimes) the best they can and otherwise muddling through a chaotic world that often seems intent on destroying them. Even on a remote island, the castaways can't escape petty problems with the neighbors or the boredom of a routine job. Like us, their world seems increasingly threatening, whether from people intent on imposing their will on others, often violently, or natural disasters. Individually and collectively, the characters continue to change in response to these challenges, just as we must continue to adapt to our ever-changing world. Seeing how these characters overcome shared fears and challenges, individually and collectively, illustrates how we, too, must work with others if we're going to survive in the modern world.

MAKING MEANING FROM CONNECTIONS

As the first season unfolded, it became apparent that although most castaways were strangers when they boarded Oceanic 815, connections between and among the passengers already existed. The interlocking connections among characters, whether important clues to their precrash lives or merely "Easter eggs" that make us laugh, continue beyond the first season. On *Lost*, truly no person is an island. Although the meaning of "lost" implies loneliness, the series shows that the castaways have links that may pave the way to their being found—at least emotionally or spiritually, if not geographically.

"Exodus" (1.23–24), more than any other single episode, provides several clues to precrash connections among the characters:

- In a Sydney hotel a harried Hurley sees that the elevator to the lobby is full; he says he will take the stairs instead of crowding inside. Just as the door closes, an annoyed Charlie shouts a sarcastic "thanks" for stopping the elevator and then not getting on.
- At the Sydney airport, Michael tries unsuccessfully on the phone to convince his mother to take Walt. Locke rolls past the phone bank on his way to their mutual flight.
- Onboard the plane, Arzt helps heavily pregnant Claire lift her bag into the overhead storage bin, and as Hurley rushes to his seat so the plane can depart, he makes eye contact with Walt and gives him a thumbs up, receiving a grin in return.
- Just before the turbulence rocks the plane, Charlie bolts from his seat to avoid being stopped by approaching crew members. He clambers over Boone and an annoyed Shannon and pushes by Jack on the way to the washroom.

These minimal contacts on the day of the ill-fated flight show that even though we often are unaware of the people we encounter, we connect with others in our everyday life. The nature of human existence is to make these contacts, even if they are fleeting and usually inconsequential.

On *Lost*, and perhaps in real life, nothing is inconsequential or random. As Locke notes in "White Rabbit" (1.5) "everything happens for a reason." This line becomes increasingly important—and frequently repeated—not only in "Exodus" but in the second season. This tag line is a focal point for the second season's advertising in the United States and indicates that one theme for the continuing story is destiny, or fate.

"Exodus" provides a multitude of connections between and among passengers, but the links between characters go beyond the day of the final flight:

- Sawyer meets Christian Shephard in a Sydney bar ("Outlaws," 1.16); later Sawyer tells Jack about the encounter, creating a friendlier bond between the two usually antagonistic characters ("Exodus," 1.23).
- When Boone pleads with a Sydney police officer to intervene in his sister's abusive relationship, Sawyer is paraded through the station in handcuffs ("Hearts and Minds," 1.13).
- Hurley's accountant assures the new millionaire of his financial worth even as he lists a litany of tragedies to befall the businesses in which Hurley has invested. Included in the list is the box company where Locke works ("Numbers," 1.18).
- Locke and Hurley share Randy as a boss, although at different companies at different times ("Everybody Hates Hugo," 2.4).
- Shannon's father dies in the emergency room where Jack meets and saves future-wife Sarah, the other victim of their joint car crash ("Man of Science, Man of Faith," 2.1). Jack walks past Shannon as she learns of her father's death ("Abandoned," 2.6).
- The TV in Sam Austen's recruitment office shows Sayid just as Kate arrives to ask for her father's help ("What Kate Did," 2.9).

- Sam Austen shows a picture of daughter Kate to Kelvin, the soldier who teaches Sayid how to interrogate prisoners ("One of Them," 2.14). Kelvin later joins the Dharma Initiative and trains Desmond in the ways of the Hatch ("Live Together, Die Alone," 2.23–24).
- At the Sydney airport, Libby intervenes when Mr. Eko sounds menacing toward Charlotte Malkin ("?" 2.21).
- Libby offers Desmond her late husband's sailboat for his use in a race that will result in his shipwreck on the same island where her plane will later crash ("Live Together, Die Alone," 2.23–24).
- Ana Lucia travels to Sydney with Christian Shephard, who may be Claire's father ("Two for the Road," 2.20).

The strangest link between characters to date takes place as one of the mysteries in the second season. Jack's first backstory in Season Two includes a brief scene with a helpful runner. Desmond happens to be sprinting upstairs in the same stadium where Jack is literally trying to run away from his failure to perform a surgical miracle on Sarah. When Jack sprains his ankle, Desmond stops to help. He idly comments as he examines the ankle that he almost was a doctor. When he asks Jack why he is running, Jack explains Sarah's desperate medical situation and his inability to fix her. Desmond asks Jack if he believes in miracles, but Jack indicates that Sarah's condition is impossible to fix. With a cryptic comment about seeing Jack in another life, Desmond jogs down the stairs and presumably out of Jack's life.

When Jack sees the miracle of Sarah's recovery for himself, he is overwhelmed with joy and surprise, but it is doubtful that he thinks of Desmond in connection with Sarah. However, when a man holding a gun to Locke's head begins to speak to him, telling Jack to drop his own weapon and threatening to kill Locke, Jack recognizes the voice. Desmond has a distinctive Scottish accent to American ears, and Jack's memory is further jogged when

Desmond steps into view. Although older and now wild-eyed, Locke's captor clearly is the same man from the stadium a few years before ("Man of Science, Man of Faith," 2.1). Logically, the two men should never meet again, but in this other life on the island, logic seems to take second place to destiny or fate.

Even when we can't see the result of our everyday encounters, perhaps the everyday run-ins with others have a greater significance. Even in a moment's time, what we say or do may influence another and ultimately cause change in someone else's life. We may consider such transitory links between real people or characters coincidental, but what if they have more meaning than we may originally think? When we search for meaning in *Lost*, we should realize that perhaps a greater force than the castaways can accept or readily understand is at play.

Links between characters also take place through dialogue, behavior patterns, or shared experiences. Structurally, the series' writers and creators enhance the links between characters by having one character repeat the dialogue spoken by another in a previous scene or episode or having one character's actions mirror another's:

- Rose tells Jack that she is letting him off the hook for his promise—to stay with her until her husband returns from the washroom ("Tabula Rasa," 1.3). Boone tells Jack that he is freeing Jack from his promise to save him ("Do No Harm," 1.20).
- Boone suggests that Jack perform a tracheotomy to save Rose, who is not breathing after the crash ("Pilot," 1.1). Ironically, Jack performs a tracheotomy to help Boone breathe after he is injured in a second plane crash—the Beechcraft's fall from a cliff ("Do No Harm").
- During a brief backstory scene in "Exodus" (1.24), Charlie struggles to hold onto his last baggie of heroin in a tussle with another addict. As the woman beats him, Charlie fends off blows as he protects the drugs instead of himself. "You're pathetic!" the defeated woman screeches in disgust. In current

time on the island, Charlie lashes out at the distraught Danielle. Although the woman has returned baby Aaron, Charlie believes that she, not the Others, set the signal fire as a ruse. Charlie scornfully denounces Rousseau—"You're pathetic"—as he clutches the child and stalks off.

- Locke's heartfelt "Don't tell me what I can't do!" ("Walkabout," 1.4) is echoed by Jack at the end of the season ("Exodus," 1.24). Jack further tells Locke "Don't tell me what to do" in the second season as he holds a gun on Desmond ("Man of Science, Man of Faith, 2.1). Mr. Eko warns Locke, "Do not tell me what I can do" ("Live Together, Die Alone," 2.23), a slight variation in wording that reflects Eko's speech patterns. Yet another variation is "You don't get to tell me what I can do," as Charlie tells Locke during their search for Eko ("Further Instructions," 3.3).
- Kelvin first awakens Desmond after his shipwreck by asking, "Are you him?" ("Live Together, Die Alone," 2.23), and Desmond echoes that line when Locke enters the Hatch ("Man of Science, Man of Faith," 2.1).
- An enthralled Locke tells Jack, "We'll have to watch that again," after he first views the Orientation video ("Orientation," 2.3), but when the second orientation film has been played, Eko asks Locke, "Do you want to watch this again?" A disillusioned Locke declines ("?" 2.21).

Characters who otherwise seem very different may share some common trait or experience, which then give us a new perspective on a "good" or "bad" character. Although Rousseau is often described by other characters as crazy or dangerous, she is, as Sayid tells Charlie ("Exodus," 1.24), also a mother who lost her baby. Claire, who seems crazed by Rousseau's abduction of baby Aaron, also is a mother who loses her baby. Whether both mothers eventually lose or are able to be permanently reunited with their children remains to be seen.

The story of the Tailies' first forty-eight days on the island parallels what the center section's survivors encounter during the same
time. Both groups face monsters—everything from the Others to
polar bears to natural dangers to the Monster. Both groups of survivors receive medical care by a trained professional who cannot
save all victims of the crash. Some people drown, although they survive the plane's destruction; others survive only after receiving CPR.
Both groups find at least one gun. Both camps are infiltrated by one
of the Others, who pretends to have been on the same flight and is
at least indirectly responsible for the kidnapping of one or more
castaways. Both groups find a research station from the Dharma
Initiative. Both locate a radio, attempt to send and receive signals,
and receive a message but fail to understand its ramifications.
Although the two new societies differ—Ana Lucia's is more of a military dictatorship compared to Jack's benevolent socialism—they
face similar dilemmas and accomplish similar goals during the first
forty-eight days ("The Other 48 Days," 2.7).

Other character similarities are revealed through additional
backstories. Charlie's problems with Claire mirror brother Liam's
early marital problems with wife Karen. Both brothers fall for
blonde Australians with a baby (Liam's biological child and
Charlie's surrogate child, respectively). Each woman believes that
the man's behavior places her child in jeopardy and banishes the
(surrogate) father from her life for a time ("Fire + Water," 2.12).
Charlie's background parallels Mr. Eko's in many ways. (See
Chapter 4 for a thorough comparison.) Sun's and Locke's wealthy
fathers become involved in shady dealings that alienate them
from their children. Because of their decisions, Jack, Locke, and
Desmond lose the loves of their lives. Desmond may be able
someday to be reunited with his love, but Jack and Locke permanently lose their significant others because they do what is in
their own best interest, instead of the relationship's. [Even trivial
actions highlight character similarities. Jack and Locke both store
wedding rings in their sock drawer (". . . And Found," 2.5;

"Lockdown," 2.17).] On *Lost*, characters have much more in common than they may ever expect.

Resonances in dialogue and situation indicate that the characters are not as isolated as they may feel. The good characters share background experiences or dialogue with not-so-good characters or those representing an opposing point of view. A seemingly throwaway line in one scene (such as Christian Shephard's "Don't cross that line" to a potentially philandering Jack) takes on new significance in a later scene (the Others' warning to Jack not to cross a line and, in effect, go to war against them) ("The Hunting Party," 2.11). These links again show the well-rounded nature of characters as well as the sense that they are all fallible humans who may need to hear repeated dialogue (i.e., advice, warnings) or repeat common experiences if they are to learn a lesson. If these characters are lost, perhaps ties to other people and situations can help them find themselves. *Lost* incorporates many such lines not only within an episode but across seasons; some lines become catch phrases for themes within the series, such as "live together or die alone." Other similarities between characters and their experiences that show the many connections among them are listed in Appendixes B and C; you can use these sections to help you make more meaning from your *Lost* viewing.

Lost also allows us to read personal meanings into the castaways' experiences. Like the characters, their dialogue or experiences may resonate with similar occurrences in our lives. Who hasn't received advice from a parent or teacher that later is given by someone else or heard a common warning ("Don't swim right after eating") repeated? One of *Lost*'s great strengths as a series is that it provides a mirror to the world and allows us to see commonalities among people and events. We often may fail to give significance to such connections in our lives, however; after all, the survivors of Oceanic 815 seem remarkably well connected to each other in small and much more important ways. Nevertheless, such unexpected connections between people do occur and make us realize that we probably do have at least a few links with at least some people we meet on the street. The authors, for example, learned only after working together for several months that we share a colleague in common at Bowling Green State University. Did we possibly pass each other in a hallway or say hello in our mutual colleague's office many years ago, long before we officially met? Was there something significant in knowing a particular professor? Such coincidences in life do take place; *Lost*, however, makes us more aware of such common experiences and heightens the significance of characters' common experiences and shared lines as important plot points. *Lost* shows not only that every character is linked to someone else but hints that these connections may someday be revealed as a factor in these interconnected characters ending up on a mysterious island.

MAKING MEANING THROUGH SYMBOLS

Another way to make meaning from *Lost* is to identify symbols and learn their significance to characters, the story, and the world at large. Symbols work on personal and universal levels. A symbol may have specific meaning to a person, but that meaning is likely hidden from everyone else. More important symbols have universal meanings—a key unlocks something on the literal level but can indicate other abstractions being revealed (e.g., the key to someone's personality).

Concrete symbols are items that can be interpreted in many ways, such as the Virgin Mary statues, monsters, and airplanes—all images that recur frequently in different settings in many episodes.

The meaning of the Virgin Mary statues varies among characters; Charlie and Eko associate them with specific drug-related experiences, but Claire at first only sees the religious symbolism. Every character has one or more personal "monsters," and terrifying events—such as toppled trees and arrival of "sentient" smoke—take on greater significance because they are (so far) unexplained, and characters attribute their worst fears to these events.

Certainly airplanes may become a symbol of terror for the crash survivors, but they also provide more layers of meaning than a form of transportation. Claire's dream image of a mobile of little airplanes ("Raised by Another," 1.10) may harken to a very real memory of such a mobile in the medical hatch ("Maternity Leave," 2.15). However, instead of representing a cute toy to attract her (as yet unborn) baby's attention, the airplanes offer a sinister premonition. Claire's baby will need to be in the Others' care before he can see the real mobile; Claire's dream airplanes fly above an empty, bloody cradle. Kate also associates toy airplanes with loss; she goes to extremes to retrieve the model airplane once belonging to deceased friend Tom ("Whatever the Case May Be," 1.12; "Born to Run," 1.22).

The Dharma Initiative's many logos contain symbols that have been interpreted by fans in dozens of different ways. The outer Dharma logo itself most often is compared with the outer structure of the Bagua of the *I Ching*. Yin is represented with a broken line or divided dash; yang is the opposite—a solid line or undivided dash. Solid and broken lines appear in different Dharma logos, and oppositions certainly are a theme within *Lost*.

The Dharma symbol is made of eight trigrams, also a key element in the *I Ching*.[8] The symbols for each hatch, such as the Swan, the Arrow, and the Caduceus, no doubt have specific meaning for the members of the Dharma Initiative who created them. However, they also carry associations with other mythologies, such as Greek.

Apollo candy bars are featured in early Season Two episodes (e.g., "Everybody Hates Hugo," 2.4), and they form an important clue-gathering activity in The *Lost* Experience. Fans who read the Apollo Candy Company's website (www.apollocandy.com) not only found the company's history and association with the Hanso Foundation but learned where in the United States and the United Kingdom they could pick up the chocolate bars, just like the ones that Kate and Hurley eat.

The Greek god Apollo represents the arts, archery, and sometimes healing and often is depicted as a wanderer. The Apollo Candy Company's commercials on TV and the website show a 1960s-style cartoon of a boy dressed like an astronaut; the space theme is prominent in all company visuals. Visiting the heavens like the wandering Apollo may be one association for fans, even if that's not the one the series' creators intended.

At least three hatches also might refer peripherally to Apollo: the Arrow (for archery), the Caduceus (for medicine), and the Swan (a bird associated with this god). The Swan also is a constellation, which again evokes the space theme. Although these symbols have meaning in themselves, their link with the big picture presented by the Dharma Initiative is still unknown. By understanding the symbols, however, we might uncover more about the Dharma Initiative and its way of thinking.

Although *Lost* provides abundant concrete or abstract, personal or universal symbols in each episode, the more often an item or theme appears, the more likely it is to be significant. Hieroglyphics in the Hatch's countdown clock (representing Hurley's numbers in the Valenzetti Equation, according to The *Lost* Experience, and signaling the world's destruction) and the many symbols on the map painted on the blast door (providing a history of the hatches and important events happening around them), as well as variations in the Dharma Initiative's logos, seem to be significant symbols that many fans have spent weeks decoding.

It would take another book to identify all symbols used in *Lost* and their many meanings. As a sample of important symbols within *Lost*, here are three common, repeated symbols used in conjunction with different characters in several Season One and Two episodes. Keys, a compass, and black and white recur frequently.

KEYS

Keys on *Lost* unlock specific items: a safe deposit box, a fail-safe device, a briefcase, an apartment door. But the events surrounding the keys and the importance placed on them by those who bestow and those who receive them increase their importance to plot and character development.

Kate commits crimes because she has a key but not the authorization to use it to unlock a safe deposit box ("Born to Run," 1.22). The key is important because it unlocks the box containing a memento of Kate's friend and first love. It symbolizes the way to open Kate's locked and heavily guarded heart; Tom is one of the few people ever to receive Kate's love, and he guarded it carefully.

Locke's key to a safe deposit box unlocks what his father really loves: money and power over his son. When Locke retrieves money for his father, he jeopardizes girlfriend Helen's love in order to gain the love of his father ("Lockdown," 2.17).

Jack wears a key around his neck for safe keeping. It unlocks the marshal's briefcase, which contains guns and ammunition ("Whatever the Case May Be," 1.12). Jack is the keeper of the key to the castaways' most coveted items: firearms. At various points in the story, the key is stolen, signaling Jack's lack of control over others. He who wears this key is the leader (at least during Season One, before other firearms are found in the Hatch).

Kelvin also wears a key around his neck; this one unleashes the pent-up energy in the Hatch. Whoever has this key is the keeper to the biggest secret (revealed to date) on the island. Kelvin loses power (and his life) to Desmond, who takes the key and stores it in a special place—his favorite book. When Desmond decides to use the key to release electromagnetic energy, he unleashes not only a vast amount of power but in essence offers to sacrifice himself to establish equilibrium. Kelvin and Desmond keep the key to the mystery of life and death in the Hatch ("Live Together, Die Alone," 2.23–24).

Keys figure in other scenes, too. Keys are among Desmond's few possessions returned to him when he leaves prison ("Live Together, Die Alone," 2.23). Locke gives a key to his apartment to

Helen; the key represents his love for her. When Locke leaves her to sit in front of his father's house one evening, she follows him, removes the key from the car's ignition, and angrily throws it over the fence separating Locke from his father ("Deus Ex Machina," 1.19). Who holds the key to Locke's heart—his father or Helen? Keys prominently indicate who's winning this tug of war.

Keys determine what a character values most, which often indicates his or her motivation for action within a scene. Kate, for example, values her now-deceased friend Tom so much that she takes the extreme measure of robbing a bank to retrieve something that once belonged to him and reminds her of better times. Desmond's actions toward the other castaways, such as running away when he thinks that the computer has been destroyed, often are suspect; we aren't sure if he's a good guy. When we know the importance of the fail-safe key, we see Desmond in a much more altruistic light. When Desmond realizes that, whatever he does, he is loved and that surviving a possible holocaust is the only way back to Penny Widmore, he becomes much more willing to use the fail-safe key as a last-ditch effort to save the island. The key to a character's motivation is often indicated by what the key physically opens.

COMPASS

The function of a compass is to indicate direction, but more symbolically, a compass can indicate someone's life direction and whether a character is off course or headed in the wrong direction. Locke decides he doesn't need a compass anymore on the island, so he gives it to Sayid, who likes to analyze maps and explore ("Hearts and Minds," 1.13). Sayid soon realizes that the compass doesn't show true north, an appropriate discovery for the way the island misleads people and strange events take place.

Sayid gives a compass to Michael when the raft sails ("Exodus," 1.23), and this may be the compass he uses as he searches for Walt ("Three Minutes," 2.22). Whatever direction

Michael believes he's headed, his compass seems to lead him directly to the Others. When Michael looks up from ascertaining direction, he sees a male Other almost directly in front of him, but he also doesn't realize that more Others see him and soon will surround him.

On *Lost*, it may be more important to follow one's instincts instead of relying on technology, which may be misleading. On this island, a compass may not indicate where one is or needs to go. Instead, it may lead directly to trouble.

BLACK AND WHITE

These colors are significant symbols during Season One but are seldom used in Season Two. Locke often is the focal point for these symbols. When he first teaches Walt to play backgammon, Locke explains that there are two sides: black and white. The larger symbolism is that in life, there are usually two sides. Locke explains the dichotomy as light and dark, good and evil ("Pilot," 1.2). However, this black-and-white approach to life, on the island or off it, is too simplistic, and *Lost* soon shows more shades of gray than purely black-and-white interpretations of any event or character.

When the bones of "Adam and Eve" are found in the caves, black and white stones are laid near them. Jack assumes some religious significance to the stones, but they hint at a possibly more sinister meaning ("House of the Rising Sun," 1.6).

Claire dreams that her baby cries from his crib (days before she actually gives birth). When she goes to him, she discovers he is missing; only blood stains the crib, and Claire's hands are bloody when she turns to Locke for help. Locke's eyes are black and white ("Whatever the Case May Be," 1.12). Perhaps because Locke seems mysterious and is associated with other black-and-white items such as backgammon pieces, Claire associates something possibly sinister with him in connection to her baby.

Black-and-white symbolism becomes less obvious by Season Three. The Dharma Initiative's two-color logo is one important use of black and white; the logo appears on everything from clothing to packages of food to hatches. Perhaps the Dharma Initiative, at least initially, offered a stark contrast to the way that most groups approached the earth's problems. Over time, as the Dharma Initiative changed, the black-and-white logo applied to everything from people to products may have taken on a more sinister meaning. The increasing emphasis on "us" versus "them" between the castaways and the Others reflects the sharp contrast between the groups and hints at the problems with black-and-white thinking.

Although oppositions, such as battles between faith and reason or good and evil, become themes running throughout *Lost*, the many perspectives on any scene, event, or character make a black-and-white interpretation highly unlikely. *Lost* symbolically sets up an easy interpretation of what's happening on the island, such as the Others being responsible for everything bad happening to the good and innocent castaways (in Season One), but then shows (in Seasons Two and Three) that this isn't the true meaning. *Lost*'s episodes provide a continuum between any pair of opposites, symbolized by black and white, and then illustrate all the gray areas between the extremes.

* * *

The castaways can only make meaning from their experiences on the island, what they see and learn about each other, and the few connections they discover between themselves and others. Viewers are much more fortunate; we have more ways to compare and evaluate clues about what's happening on the island and why.

Lost presents us with multiple opportunities to make as much (or as little) meaning as we like, from episodes or other multimedia information that supplements the text. More than any series to date, *Lost* provides a wealth of additional materials to help us uncover more layers than can be revealed upon a single viewing of episodes. Through further research, fan-scholars gain insights into symbols and connections that may be difficult to understand on more than a superficial level without time-consuming extracurricular research.

Lost offers even more than excellent storytelling; it can be an interactive experience that allows us—if we choose—to become one of the castaways and experience the mind-boggling mysteries for ourselves. With *Lost* we can be more than passive watchers and interpreters; through extracurricular activities such as The *Lost* Experience, we can become active investigators and information sharers. We can even uncover clues that may help "dissidents" such as Persephone/Rachel Blake fight against the Hanso Foundation. As the series progresses, the layers of meaning become deeper, and connections between and among characters and events increase in complexity.

We may never find one all-encompassing theory to explain everything on *Lost*; perhaps even the series' creators haven't pinned down that one. We may be reading far too much into some symbols and looking for minutiae that really lead nowhere. Because *Lost* is more complex than the average television program, its stakes are greater. It risks alienating fans with too many unanswered questions or dead-end plot points. However, the search itself explains a lot about us as a viewing audience and how we take in information today.

Perhaps because the world seems ever more frightening, many of us look for proof that everything can be explained or understood, that there is meaning behind even the smallest detail. Because information is the most important global commodity today, we become accustomed to feeling overwhelmed by the bombardment of new information available in multiple media wherever we turn. We often find it impossible to separate the important from the merely interesting or quirky, and it's difficult to know today just which facts and news items will become most important to our survival tomorrow. So it is with *Lost*. Only in hindsight are we able to see which plot threads or themes give us a greater understanding of characters or the island. As we watch episode by episode, we might easily be misled about the overriding importance of one week's dream sequence or popular culture reference; we might attribute greater significance to something than it really deserves.

Although that's frustrating to us as *Lost* fans, the very act of searching for meaning in everything, comparing notes on the Internet and in person around the water cooler, and trying to find the real story amid gigabytes of data is part of our modern lives. This is the way we know how to make meaning; the act of researching and comparing—especially on the Net—is now familiar and expected. *Lost*, to a greater extent than any other Net-savvy series, not only allows us to think about the series after an episode airs—it almost demands that we take it as seriously as we take our jobs or any other aspect of our lives if we're going to get the most out of the series.

Lost helps us find ourselves as viewers and participants in the ongoing mystery by providing us with starting points and letting us do the work of making meaning. The act of making meaning also makes the series personal and memorable to us. Five years from now, even if *Lost* is off the air, what we'll remember about the series may not be a clue from episode 4.15. It's more likely to be bits of research gathered in conjunction with the series—perhaps a new appreciation of a book that we read because Sawyer did, or a study of the *I Ching* because it interested us beyond the Dharma logo. We might develop friendships that span more than a single fandom, or we might even change as people because we confronted our life issues while the castaways confronted theirs. Perhaps a strength of *Lost* isn't in uncovering the same meanings that the writers had within a given episode or that the series' creators intend with the whole of *Lost;* the series' lasting value comes from allowing us to make multiple meanings that are important to us, collectively or individually.

Notes to Chapter Three, "Finding *Lost* Meanings"

1. *Lost:* The Complete Second Season DVD, 2006.

2. "The *Lost* Survival Guide." ABC, September 9, 2006.

3. Jeff Jensen, "Gone (for Now) . . . but Not Forgotten!" Retrieved November 14, 2006, from http://www.ew.com/ew/article/commentary/0,6115,1559558_3_0,00.html.

4. Elizabeth Vargas, "*Lost* Special." *20/20*. ABC, May 6, 2005.

5. John Stossel, *20/20*, September 8, 2006.

6. "2005's Sexiest Men Alive," *People*, November 21–28, 2005.

7. Vargas, "*Lost* Special."

8. Several scholarly fan sites and discussion boards discuss meanings behind the Dharma Initiative's logos. The Fuselage maintains threads discussing the logos throughout Season Two, and Wikipedia offers many examples and illustrations of the logos and comparative symbols within the *I Ching* (http://lostpedia.com/wiki/DHARMA_logos).

PART THREE

SPIRITUALITY

On *Lost*, spirituality takes many forms, not all of them within traditional or recognized religious expression. Locke is one of the most spiritual characters on the series, one who wrestles with his own battle between belief in science and the need for proof versus faith in the island and its many signs. Especially during Season Two, Locke faces a spiritual crisis, although he, to date, hasn't mentioned past or current affiliation with a specific religion; Season Three sees a return to Locke's spiritual roots.

Characters like Rose, Mr. Eko, and Charlie identify spirituality with a specific religion. Rose is clearly Christian and most likely Protestant, which might bring an interesting dynamic in future episodes; husband Bernard is Jewish, but so far he hasn't shown any outward expression of his religion. The fact that Rose's marriage is "mixed," at least racially and religiously, would be another interesting aspect to analyze in upcoming episodes. Eko and Charlie are Catholic, Eko so much so that he calls himself a priest and largely takes on that role in Season Two before once more relinquishing it in Season Three. Even Claire, who seems leery during much of the second season of Charlie's Catholicism, to the point of asking Locke whether Charlie might be a "religious nut," asks Eko to baptize herself and her baby.

Sayid, who in Season Two professes more interest in his old job as "interrogator" than living a life freed from his past, occasionally reveals his belief in Islam. The Season Two finale, for instance, shows Sayid praying as Desmond's sailboat carries him to a rendezvous with the Others.

Perhaps the most intriguing example of the diverse spirituality of characters is illustrated through Henry Gale/Ben Linus, a leader of the Others. Gale shows almost a religious fervor when he tells the castaways that the Others are really the good people on the island.

Spirituality on the island, as in our outer world, includes many different beliefs, and the expressions of spiritual faith vary as much as the individuals who profess these widely ranging beliefs. *Lost*'s many characters wrestle with their interpretations about what is happening on the island and whether a Divine Creator, a large corporate entity, the Dharma Initiative, the Others, the Monster, or nothing at all is running the show. As is common with any of the series' mysteries, it's left to us—as well as individual characters—to determine which is the "correct" way to interpret scenes and events.

During Season Two, spirituality largely concerns the battle between science and faith. The battle is best illustrated at first through "discussions" (some of them very loud and angry) between Jack and Locke, although other characters, including Desmond, Charlie, and Mr. Eko, also begin to question what they believe. During this season, the characters come to some surprising and life-altering conclusions, which change them and thus the makeup of the castaways' new society.

At the beginning of Season Three, as the castaways deal with the dispersion of their society into smaller groups (held captive by the Others, on the beach, and on Desmond's sailboat), they need to rely on each other even more and may question the direction their fledgling society should take. They must come to grips with their fear and animosity toward people who've lived on the island far longer than they have.

In this section, the battle between "men of science" and "men of faith" is discussed, as are characters' spiritual expressions of their beliefs and the many life themes and questions they face. As the series reveals more mysteries, characters and fans are likely to confront their own belief systems and perhaps come to a better understanding of why as well as what they believe and how that belief translates into daily action. Although *Lost* doesn't "preach" religion, it explores concepts like faith, the nature of love, redemption, fate, and destiny—issues that bear a further analysis in this section.

SPIRITUAL PRACTICES ON THE ISLAND

A first-season poster, distributed initially at Comic Con in San Diego in July 2004, boldly announces that "The crash was only the beginning." What seems like a final act, or at least possibly the most traumatic event in most survivors' lives, truly is the starting point for the *Lost* castaways. As impossible as it may seem, in many cases their lives are changed for the better. The castaways all have the ability to start over, especially when, during Season Two, it becomes ever clearer that they are going to be stuck on the island for a long time, perhaps the rest of their lives.

Season Three marketing during summer 2006 indicates the direction that many characters would explore in upcoming episodes. In a commercial on U.S. television, Locke explains what brought him to the island; "destiny" is his keyword. In another ad, Charlie ponders whether he can be redeemed. Even the tagline used in television and print promotions touts the destiny-friendly pronouncement that "everything happens for a reason" (a line first spoken by Locke in "The Moth," 1.7).

In the Season Three TV promotion, several characters ask in voiceover, "Who will I be?" The island provides the possibility for them to have a fresh start, but they often are reluctant to take it. Each season's U.S. promos are logical follow-ups to the previous season's. Not only is the serial leading us sequentially through the multilayered plot, but characters are furthering their exploration of who they are and who they would like to be. This logical progression from recognizing an opportunity for "rebirth" on the island, finding meaning in that new beginning and coming to an understanding that they *can* take that opportunity to become better people, and in the third season, deciding who to become and how to do that is a tortuously slow process. However, it may lead to greater spiritual development for many characters.

Although different characters are included in these promotions across the years, Locke and Charlie are two constants, and, probably not coincidentally, they are two of the most spiritually questioning and questing characters on *Lost*. Bad-boy Sawyer also is prominently featured, but he often proclaims that the castaways haven't yet seen who he really is and don't know all that he's capable of doing. Sawyer doesn't seek redemption, and he seems adamantly confident that he can deal with whatever dangers arise.

In the Season Three promo, new regular character Desmond makes an appearance; with the destruction of the Hatch and his new status as island (and castaways') savior, he may take on a different role in his life (and a larger role in the series). Even Claire, absent from earlier new-season promos, asks, "Who will I be?" before Season Three. As a woman becoming more accustomed to her role as mother, and as a renewed friend and Charlie's possibly future lover, Claire may explore more aspects of island life. This season really represents the first time she can determine the direction of her postpregnancy, post-Thomas life.

Of course, not all new opportunities or possibilities for character development are of a spiritual nature. With such a large group, not every character can receive the same amount or type of development. As characters confront life issues, however, they often wrestle with the basic question of whether they should seek spiritual answers to other questions or if secular sources seem more logical in providing them answers.

The series' creators and writers ask recurring questions about redemption and the meaning of life. They ask perhaps the most important question to *Lost* fans: Who or what is behind everything that happens on the island? That question can be broadened to Who or what makes events occur in our lives? Is life logically run—a series of predictable causes and effects, even if we may not always understand just how far reaching some effects may be? If so, the fault of not understanding or planning for the effects is ours; we simply don't know enough yet, but facts *can* be uncovered and everything known—someday.

Do we need faith rather than knowledge to be able to live fully? If so, a greater presence influences and intervenes in life, and we don't need knowledge so much as faith that situations work out as they should. These questions and responses are pertinent not only for the *Lost* characters, but for us. No matter what religion the characters follow—if, indeed, they adhere to a religion—they are dealing with these crucial life questions while they investigate the island's mysteries.

In *Lost*, a character's philosophy and spirituality (or lack thereof) are often closely linked because the castaways face life-altering experiences almost daily. They need some foundation for their lives, some approach to making sense of what often seems not to make any sense at all.

A typical situation: During the first-season finale, "Exodus" (1.24), Hurley spies the Black Rock, which, in typical *Lost* fashion, is neither black nor a rock, but instead a wooden sailing vessel grounded several miles inland. "How can something like that happen?" he questions aloud. Rousseau, guide for the expedition, merely quirks an eyebrow. "Do you live on the same island I do?" she replies as an explanation.

The inexplicable merges with the unpredictable throughout the series. Shortly after the survivors arrive at the Black Rock, science teacher Leslie Arzt suddenly gets blown up while attempting to give a lesson about handling dynamite safely. Hurley reels from the death of a man with whom he has just had a conversation. On the same trek, the group encounters the Monster once more, and Locke nearly lets himself be carried away. In this scene, Locke displays the faith he has begun to proclaim so loudly; he trusts the island and is more curious than fearful about what it may hold. The other survivors, however, don't share his unlimited curiosity.

On *Lost*, this is simply an afternoon on the island. Even more so than in the real world, which has its own sudden, terrifying events, the island exploits every human fear. Natural disasters, humans bent on murder and destruction, and "monsters" that defy definition all prey upon the survivors' sanity.

During the first season, the search for food, water, and shelter is an additional worry; the castaways first have to figure out how simply to survive in the jungle. During the second season, the Hatch provides some comforts, and food sometimes is parachuted near it ("Dave," 2.18). For a while, the Hatch is nearly as convenient as the local 7-Eleven; it provides the basics of food and supplies as well as a meeting and work place. Not all castaways visit the Hatch often, but it becomes something of a social center. It's a pantry, living room, gym, bathhouse, laundry, office, and jail, all in one. The discovery of the Hatch eases the castaways' struggle for food, shelter, even entertainment, but it can't provide everything the new little society needs. Instead, it also invites yet more potential dangers—Desmond, the button that needs to be pushed every 108 minutes, plunging blast doors, strange electromagnetic fields. It becomes a place of both secrets and revelations.

With the destruction of the Hatch at the end of the second season, the castaways again need to return to hunting, fishing, and foraging as well as dealing with the accompanying anxieties. Season Three episodes airing in late 2006 present a well-organized beach community. When Locke and Charlie carry the injured Eko back to camp, Locke orders people to bring bandages and medical supplies ("Further Instructions," 3.3), which they do. Eko's hut mysteriously catches fire, and several castaways rescue him from the blaze. While Locke later gathers a search party to track the missing Eko, the castaways are busy with everyday life; Hurley, for example, chops fruit ("The Cost of Living," 3.5). Although the remaining medical supplies may run out and food drops end, beach life is becoming normal for many castaways. They seem much more capable of taking care of little crises, such as fire in camp or injuries.

An even greater danger may be lurking, however. Walt, held captive for several weeks by the Others, warns his father that his captors aren't as rustic as they seem ("Three Minutes," 2.22); in Season Three, with more information forthcoming about this group, the castaways are exposed to new dangers. Although home for the Others looks like typical suburbia, with book club meetings and friends who moonlight as plumbers to help fix leaky pipes ("A Tale of Two Cities," 3.1), the group also runs a research compound/prison. In what appear to be remnants of the Dharma Initiative's experimental labs, the Others "retrain" or "punish" members of their group or captured "guests" Jack, Kate, and Sawyer. Henry Gale, also known as Ben Linus, thinks his friends are good people who merely need to convince Jack, in particular, to join them, but the early Season Three episodes emphasize mind games, punishment, and even torture.

An intriguing breakout character, Juliet, says she is a fertility doctor, presumably taking an oath to first do no harm to patients. Of course, Kate isn't one of her patients when Juliet threatens to kill her. This act coerces Sawyer to give up his bid to escape ("The Glass Ballerina," 3.2); the con man/murderer knows that Juliet would shoot Kate without hesitation. Even Elizabeth Mitchell finds her character cool, calculating, and not the typical doctor: "She's so good at reading other people that she knows how to block [them] from reading her."[1] Juliet seems sincere and trustworthy when she personally makes Jack a meal and talks with him, but she also tries to get him to agree to kill Ben during surgery ("Every Man for Himself," 3.4).

Season Three portrays the Others in greater depth. As Damon Lindelof aptly summed them up: "The Others emerging as a less mysterious and more significant threat is very significant in the evolution of the show."[2]

The castaways may have to work more closely with the Others in order to survive, a truly frightening prospect judging by the limited information gathered about them so far. Just as one set of terrors abates, new crises arrive with different potential traumas. In order to survive mentally and emotionally as well as physically, the castaways need a way to cope with the chaos that seems a regular feature of island life.

The castaways also naturally question the foundation of their previous lives and wonder if they need something more in order either to escape the island or to survive the experience. Whether these people are religious or merely question what brought them to the island, they look for answers to life's larger questions, such as

- What is my purpose?
- Will I, or how will I, be held accountable for my actions?

As with most aspects of *Lost*, each character has a different answer to life questions or searches in different places for the answers. A *Time* article in January 2005 suggested that like "a religious text, *Lost* is open to endless interpretation."[3]

Lost is a nonreligious program, at least compared to such other U.S. predecessors as *Highway to Heaven, Touched by an Angel, Joan of Arcadia,* and *Seventh Heaven.* These programs emphasize one religion more than others. When we sit down to watch them, we know what to expect in the episode's content; the program's themes will affirm a specific belief system. In fact, that's why we watch spiritual shows; they illustrate our beliefs. *Lost* is closer to real life—as strange as that seems—when it comes to spirituality. *Lost* can't be limited to one genre; although it slips in spirituality in some episodes, the series does more than base stories on a religious context. *Lost* doesn't guide us toward a particular belief; it asks lots of questions and shows us what different characters believe. Spirituality as described in *Lost* doesn't rely only on a Christian belief system, although during Season Two Christianity (specifically, Catholicism) is shown more than any other religion. Spiritual expression may be more personal than ritualized, more self-defined than ordained, more universal than unicultural.

Nevertheless, series co-creators Damon Lindelof and Carlton Cuse make it clear that addressing life issues is part of their agenda for *Lost*. They "aspire to use *Lost* as a vehicle to tell stories of redemption and, according to Cuse, explore the question of "how does one lead a life.""[4]

Spirituality requires a belief in something beyond oneself—some higher power or supernatural being who does have the answers. Omniscience is an important role for whatever deity is revered. For some characters, God is that deity; for others, Allah; for at least one survivor, the island.

Spirituality also requires people to act based on their beliefs—to define what is right or wrong, to determine what is important or valuable. Within the range of 14 characters prominent during the first season, and with new characters added during the second and third, we see a wide range of belief systems at work, from those who frequently express their spiritual beliefs to those who seem to have none or who follow only their own counsel. Conflict between potential leaders with different beliefs becomes important during Season Two as Jack and Locke often argue about what's best for their new society.

THE BATTLE BETWEEN SCIENCE AND FAITH

One significant element of *Lost* is the battle between reason (or science) and faith. From the first episode of the second season, "Man of Science, Man of Faith" (2.1), through the season's finale, "Live Together, Die Alone" (2.24), questions of faith resonate in several episodes. Locke, in particular, begins as a self-named man of faith, but events in the Hatch and revelations about experiments taking place on the island bring him to a spiritual crisis. Locke, however, isn't the only character who seems to be questioning whether every mystery has or needs a logical explanation. During Season Two, Locke, Mr. Eko, and Charlie illustrate varying degrees of faith and the struggle to find answers to their questions.

Both science and faith can have a place in modern society—whether on the island or in real life. The extremes of either position, as evidenced by Jack and Locke, often cause heated debates about the direction that a society should take. In that respect, *Lost*'s budding society is no different from ours. In Season Two, men of science and men of faith often square off against each other.

As a surgeon, Jack believes in the power of advanced medicine and the technology used to prolong human life. He's seen the miracle of modern medicine—or so he believes—with the healing of Sarah, the woman who becomes his wife. When he believes that she will be paralyzed for the rest of her life after a car wreck, despite Jack's best efforts in surgery, he is told (by Desmond) to believe in miracles. But when Sarah awakens from surgery able to wiggle her toes, Jack believes not so much in a religious miracle as a technological one ("Man of Science, Man of Faith," 2.1). Through later flashbacks ("The Hunting Party," 2.11), we learn that Jack often has trouble letting go of patients and takes on cases that no one else will take. He does so not so much for his own vanity but to confirm his belief that a modern surgeon should be able to save everyone. When a patient dies, Jack is devastated. He bases his beliefs on facts and knowledge, and this belief system operates in every facet of his life.

Jack's need for hardcore facts to justify his actions often pits him against Locke, especially when Locke is in true-believer mode. During the first season, Locke relies on signs, such as a vision of his mother telling him which direction to go and one of Boone talking about his dead nanny—a part of his past that

Boone hadn't previously revealed to Locke ("Deus Ex Machina," 1.19). By following this vision, Locke finds the drug runners' plane. Although Boone's resulting death after that discovery rattles Locke and makes him question his faith in the island, he soon gets another sign from the island: a light in the Hatch.

Locke's past also provides fuel for his willingness to believe in his destiny on the island and thus in its ability to send him signs that he can interpret. When Locke boards Oceanic 815, he is in a wheelchair. When he awakens after the crash, he can walk ("Pilot," 1.1). He and other characters, such as Rose, have found healing on the island. Even when Locke's leg is wounded during the second season, Rose reminds him that his healing will be accelerated—and it is ("S.O.S.," 2.19).

This accelerated healing doesn't seem to be based on our idea of normal, scientific medicine—if anything, a bloody wound not treated with the best antibiotics might not heal properly in the humid tropical jungle. But Locke soon walks around without a crutch or even a splint to bind his broken leg. He interprets his experiences as more than explainable by fact, logic, or science. Locke believes that something else is at work, and he has faith in it.

LOCKE'S CRISIS OF FAITH

When Locke names himself as a man of faith, we might expect him consistently to believe in the island, no matter what occurs. Throughout Season One, he displays just this kind of faith and places his trust in the island, because he feels it is his destiny. Once Locke opens the Hatch and begins a more mundane life there, he begins to question his destiny, a process that lasts until the end of Season Two. Although Locke is a spiritual man, his faith is not blind, and he often questions what he sees.

Despite questioning his destiny and the island's guiding signs, Locke is a pivotal character in any discussion about reason and faith. The beginning of the second season pits Locke against Jack in their understanding of the Hatch and the importance of pushing the button, supposedly to stave off the end of the world ("Man of Science, Man of Faith," 2.1). However, late in the second season, Locke himself begins to doubt the value of button pushing.

When he and Mr. Eko discover the Pearl hatch and see a second orientation video, Eko believes that pushing the button is a divine job, whereas Locke thinks he's been tricked—his role as button pusher is only part of an experiment ("?" 2.21). Locke then accepts the "logical" argument against Mr. Eko's faith-based interpretation of the importance of pushing the button.

Eko doesn't need to know why the button must be pushed, only that it is an important part of their cosmos. For Eko, pushing the button becomes a spiritual act of faith. His job is important, even though he doesn't know why. He takes the job on faith, and it becomes his new calling. During the Season Two finale, Locke comes around to Eko's point of view, but only after dire circumstances prove to Locke that his initial faith is justified. Locke first destroys the computer and makes it impossible to push the button, thus starting the Doomsday scenario ("Live Together, Die Alone," 2.24).

Only when Desmond seemingly sacrifices himself to save the island by using the fail-safe device that only he knows about does Locke understand that the button really needs to be pushed. Locke's faith has been restored.

Locke has a need to be proven right, to know the answers to all his questions. His faith often is conditional—he needs to see the proof to justify his emotional investment in believing something. Actor Terry O'Quinn, who plays Locke, reportedly held discussions with Cuse and Lindelof about the direction his character should take in Season Three. O'Quinn was unhappy with the Locke who pushes the button, drinks a lot of coffee, and sits around the Hatch.[5] Locke is complacent in his faith-based approach to life when things are going well. As a result, he becomes boring and predictable.

He also returns to his pre-island need for anger management

sessions. Locke-of-the-Hatch is "interesting" only when he becomes agitated as the pawn between Jack and Henry Gale; he angrily swipes his arm across a countertop, scattering objects in the wake of his frustration. Finally he decides to force the Doomsday scenario to prove that the button doesn't need to be pushed for the island to remain safe. However, when Locke questions his faith or is motivated by it to actions deemed rather questionable by the other castaways, he becomes a much more interesting character to watch and, presumably, to play. Locke-of-the-jungle is a dynamic, unpredictable character who makes events happen instead of watching events happening around him.

Now that his faith has been tested several times and he has once relied on scientific proof instead of faith regarding the Hatch, a humbled Locke once again believes in the island and the signs it sends him. "Further Instructions" (3.3) is another apt episode title; in this episode, Locke receives his next instructions not from a returning Hurley with information from the Others, nor from any other castaway. Locke turns straight to the island.

Instead of waiting for a sign, Locke becomes proactive by seeking guidance and forgiveness for his reliance on science instead of the island. Locke builds a sweat lodge to purify himself and seek inspiration, although he's not sure what he'll receive. In a reversal of their previous roles a few months earlier, spirit guide Boone returns from death to make Locke figure out what he needs to do next. Although Boone seems to be forgiving and pushes wheelchair-bound Locke through much of his vision/dream, he also forces Locke to drag himself up an escalator before he receives his instruction: Find and help Eko.

When Locke accomplishes this mission—after fighting off a polar bear, no less—the next message from the island comes through an apparently unconscious Eko. For a few moments, Eko talks to him and presents him with his next challenge: Free Jack, Kate, and Sawyer from the Others. This action will bring together

Locke's "family," which Boone earlier says needs to be drawn together once more. Locke accepts this mission with the same fervor that he searched for Eko.

Once Locke again receives instructions from the island, he can act confidently and forcefully. His faith in the island has been restored not only because he realizes his own shortsightedness in the "Hatch incident," but also because the island provides him with instant gratification this time. In contrast to his directive to open the Hatch and push the button, rather time-consuming events, Locke successfully rescues Eko less than a day after receiving this mission from a sweat lodge encounter with Boone. Although the rescue of his other friends should take longer, a cheerful Locke announces to the castaways on the beach that he'll bring their friends "home."

Locke's "home" and "family" provide a distinct contrast to Ben Linus's. Henry Gale/Ben and Ethan also use these words to describe the Others; Ben tells Hurley that his friends are coming home with the Others ("Live Together, Die Alone," 2.24); Ethan explains that Claire's baby will be reared by a good family ("Maternity Leave," 2.15). Like other aspects of the man of science–man of faith contrast, Locke likens "family" and "home" to a benevolent commune, where friends share in the bounties of nature and interact spiritually with it; his Season Three backstory in "Further Instructions" (3.3) provides a model on which to base his island home life. Locke seems to be a good candidate for leading a participative, socialist community.

The Others' home is based on the (to most of us) traditional realm of science and technology. Not only do the Others own and use more technology, but they show a Big Brotherly love for monitoring everyone's behavior. They seem to prefer a highly structured, almost dictatorial society with well-defined levels of command. In this environment, perhaps it isn't so strange to see how "good people" may need to show "sinners" the error of their ways.

With Locke's certainty in his destiny once again, he may be

able to establish a society very different from the Others', or even the one Jack once led. Each leader and little society likely would claim that theirs truly is the "good" one.

A faithful Locke, especially one who basks in the island's good graces, is an effective man who becomes focused on his mission. His faith, bolstered with information from his deity, provides him with purpose and gives meaning to his life.

"Faithful" versus "Logical" Interpretations of Important Events

Lost presents interesting scenarios that intertwine characters' interpretations of one event. Initially interpreting events as divine intervention, characters may change their interpretation when they later uncover more mundane explanations. Which interpretation is correct, however, is left up to each character, and to us in the audience.

In Season One, Locke pounds in frustration against the Hatch's window and asks why his faith hasn't been rewarded ("Deus ex Machina," 1.19). Seemingly in response, a light in the Hatch comes on. Locke takes this as a spiritual sign, and it motivates him to continue the quest to open the Hatch. This answer to his question also makes him believe later in the importance of pushing the button—the Hatch, to him, is almost a sacred space, and his destiny is to open it and do what is required of him there.

In a Season Two revelation, we learn that Desmond had been at the point of committing suicide one evening because he is all alone on the island and faces a bleak existence of pushing the button for the rest of his life. Before he can kill himself, he hears knocking somewhere in the Hatch. When he investigates, he turns on a light ("Live Together, Die Alone," 2.24)—the light that Locke sees. Desmond doesn't yet know that Locke is going to be able to enter the Hatch, or even that someone else is on the island. He believes that some higher power saves him from suicide, but it turns out that Locke has been pounding on the window.

Locke initially believes that the Hatch is his reward for following a higher power, but he becomes disillusioned when there seems to be a logical/scientific explanation to the Hatch's mystery. Pushing the button is part of an experiment, or so Locke interprets the (Pearl) observation hatch and its monitoring of activity in "his" Hatch (the Swan).

In his version of an experiment, Locke attempts to prove that pushing the button isn't necessary, but Desmond knows from prior experience that, indeed, the island will be torn apart by electromagnetic forces. Button pushing is one means of establishing equilibrium, but if the button isn't pushed in time, there's another way, one only Desmond knows.

We can play the "What if?" game to analyze the interlocking actions of Locke and Desmond. (Of course, Jack, Henry Gale, Mr. Eko, and even Kelvin also are factors in the "What ifs." To simplify the analysis, however, only Locke and Desmond are considered.) If Locke hadn't knocked on the Hatch, Desmond would have committed suicide. Without Desmond's knowledge and decision to sacrifice himself, if necessary, to operate the failsafe, everyone on the island would have been killed when the button wasn't pushed. But if Desmond hadn't flipped the light switch, Locke might not have opened the Hatch and learned about the button. Eventually Desmond would have died, and no one would have been around to push the button or operate the fail-safe.

If Desmond or Locke hadn't interpreted their experiences as spiritual responses to their individual crises, they might have acted very differently. Locke might have decided to abandon button pushing much earlier, long before Desmond returned. (If Jack had been in charge of button pushing first, the activity likely would have stopped soon after Desmond left; Jack doesn't believe that the button has anything to do with a Doomsday scenario.) Even when the electromagnetic storm was building, Desmond might have decided that he might as well end his life now, instead of holding onto the newly discovered possibility that his and Penny Widmore's love will conquer all.

So how should we interpret these events, especially when given more information about what happened that night at the Hatch? What made the separate actions of these two characters come together in a meaningful way, with such long-ranging consequences? Is it fate? destiny? serendipity? coincidence? divine intervention? random action? logical cause(s) and effect(s)? To what should we, or Locke or Desmond, attribute this series of actions? For example, we could conclude that Locke's or Desmond's acts are mundane—who wouldn't turn on a light to help illuminate the unexpected source of a noise? Are we giving too much emphasis to an everyday act? Or is Providence at work here? How we interpret this sequence of actions and whether we give spiritual meaning to it may determine how we'll look for meaning in future scenes.

Hindsight and multiple viewings can influence our interpretation of what's happening on the island. Locke and Desmond interpret the significance of their experiences on the fly—they, like real people just living their lives, don't have our luxury of analyzing every on-screen moment and replaying scenes showing different characters' perspectives. For them, the "logical" or "spiritual" meaning of an immediate event carries more weight.

For example, if Desmond occasionally heard weird knocks around the Hatch and routinely turned on lights to look for problems, he might not even recall the night that Locke knocked on the window. But the night we've seen replayed from different perspectives is the night that Desmond almost killed himself but was distracted—probably not a common experience in his life. Desmond then attributes more meaning to this night and the event that dissuaded him from suicide. Some characters, more so than the audience, may find spiritual meaning initially in certain acts or events; by watching characters' reactions to and interpretations of events, the more skeptical in the audience may be persuaded to look at scenes in a new way when characters become convinced of the intervention of a higher power into their lives.

Lost is good at presenting these types of situations that make both characters and viewers question how events should be interpreted. They provide discussion topics for countless fan forums and have even led to sermons in churches across the United States. In an age in which spiritual issues are often hot political and social topics, *Lost*'s storytelling touches a national (even international) nerve. Are the characters' actions predestined, and if so, what does that say about science or faith? Are some things unable to be explained—ever, and some mysteries never to be revealed? Can everything be explained purely by science, or is faith a necessary component of island—and modern—living? Perhaps most important, does there need to be one type of answer, based solely on faith or science?

This is the beauty of *Lost*. One scene or event can be interpreted many ways, and, according to the series' creators and writers, there isn't only one correct interpretation. Thus, the characters—and we in the audience—must rely on our own belief systems to determine whether reason or faith, chance, or a divine being, is the prime mover behind the event. *Lost* makes us, as well as the characters, confront and reaffirm the reasons we believe in science or have faith. But the middle ground—that both science and faith are necessary for a full life—is something that society, either on or off the island, is slow to grasp. When Locke wavers between absolute faith in the island and his need for proof that this faith is justified, we see the battle between faith and science within Locke's dilemma in reconciling these extremes.

Lost successfully blurs divisions between faith and science and forces us to decide for ourselves what's at work on the island and how mysteries are best acknowledged. We only know from what Lindelof and Cuse have said that "life themes" such as the battle between faith and science are consciously added to plot and character development. This battle undoubtedly will continue to be waged throughout the series.

GOOD VS. EVIL

Many religions teach that the basic struggle is between good and evil. Hints that such a larger battle may be shaping up on the island begin in "Man of Science, Man of Faith" (2.1). New character Desmond helps Jack when, in a precrash flashback, he injures his ankle as both men run the steps in a stadium. From their conversation we learn Desmond is training for a world race, almost became a doctor, and likely has a spiritual bent. He tells Jack to "lift it up," a double meaning to elevate the injured ankle and to pray for a miracle for accident-victim Sarah. "What would you do if a miracle were possible?" Desmond asks Jack.

Whereas Desmond is more ambiguously good in this first episode, he becomes a sympathetic character in the Season Two finale. According to the cliffhanger, he (seemingly) sacrifices himself by operating the fail-safe in the middle of an electromagnetic storm. However, in true *Lost* fashion, Desmond may not be a completely good or bad character. His later actions may redeem him from previous misdeeds, including a stint in prison and the manslaughter of Kelvin ("Live Together, Die Alone," 2.23–24).

Desmond helps Locke open the Pandora's Box—the castaways' mystery of the Hatch. Although it provides benefits to the survivors' new little world, it also unleashes a host of ills. The benefits are many—food, shelter, medicine, tools, and weapons; luxuries such as a washer, dryer, shower, record player, exercise bike, books, and a film projector are bonuses. However, the Hatch also supplies Knowledge, a valuable but potentially terrifying commodity. It provides more (and sinister) clues about what's happening on the island. It introduces the need to push the button, an act that Locke later terms enslavement ("Live Together, Die Alone," 2.23). Perhaps ignorance is truly blissful—the castaways' pre-Hatch life is relatively less complex, and they didn't realize quite to what extent they might be manipulated.

Pandora's Box once provided the inquisitive Pandora with more knowledge of evil now set free in the world, but hope also

was found in the box. Not so surprisingly, even before he opens
the Hatch, Locke tells Hurley that he believes hope will be found
within it ("Exodus," 1.23).

Modern-Pandora Locke opens the Hatch and unleashes fuel
for petty arguments and discontent among the castaways (e.g.,
having to go to work as button pushers, fighting over food parachuted nearby, setting and resetting the combination lock to the
arsenal, deciding who has access to the luxuries). Locke and Eko
together also unleash more knowledge into their society (with the
discovery of the Pearl hatch in "?" 2.21), which causes Locke to
question his purpose in life, Eko to discover his purpose, and Jack
to battle Locke over the direction their society should take, for
example. Like Pandora, the castaways can't now return to a more
peaceful life ignorant of the darker side of the island.

Perhaps a religious metaphor works as well as the analogy of
the mythical Pandora's Box. During Season Two, the castaways
sample the fruit of their garden paradise, and their eyes are
opened to other people and their agendas. They realize they're
not alone and must deal with a larger world than their little beach
encampment. The castaways of Oceanic 815 survive another
"fall" in their tropical Garden of Eden.

A more sinister presence than Desmond, who, innocently or
not, introduces Locke to the intricacies of the Hatch, is Henry
Gale, or "fake" Henry Gale, as fans call him. [The real Gale lies
buried beneath the tree that snagged his hot-air balloon ("The
Whole Truth," 2.16).] Gale insists that the Others are the good
people, but the castaways' experiences make them seriously question that statement. During Season Three, even as the Others
interrogate the captured Jack, Kate, and Sawyer, our assessment
of them may change. After all, our favorite castaways have a lot of
sins among them—adultery, murder, theft, gluttony, and so on—
let's face it, they easily illustrate the Seven Deadly Sins. Are the
Others worse than that? Although pitted as opposites of the castaways, they are being shown as somewhere between the great evil

perceived by the castaways and Rousseau and the great good proclaimed by the Others themselves.

Spirituality is indeed an active force on the island, and as the
series progresses, the castaways' belief systems will be tested.
Whether they follow the tenets of a specific religion or blend
concepts from the beliefs of those around them is yet to be seen.
As more characters look for spiritual responses to the island's
challenges, even more examples of spiritual or explicitly religious
symbolism are likely to make their way into *Lost*'s multiple layers
of meaning.

What's in a Name?

Names are often symbolic on *Lost*. Damon Lindelof conceded
that "[e]very single name . . . has purpose and meaning."[6] Some
names are more whimsical than others—Pace, for example, might
help remind Charlie to stop veering from one emotional extreme
to another and to pace himself. But other names, especially those
with philosophical or spiritual resonances, hint at more significant aspects of the characters' roles or personalities. (Other interesting coincidences with names are listed in Appendix C.)

Jack and Christian Shephard

The writers' clues about characters point to Jack Shephard as the
hero of *Lost*. "[Jack Shephard] is the de facto leader of the island's
society, thus his appropriate surname is . . . one who tends the
flock."[7] Jack acts as a savior from the moment we see him open
his eyes on the island. During the first fifteen minutes of the pilot
episode (1.1), he frantically runs from crisis to crisis, directing the
physical salvation of many people. Seemingly capable of saving
everyone, almost by himself, he only delegates tasks once he
averts danger or solves a problem. Jack, often dubbed the show's
"moral center," grows into his job as the survivors' leader.
However, as Matthew Fox has explained, Jack becomes more
human and less like a savior as the first season progresses and his

beliefs come into question. According to Fox, Jack "is not always going to be good. He is going to be tested to go into very deep-gray areas." In the real world, a leader's morality or judgment is sometimes called into question, and the concept of a leader as a model of virtue is outdated. Jack seems more flawed, and thus more real, as he begins to deal with these gray areas.

Surprisingly, moral-center Jack professes no religion and is labeled a "man of science" by Locke, a self-described "man of faith," during the first season's finale ("Exodus," 1.23–24). At times Jack reverts to some earlier religious training, but he keeps his spiritual beliefs, whatever they may be, to himself. He explains to Claire that he doesn't feel comfortable leading the memorial service for the numerous dead ("Walkabout," 1.4). Although he allows that others may need a religious context for the deed, he isn't one of them. His need to make scientific, logical meaning out of island experiences, to analytically assess the information he receives, makes him the opposite of Locke.

Jack's need for facts before he commits to action may make him a prime recruit for the Others. As a doctor and now an island leader, this Shephard's valuable skills and analytical personality indicate that he might be a highly anticipated new "family" member for the Others ("Live Together, Die Alone," 2.24). His ability to perform spinal surgery on Ben certainly is a worthwhile reason to "recruit" him, but as early Season Three episodes show, Jack can be as manipulative and calculating as any Other "man of science."

Jack's father is even named Christian, an ironic choice considering that his professional life as a workaholic and eventual life as an alcoholic seem far removed from a religious role model. However, Christian Shephard often acts as a father-advisor to those who cross his path, not only son Jack, but Ana Lucia and Sawyer. Christian may even have taken his role as father further than we originally know, for Claire may be his daughter ("Two for the Road," 2.20). For a character who lives on screen only through backstories, Christian Shephard influences many. (Could

J. J. Abrams be playing "six degrees of Christian Shephard"? In September 2006 Abrams's series *Six Degrees* debuted. In a strange twist, perhaps every *Lost* character will end up having a tangential relationship to Jack's father.)

Lost's writers carefully select names for each character, which provides hours of fan speculation about the exact meaning of each new character's name. Even a brief comment about "Jacob's list" ("I Do," 3.6) prompts fans to search the biblical and linguistic sources of Jacob to learn more about a character who, as far as we know, hasn't even received screen time. By choosing significant names, the series' creators and writers add another layer of meaning to *Lost* and help us see connections among characters.

THE PHILOSOPHERS—JOHN LOCKE, ROUSSEAU, AND (DESMOND) DAVID HUME

The castaways' other (first-season) leader is John Locke, the name of a prominent British philosopher (1632–1704) who argued that the origin of faith is not in reason but in extraordinary communication—such as a spiritual revelation. Some things cannot be empirically proven; they cannot be known as fact. Those areas of knowledge are not based on experience but can be based on revelation. People have faith that this knowledge is correct, even though they cannot prove it by experience.[8] (An interesting choice of title for a "recap" episode is "*Lost:* Revelation," shown in early January 2006 right before the U.S. debut of "The 23rd Psalm" after a long hiatus. Perhaps *Lost*'s creators want us to believe in the series, no matter how farfetched some story arcs might seem.)

As the first season progresses, the island's John Locke increasingly relies on revelation. In "Deus Ex Machina" (1.19), he follows the symbols and information provided in a dream/vision to guide him in his next actions. He tells Boone that the island will provide him with the knowledge he needs. After Boone's death ("Do No Harm," 1.20), he visits the Hatch to beseech the island about his lack of understanding. He has clearly done the island's bidding but is unsure why Boone needed to die. His momentary lack of confidence is restored when a light shines from the Hatch's window. This moment of revelation seems to fuel his enthusiasm for opening the Hatch and uncovering the hope he is sure is contained within ("Exodus," 1.24).

Locke seems much more interested than Jack in exploring the Hatch ("Man of Science, Man of Faith," 2.1). He wants to uncover the mystery by going inside the Hatch. After only a few days, he lives comfortably in the Hatch and seems to have taken Desmond's place in charge of button pushing.

For all practical purposes, Locke becomes the Dharma Initiative's recruiter for maintaining Station Three. He often tells the survivors about his schedule for pushing the button. In "Orientation" (2.3), he tells Jack that he will set up a schedule. In "Everybody Hates Hugo" (2.4), he entices Charlie with promises of music in the Hatch and reminds Hurley that he has a job to do, whether he likes it or not. During "What Kate Did" (2.9), Locke explains the schedule to Michael and Mr. Eko and sips a cup of coffee and sets up the orientation film so they can learn about the Dharma Initiative.

Eventually, Eko will help Locke reconnect his spiritual, or island-given, connection. He provides not only a missing segment from the orientation film but also an Old Testament story to compare the King of Judah's actions and motivations for rebuilding the temple at Jerusalem with the castaways' recent events and possible "rebuilding" of Station Three ("What Kate Did," 2.9). His response to the second orientation video in the Pearl hatch eventually points Locke back toward a more spiritual interpretation of events in the hatches and on the island ("?" 2.21). "Revelation" truly is a keyword for philosopher John Locke and *Lost*'s Locke, and early Season Three episodes provide yet more revelations.

Danielle Rousseau shares a surname with Jean-Jacques Rousseau (1712–1778), and the two seem to share an appreciation for the "noble savage" who lives well outside modern society or governmental rule.^{9} However, there is less of a philosophical connection between the two Rousseaus than between the Lockes, or between Desmond David Hume and philosopher David Hume.

The Scottish philosopher David Hume (1711–1776) theorized about reason and discussed the moral implications of an individual's reactions to others. The relationship between an individual and other people is especially interesting to study if the individual has no real connection to them. For example, if someone sees a speeding car approach a stranger crossing the street, will he or she try to push the stranger out of the way, shout a warning, watch the accident take place, turn away, or react in another way? Hume believed that a moral person would help strangers, even if by doing so that person wouldn't benefit from providing aid. The help would be given simply because it's the "right" or moral way to behave.^{10}

In the last scenes of the Season Two finale, in true cliff-hanger fashion, Desmond decides to operate the fail-safe, an act that likely will cause his death ("Live Together, Die Alone," 2.24). Although he knows many of the castaways from his few interactions with them in the Hatch and on the beach, they aren't his closest friends. Still, he decides to sacrifice himself, if necessary, to keep the island from being torn apart.

Aside from being an interesting experiment to test Hume's philosophy, Desmond shares a few other similarities with this philosopher. Most superficially, both are Scottish. They enjoy reading the classics of their age; Desmond, in particular, values the works of Charles Dickens (a connection that is continued with the title of the Season Three opener, "A Tale of Two Cities"). They are both influenced by John Locke—Hume by the philosopher Locke, Desmond by his fellow Hatch dweller.

Characters who share names with philosophers don't have to share their philosophies, but Locke, Rousseau, and Hume provide fan-scholars with additional insights into the possible spiritual and philosophical makeup of *Lost* characters.

Literary Characters (Penelope and Henry Gale)

Literature as well as philosophy is fertile ground for *Lost*'s writers. Whereas Sawyer might have no discernible link to Tom of the same surname, Henry Gale and Penelope Widmore bear more resemblance to the characters who share (at least part of) their name.

Dorothy Gale's Uncle Henry is best remembered from the 1939 movie version of *The Wizard of Oz*, a shortened version of the many *Oz* books written by L. Frank Baum in turn-of-the-20th-century United States.[11] During this period in U.S. history, the rural farms began to lose ground to urban industrialization. On *Lost*, the dichotomy between rural island life on the beach and in the Others' (probably sham) ramshackle buildings contrast with the technology available in the series of hatches. The tension between nature and technology is an important background for both *The Wizard of Oz* and *Lost*, and Henry Gale figures as a key background player in each.

Dorothy's Uncle Henry is a hardworking Kansas farmer devoted to his family. Although not the smartest man in Kansas, he is a good-hearted man and the head of his family. The "fake" Henry Gale is much craftier than his Kansas "ancestor"; in fact, he acts much more like the mysterious eponymous Wizard of Oz himself, who conceals his true identity and directs others on quests or missions. Gale's last on-screen act during Season Two is to send Hurley on a mission—to tell the beached castaways to stay away from the Others ("Live Together, Die Alone," 2.24). His mission for Jack, Kate, and Sawyer is revealed during the third season. Gale, who leads his "family" of Others, believes they "are the good guys," as he tells Michael ("Live Together, Die Alone," 2.24).

There's even a hot-air balloon in both stories, just to seal the connection. However, it's unlikely that island-dweller Gale needs to resort to a balloon to make his way back home; Gale tells Michael how to return home, and unless he lies or conceals the true path home, this "wizard" also knows how to get back to Kansas.

As with Ethan Rom, whose name is an anagram for "Other Man," "Henry Gale [from] Minnesota" becomes an anagram for "See an Other Man Lying."[12] A "cult" leader who lies to his "family" and outsiders isn't a new character, but this inclusion calls into question just how far a leader who devoutly and unswervingly believes in a cause will go in the name of "the greater good."

Penelope in Homer's *The Odyssey* also is well known for her faithfulness to the wandering sailor Odysseus. Despite their separation of many years, during which Odysseus's journey is prolonged many times, Penelope waits for her husband. She cleverly avoids suitors who think Odysseus long gone. Desmond's Penelope seems equally faithful, and she has at least one other suitor. However, Penelope waits for Desmond and has promised to continue to do so for however long it takes for them to be reunited.

These secular stories are well known to many readers, moviegoers, and TV audiences. They've taken on epic proportions and achieved mythic status, as have the depictions of many religious stories shared across media worldwide. However, they also can symbolize some important spiritual principles. Uncle Henry and Penelope are steadfast in what they do—Gale as a farmer and doting uncle, Penelope as a loving wife. *Lost*'s Henry Gale clearly believes in his mission or duty to do what's right and is steadfast in his beliefs. To date, he is the only character who seems to know how to get off the island; he can point the way to the true path home. Penny Widmore's love takes on a spiritual dimension when she reminds Desmond that it can sustain him through anything and is eternal. In choosing literary allusions, *Lost*'s creators and writers blend popular literary characters with more philosophical or spiritual dimensions to their portrayals.

BIBLICAL NAMES (ISAAC, DANIEL, AND AARON)

Lost also uses the Christian Bible as a source for other symbolic names. Of course, many popular given names in Western countries have biblical origins: Michael, John, and James, for starters. *Lost's* Michael Dawson, John Locke, John/Jack Shephard, and James Ford (Sawyer) may not stem from biblical names as much as other sources. However, less popular U.S. choices of names that have biblical origins may offer insights into their characters' purpose.

Isaac, although a minor character in a backstory ("S.O.S.," 2.19), plays an important role in that episode. In the Bible, Isaac is the beloved son of Abraham who helps prove his father's obedience to God. In a rough comparison, *Lost's* Isaac does the same for Rose, who contracts a terminal illness but is still faithful to God. She accepts the diagnosis and is at peace. Healer Isaac can't cure Rose, but his comment that the particular magnetic forces in his region of Australia won't work for her hints that magnetic forces elsewhere might heal Rose ("S.O.S.," 2.19). Both Isaacs seem to be favored by God as spiritual messengers to others.

Daniel and its variations become popular names throughout the series; Danielle Rousseau is the important first "new" person the castaways encounter fairly early in the series. Although "Rousseau" seems to be the more important name, her first name still counts as a variation of Daniel. As a man's name, Daniel is featured more prominently early in Season Three, although it comes up conversationally during Season Two (e.g., Ana Lucia's partner Danny is mentioned in "Collision," 2.8). One of the Others, Danny Pickett, also is referenced by name a few times in the first six episodes of Season Three. However, the Biblical connotation becomes more pronounced when a young altar boy, Daniel, questions whether Eko is a good or a bad man ("The Cost of Living," 3.5). Although the "priest's" actions initially indicate that he's good, Daniel later determines that Eko's actions mark him as a bad man. In the Bible, Daniel finds himself caught in the lion's den; Nigerian Daniel is trapped between Priest Eko and the drug lords who threaten the church.

Claire's baby Aaron may eventually lead "his people" (i.e., the surviving castaways) out of the wilderness, just as Moses's brother-in-law led the Israelites during their exodus. Although Claire chooses "Aaron" simply because she likes the name, she later discusses the name's significance with Mr. Eko ("Fire + Water," 2.12). Fans speculate that this choice may have greater significance later in the series. When grown, Aaron may be a pivotal character. However, that may not occur for many seasons to come.

Names, whether secular or religious in origin, illustrate the wide range of spirituality on *Lost* and help us connect what we know about characters from other sources with what we learn about the lost souls on the island. The similarities and analogies provide us with the writers' clues about each character's life path.

DEALING WITH DEATH

One major role of spirituality has always been to help people deal with death. On *Lost*, as in life, there are many different reactions to death.

As noted earlier, Jack seems to believe his purpose in life is to save everyone. When he loses a patient, he takes it personally and has difficulty dealing with the finality of death. Jack lacks words at Boone's funeral, and Sayid steps forward to honor Boone when Jack and Shannon say nothing ("Exodus," 1.23). Jack does slightly better at Shannon's funeral ("Collision," 2.8) when Sayid is unable to continue the eulogy and leaves the gravesite. Jack doesn't speak, but he begins the ritual of placing a handful of earth into the grave. Reluctant Jack says a few words over Ana Lucia ("Live Together, Die Alone," 2.23); he accepts that task as part of his role as leader. Jack understands the significance of burial rites and gradually takes on a greater role as the number of fatalities rises. Nevertheless, dealing with funerals, including his father's planned interment, seems difficult for Jack, who as a healer wants to save his patients. He defies death frequently, and acknowledging its victory is something he is loath to do, even from a spiritual standpoint.

However, Jack takes complete charge of one burial. When the marshal dies, Jack calls on some type of religious upbringing to bury the man and mark the grave with a cross, the most important Christian symbol. (In "Whatever the Case May Be," 1.12, Jack tells Kate he buried the marshal.) He probably feels guilt at the marshal's death—not only is he unable to save the man from his injuries, but he apparently euthanizes him after Sawyer's botched attempt to end his suffering. Perhaps providing a Christian burial is the only way Jack can atone for the man's untimely death.

In a similar way, Charlie seems obligated to bury Ethan, the "monster" he gladly shoots multiple times in "Homecoming" (1.15). He feels no moral dilemma over killing Ethan, but he nevertheless takes responsibility for burying his enemy. Hurley humorously questions whether monstrous Ethan, just like the undead in horror movies, will rise from the grave to chase them. Charlie, however, does not respond to such humor. Perhaps if he keeps telling himself Ethan's death is necessary, he can keep at bay any spiritual guilt from committing murder. Perhaps he merely wants to make sure Ethan is dead and gone—out of sight forever. Whatever his motives, Charlie ensures Ethan gets a proper burial when he simply could have dumped the body elsewhere.

As the series continues, most likely the cemetery by the sea will grow. The crosses marking the graves of Joanna, Boone, and Shannon are a touchstone image for several Season Two episodes. Before Shannon searches for Walt, she sits beside Boone's grave ("Abandoned," 2.6). When, after seeing ghosts and receiving messages from the dead, Kate questions her sanity, she is sitting at the edge of the cemetery ("What Kate Did," 2.9). Questioning the reality of images of the dead (such as ghosts or spirits) or seeking some solace by remembering the dead is becoming the focal point of scenes set in the cemetery. The ritual of burying the dead and honoring them with crosses seems to have a significant spiritual impact on the surviving castaways.

This ritual gains momentum in the second season, with the double funeral of Libby and Ana Lucia. Funerals sadly become a gathering place for most castaways, a gruesome social event that pulls the majority of survivors together. The combined funerals of the two young women make Claire aware of her mortality, and she impulsively reaches for Charlie's hand during the brief ceremony. The solidity of a surviving friend comforts her ("Live Together, Die Alone" 2.23).

Surprisingly, priest Eko declines to attend Ana Lucia's and Libby's funerals, although he knew both women well and was especially close to Ana Lucia. She even tells him of her death when she appears in Eko's dream, long before anyone else notifies him ("?" 2.21). Although he prepares Ana Lucia's body for burial and prays over her, his job in the Hatch is more important than attending funerals. A higher spiritual calling for the living takes precedence over rites for the dead. Eko lets the other castaways perform that task, even though he acknowledges that he will mourn his friends.

Locke hears Eko's last words, gently closes his eyes ("The Cost of Living," 3.5), helps to bury him, and gives a heartfelt eulogy ("I Do," 3.6). Locke alone takes charge of the ceremony and determines that Eko should be buried in the jungle, rather than the "family" cemetery near the beach. He explains that another death might be upsetting to the other castaways. Although Locke's demeanor suggests that he wants to give Eko a proper burial, his choice to isolate the grave of a man who touched so many lives in his final days seems odd. All castaways must deal with Eko's death, sooner or later; hiding the grave in the jungle only postpones what must take place.

Perhaps Locke somehow feels differently about Eko's death than he does about those of other castaways and therefore is compelled to bury Eko in the jungle. Jack buries the marshal in a different location than the "family" cemetery later established on the island; the marshal is thus forever isolated as an "outsider" from those who die shortly thereafter and from the mass cremation of those killed in the plane crash. Charlie also buries Ethan in a grave far away from those of his friends. In the same way, Locke chooses to bury Eko separately instead of bringing the body back to the castaways' camp.

Whether feeling some responsibility in the death of another man and burying him outside the community cemetery is significant in *Lost*'s master plan (e.g., all those buried outside the community cemetery are "bad" in some way), this action is yet another common experience that connects Locke, Charlie, and Jack.

The Others have their own type of funeral—one resembling the pyres set adrift in Viking or even King Arthur movies. The ritual of placing the body on a raft, setting it aflame, and then watching it drift away as it burns definitely isn't a Christian ritual, but it seems one with which the Others are familiar. The mourners dress in white, perceived as a color of purity in many Western cultures but as a color of death in many Eastern ones ("The Cost of Living," 3.5). The music is definitely Western; Brenda Lee's "I Wonder" plays as the pyre is launched. Everyone seems to participate in the solemn ceremony, gathering by the water to see Colleen off. Like Locke, the Others may combine symbols and rituals from many religions to form their own traditions.

Facing the reality of loss, including death, how do *Lost*'s characters deal with impending doom? Those with strong religious beliefs have faith that they will have what they need to survive. However, some characters without such a foundation feel overwhelmed when a crisis occurs.

Self-centered Shannon denies that she may not be rescued soon and relies on old patterns of behavior to manipulate others into helping her. After a few weeks, however, she develops more independence and self-esteem as she translates Rousseau's notes from French ("Whatever the Case May Be," 1.12) and builds her own shelter ("In Translation," 1.17). As she spends more time with Sayid, she reveals she can take care of herself. But she also falls in love. This positive progression into self-reliance and openness with others abruptly ends, however, with Boone's death. She deals with this loss by returning to her manipulative ways. When Locke asks her forgiveness for his part in Boone's death,

Shannon ignores him. After Sayid refuses to kill Locke for her, she takes matters (and a gun) into her hands as she attempts to kill Locke herself ("The Greater Good," 1.21). Instead, the bullet only grazes him, and Shannon becomes angry and isolated for a few episodes. Her ability to deal with loss is devoid of a spiritual context; she tries to solve problems herself, and when that does not work as she wants, she becomes bitter.

In "Exodus" (1.24), Shannon seems genuinely concerned for Sayid's welfare and relieved by his safe return after a confrontation with Rousseau; she thinks of another instead of herself. At times, however, she still seems overwhelmed by grief. As the castaways retreat to the caves to hide from the Others, she struggles to haul Boone's as well as her own belongings. Sobbing, she tells Sayid she needs Boone's clothes, her only link to her brother. In agreeing to help her carry her spiritual as well as physical baggage, Sayid helps her heal, a process she seems incapable of beginning alone.

Walt also facilitates this healing by giving Vincent to Shannon before he leaves on the raft. During Season Two, Shannon takes more responsibility for Vincent, who helps her focus on something beyond herself. Vincent also guides her toward "visions" of Walt, but these visions ironically lead to both her redemption and her death. Although she never looks to formal religion for guidance, she allows her unexplained "mystical" visions to guide her during the last days of her life ("Abandoned," 2.6; "Collision," 2.8).

Sawyer is also self-absorbed and often finds enjoyment in tormenting other survivors. On their first night on the island, he runs into Jack as they search the fuselage (including deceased passengers and storage bins) for salvageable materials ("Tabula Rasa," 1.3). Jack looks for alcohol, medicines, and tools that might be useful to treat the survivors; Sawyer gathers whatever will make his life easier or may be useful in trade. During the first season, his stash of goodies almost becomes a running joke; whatever is needed can be found within his makeshift tent. The con man justifies his actions by reminding Jack they are far from civilization and truly "in the wild." Without human-made laws, each castaway theoretically can do whatever he or she chooses without consequence. Whereas Jack tells Kate each person has a clean start on the island ("Tabula Rasa," 1.3), Sawyer takes that message to mean "each person for himself" at whatever cost to the rest of the castaways. He remakes himself as the rich man who owns the few remaining luxuries and is thus more powerful.

Sawyer mellows over time, but he usually follows his own rules and cares little about anyone else, except as they affect what he does. His prime objective in his precrash life had been to murder the man he blames for destroying his family; on the island he lacks even that purpose for his life. He may suffer somewhat for being perceived as an outsider who only occasionally helps others, but he doesn't seek redemption. Occasionally he is magnanimous, as when he finally tells Jack about an encounter with his father in a bar in Sydney ("Exodus," 1.23). Jack has long awaited the validation the story of a father's pride in his son provides, and the fact it comes from Sawyer, who typically keeps such information to himself, presents a redemptive moment for the con man. Nevertheless, later in the same episode, Sawyer assures Michael that he is "no hero." He seems content to rely on himself and disregard any spiritual, as well as many human, laws.

Yet he is capable of compassion, even at his own expense. As Libby lies dying, Jack knows he lacks the technology to repair damage from the gunshot or even strong enough medicine to ease her passing. There is nothing he can do but watch her in agony, a deathwatch shared by Hurley. Jack asks Sawyer for the heroin he stole from the Hatch. Sawyer realizes that he'll lose his wealth if he returns the heroin; someone will learn his hiding place for guns as well as the drugs. Nevertheless, he gives the drug to Jack so that Libby's death is easier for her, and for Hurley to watch ("?" 2.21).

This subtle softening doesn't last long. Sawyer soon joins Kate in killing two Others who trail Michael and company on their trek to bring Walt home ("Live Together, Die Alone," 2.23). He shows no remorse in killing those perceived as enemies, but he seems more susceptible to grief when he knows or likes the person who dies, such as Libby or Ana Lucia. He doesn't turn to spirituality during hard times, but he occasionally reveals a more compassionate or moral side. He is capable of feeling gentler emotions, but his past experiences have taught him to rely on no one but himself. Sawyer can't trust God because he's never learned to trust anyone else.

During Season Three, living in a cage under constant threat of death, Sawyer finally shows just how much he loves Kate: he would die for her. He tries to give her hope even when they face bleak conditions with no real possibility of escape. He may even trust as well as love Kate, although they both are commitment-shy. Loving Kate may not redeem Sawyer, but it allows him to open his life in a more positive, life-affirming way ("I Do," 3.6).

* * *

Traditional expressions of religious belief provide solace to the faithful, but the castaways on *Lost* without a belief system often are shown having difficulty dealing with crises or shifting back and forth between emotional extremes. Belief in a higher power doesn't seem to protect anyone on the island, but those with a solid spiritual foundation are portrayed as less "lost" and more likely to emotionally survive the island's challenges. Redemption is a possibility for those who seek it, but it isn't easy. Inner peace dearly costs those who want to be "found."

NOTES TO CHAPTER FOUR, "SPIRITUAL PRACTICES ON THE ISLAND"

1. Snierson, "Spotlight: Elizabeth Mitchell," 28.

2. Terry, "Second Sight," 34.

3. Poniewozik, "Welcome to His Unreality," 61.

4. Jensen, "War of the Worlds," 35.

5. Todd Gilchrist, "Interview: Terry O'Quinn," Retrieved November 30, 2006, from http://dvd.ign.com/articles/728/728420p1.html.

6. Matthew Gilbert, "The Games People Play with Names," *Boston Globe*, February 10, 2005. Retrieved February 16, 2007, from http://www.boston.com/ae/tv/articles/2005/02/10/the_games_peo ple_play_with_names?pg=full.

7. Hatty, "Matthew's Moral Center," 9.

8. Several books provide biographies of Locke, including Maurice Cranston's *John Locke: A Biography* (London: Longmans, 1959), Nicholas Wolterstorff's *John Locke and the Ethics of Belief* (New York: Cambridge University Press, 1996), and John Dunn's *The Political Thought of John Locke: An Historical Account of the Argument of the 'Two Treatises of Government'* (New York: Cambridge University Press, 1983). These and other references are listed in Works Cited.

9. Biographical information about Rousseau comes from a variety of books, including Jean Starobinski and Arthur Goldhammer's *Jean-Jacques Rousseau: Transparency and Obstruction* (Chicago: University of Chicago Press, 1988) and Maurice Cranston's *The Early Life and Work of Jean-Jacques Rousseau, 1712–1754* (Chicago: University of Chicago Press, 1991). These and other references for Rousseau are listed in Works Cited.

10. Insightful biographies of David Hume include David Fate Norton's *David Hume: Common-Sense Moralist and Skeptical Metaphysician* (Princeton, NJ: Princeton University Press, 1982), Peter Millican's *Reading Hume on Human Understanding: Essays on the First Enquiry* (Oxford, UK: Oxford University Press, 2006),

and Norman Kemp Smith and Don Garrett's *The Philosophy of David Hume* (New York: Palgrave Macmillan, 2005).

11. *The Wizard of Oz*, MGM, 1939. The original series of *Oz* books on which the movie was based was written by L. Frank Baum.

12. "*Lost*: Everything You Need to Get Ready for Season 3," *Entertainment Weekly*, September 29, 2006, special insert, 21.

CHAPTER FIVE

FORMAL RELIGION AS A WAY TO UNLOCK MEANING

Formal religion can be a powerful influence on one's life and worldview. Rose's Christianity (most likely Protestant); Mr. Eko's, Charlie's, Hurley's, Desmond's, and perhaps even Claire's Catholicism; and Sayid's Islam affect the characters' actions and provide them with a framework for understanding the world. Although no characters thus far have identified themselves as pagan, elements of that spiritual expression also arise on *Lost* during the first season, although other religions dominate the castaways' spiritual practices in Seasons Two and Three.

Even if characters don't consider themselves religious now, they still may react to the world based on earlier religious influences. People in danger often call on their religion to help them through a difficult time, even if they act noticeably less religious when life is going well. Through the snippets of religion interspersed throughout several episodes, we can see its influence on a character.

ROSE AND PROTESTANT CHRISTIANITY

Of all the characters on the island, Rose seems most at peace. Her faith in God seems unshakable, even if her faith in others sometimes is questioned. Like many women, she sometimes becomes annoyed with her husband. She is argumentative with Bernard when he forgets her birthday ("S.O.S.," 2.19), and she may not agree with everything the other survivors do, but Rose brings a measure of grace and harmony to the lives of others.

Midway into the first season ("Whatever the Case May Be," 1.12), Charlie reaches a crisis point. He has given up heroin and begun a friendship with Claire. He very much wants to protect Claire and her unborn baby, but when he is tested as a protector, he fails, and Claire is abducted. Charlie questions how Rose can be so cheerful when danger and death surround them. But Rose doesn't let Charlie wallow in self-pity. She spends time with the young man, who is doing his best to isolate himself from the other castaways. Rose tells Charlie that he needs to seek help. "Who's going to help me?" he asks. As a new segment in the episode begins, the scene cuts to a close-up of the cross adorning the marshal's grave. The answer to Charlie's question is clear. For him, as for Rose, the answer lies in Christianity.

At the end of the episode, Charlie asks Rose how she can be so certain that she will see Bernard again; the couple is separated during the plane crash, and Bernard's whereabouts are then unknown. Charlie doubts whether he will be reunited with Claire. "It's a fine line between denial and faith. It's much better on my side," Rose assures him. A tearful Charlie, his troubles seeming too great to bear, asks Rose for help. She prays with him, beginning with a familiar Christian phrase, "Heavenly Father" ("Whatever the Case May Be," 1.12). Rose practices what no doubt she has often heard preached; her spirituality makes her who she is and gives her the confidence to live fully, even on an island of mystery and uncertainty.

Rose quietly influences those around her. Her faith that she and Bernard will be reunited is rewarded when, indeed, Bernard and the other Tailies show up on the other side of the island one afternoon ("Collision," 2.8). Rose isn't an "I told you so" type of woman, but the castaways undoubtedly will remember that Rose was right in believing Bernard alive. She has a strong spiritual foundation, and she doesn't seem to rely on facts or others' ideas of what is logical or likely. She lives her life confidently and does what she believes is right.

Rose's personal battle between science and faith involves Bernard's reaction to her impending death and her own ability to come to terms with disease (likely to be cancer, although that's not specifically said in the episode; "S.O.S.," 2.19). Modern medicine fails Rose; there is no cure for her disease, and she has only months to live. But live she intends to do for as long as her physical body allows; Rose plans to spend all her remaining time with new husband Bernard. However, Bernard is so sure that there can be a cure for Rose that he drags her halfway around the world from their New York home to find it. Ironically, faith is an important component in the "cure" that Bernard has researched. He locates an Australian healer named Isaac who facilitates miracles for terminal patients. When Rose visits Isaac, she and he both know that he can't help her.

After science fails Bernard in healing Rose, she won't let his faith in this healer also be destroyed. She asks Isaac to tell Bernard she has been cured, even though that's not the case. However, when she lands on the island, she, like Locke, finds physical healing. When she finally confides in Bernard that she won't ever leave the island because it has healed her, Bernard finally accepts that he has lost his battle for a scientific cure. He sees no need to seek a way off the island. Bernard believes in her healing because Rose believes, and the couple must stay on the island for the rest of their lives. Whereas this might be a tragedy for some people, Rose and Bernard seem content because they have each other.

Rose stands out as the most prominent religious character during the first season, and she and Bernard take on larger roles in the second season, even receiving their own backstory. According to the axiom, actions speak louder than words, and Rose's daily faith in God perhaps is the strongest argument this woman could make for her religion.

CATHOLICISM

Catholicism seems to be the dominant religion among surviving castaways and new characters who clearly indicate their current or former religious practice. Of the original fourteen major characters, Charlie and Hurley are shown talking with or refer to their parish priests; both have been reared in the Catholic Church. During Season Two, new regular character Mr. Eko and recurring character (and Season Three new regular) Desmond also are Catholic. Perhaps Claire may even be slowly turning toward the Church; she asks Eko to baptize her and her baby, but she may turn to Eko only because he is the only "real" holy man around. These characters display, even within a single season, varying degrees of devotion to Catholicism, as they have epiphanies, confront opposition to their beliefs, and seek redemption for their pasts.

CHARLIE AND MR. EKO

Charlie and Mr. Eko illustrate faith that's tested by disappointment and a lack of personal fulfillment. As they grow as characters during Season Two, they begin to do what is right simply because that's the right thing to do instead of doing what's right because it'll get them what they want. They begin to find fulfillment in quieter, but more meaningful lives—after all, both achieve a level of notoriety and fame in their pre-island lives, but fame and fortune do little to help them long term.

These characters, who look and respond so differently, share surprising similarities. Both had a religious youth in the Catholic Church—Charlie as an altar boy ("The Moth," 1.7), Eko as seemingly the only boy in his group of friends to wear a cross ("The 23rd Psalm," 2.10). Both seem marked as the "good boys" in their family until their childhood faith is severely tested.

Eko may not take drugs, as Charlie has, but his pre-island business requires him to deal them, and to deal with the smugglers and thugs who make up his trade. On the island, both Charlie and Eko reject the role that drugs have played in their pasts.

Both men probably blame their brothers for leading them astray. If they didn't love their siblings, they wouldn't have tried to protect and help them. However, in doing so, they make decisions that separate them from the good life sanctioned by the Church. When Eko's and Charlie's lives end up being less than perfect and they recognize what they have become, they likely resent what they feel they had to do for their brothers. Only when they become their own men—or believe they can be God's children again—do they take responsibility for their lives and look for ways to help others.

Late in Season Two, Eko and Charlie work together to build a church. What is surprising is that when Eko abandons this job in favor of button pushing, Charlie continues to work on his own, although the job is much more than one man can handle ("Three Minutes," 2.22).

Each man has an epiphany that makes him decide to change. Charlie "sees the light" when he saves Jack from a cave-in and realizes that he is strong enough to give up heroin and go through withdrawal by choice, rather than waiting for the drug to run out ("The Moth," 1.7). Eko's epiphany occurs when he finds his brother's body in the downed plane on the island. By again donning the crucifix, he takes on his brother's role as a priest ("The 23rd Psalm," 2.10). His duties include some impromptu counseling, baptisms, and prayers for the dead.

Both characters share one more similarity—dreams that seem to be prophetic. Charlie dreams that he must save baby Aaron. A bizarre dream sequence in which Hurley, Claire, and Charlie's mother wear biblical clothing and Charlie swims to a floating piano with Aaron inside motivates Charlie to do everything possible to have the baby baptized ("Fire + Water," 2.12). Religious symbols (e.g., a white dove, a portrait of John the Baptist, chants of "save us" and "save the baby") abound in each backstory segment and dream sequence in this episode.

Eko also follows a dream and has faith that it, not logic or facts, should direct his life. In a dream, Yemi directs Eko to the location of the previously hidden Pearl hatch, which seems to be an observation area for an experiment taking place in Locke's Hatch ("?" 2.21). This discovery leads Eko to believe that the button is so important that he is willing to sacrifice himself to blow up the locked door that prevents him, or someone else, from pushing it ("Live Together, Die Alone," 2.24).

Very late in his life, Eko turns away from being a priest. He fails to keep pushing the button and save the Hatch, thus failing his sacred mission. He is injured and dragged to a polar bear's cave, where he is saved by Locke ("Further Instructions," 3.3). Eko seems unable to save himself, spiritually or physically. He loses his faith. During this low spiritual ebb, Eko again sees Yemi in a dream, urging him to come to his brother. He obeys this command, only to discover he no longer can discern the "real" spirit of Yemi from a more sinister imposter ("The Cost of Living," 3.5). When Eko faces the monsters of his past, embodied in the image of Yemi, the former warlord expresses pride in his past actions. He dies without repenting his former life as a warlord.

Although Eko's spirituality is sincere, he also wars against himself because circumstances often force him to rely only on himself (or so he likely believes). He may question God's wisdom in taking him from his brother and home to become part of the drug runners' violent world, an act that drastically changes both his and Yemi's lives. Eko's faith is similar to that of many "self-made" people who want to believe in the benevolent God whom they revered in their youth, but whom they don't find particularly helpful in dealing with a ruthless world.

If Charlie's spiritual growth and backsliding parallels Eko's, will he, like Eko, revert to a less spiritual persona, or will he decide to stay on a spiritual path? Charlie's past seems much less violent than Eko's, but his need to make everything right for his family (and himself), no matter the cost to his soul, seems likely to make him once more seriously question his faith.

HURLEY

Also raised Catholic, Hurley harbors memories of frightening recent religious experiences. During Hurley's beloved grandfather's funeral, the family's priest dies suddenly—struck by lightning at the grave site ("Numbers," 1.18). Perhaps events like these turn Hurley from traditional spiritual beliefs toward a certainty that a curse plagues him for using the mysterious Numbers for personal gain. Being cursed and facing fate's retribution are not Church tenets, and Hurley seems to fall away from his religion and under the spell of superstition after a series of improbable coincidences.

During the second season, Hurley is certain that the curse leads to such bizarre events as seeing a former friend from the mental institution ("Dave," 2.18) and vowing to give up his food addiction only to discover a cache of food dropped nearby. Hurley's fear of being rejected by his new friends turns into a self-fulfilling prophecy when he tries to please everyone at the cost of doing what he feels is right ("Everybody Hates Hugo," 2.4).

Only when Hurley acts truly like himself is he able to find a closer friendship with Charlie ("The Long Con," 2.13) and, more significantly, Libby. Hurley's crush on Libby blossoms into love just before Libby is killed, and Hurley—for the first time on the island—is angry. How Hurley deals with these emotions, especially grief, is yet to be seen, but during Season Two Hurley tries to solve his problems all by himself. Two women—Rose and Libby—

help him through crisis points, but Hurley so far hasn't turned to religion, even at the height of his turmoil. His belief in the Numbers' curse is stronger than his belief in himself or in God.

Hurley might even find himself becoming a follower of Desmond, who seems to have developed the ability to know the future. When Desmond appears in the jungle after the Hatch's implosion, nude but otherwise unharmed, Hurley donates a shirt to clothe him. During their conversation, Desmond repeats something Locke will soon say; Hurley recognizes the words when he listens to Locke address the castaways ("Further Instructions," 3.3). Soon after, Desmond tries to convince Claire to move temporarily from her hut. Seeing no reason to do so, she declines. Desmond spends the day building a lightning rod, setting it close to Claire's home. During a sudden downpour, Claire huddles over baby Aaron. Desmond, nonchalant, leans nearby, specifically telling Hurley to watch what happens. Lightning strikes the makeshift rod, saving Claire and her child from a fiery death ("Every Man for Himself," 3.4).

Hurley, of all castaways, can appreciate the significance of lightning. Seeing Desmond's "power" and probably wishing someone like him could have saved the parish priest at the funeral may make Hurley believe in Desmond as a supernatural human.

Lightning also is a prop for numerous comedy routines, usually starting with, "May God strike me dead if . . ." *Lost* turns these jokes into reality. That a priest and Aaron might attract lightning, and Desmond might know how to stay safe from God's wrath, are bound to make an impression on Hurley.

DESMOND

Down the Hatch, when Desmond desperately hopes that his repair job has fixed the computer needed to "save the world," he crosses himself before rebooting the system ("Orientation," 2.3). Although Desmond may never have strayed from his religion, his secular passion is channeled into training for an around-the-world race. Whether Desmond is truly good, as he seems in current time, or bad, as his cryptic messages to Jack during a backstory segment may lead us to believe at the beginning of Season Two ("Man of Science, Man of Faith," 2.1), he expresses a need for divine intervention when he faces a crisis.

Desmond becomes a more sympathetic character in the Season Two finale when we learn that he has lost the love of his life, Penny Widmore, during his long stint in a Scottish military prison. Upon Desmond's release, Penny's father ensures that the couple remain separated. Desmond becomes determined to gain Penny's attention and prove to Widmore that he is worthy of marrying his daughter. However, when these plans fail abysmally with Desmond's shipwreck on the island, he eventually despairs.

At one point he plans to commit suicide, certainly a huge break from the beliefs of the Church. Desmond's next attempt to sail away from the island proves futile, and the despondent sailor decides to drink himself into oblivion. Desmond shows a capacity for great joy and great sorrow, extremes that don't seem motivated or mediated by religion. Only love—which may move beyond the secular toward what Christian theology calls agape—may be Desmond's link to the formal religion of his earlier life.

Desmond's religious training involves respect for priests. Locke explains that Eko, whom Desmond locks out of the control room after hot-wiring the blast doors, is a priest. This news stops Desmond in his tracks. "We locked out a priest?" he asks ("Live Together, Die Alone," 2.24). Under most circumstances, Desmond wouldn't go against a priest's wishes, and Eko clearly wants to be inside the now-locked room.

Desmond also believes in the balance of life—what others might deem karmic. As he descends to the fail-safe, he tells Locke, "You saved my life, so I could save yours" ("Live Together, Die Alone," 2.24). This balance seems fair to Desmond, who doesn't hesitate to open the fail-safe and release what should be a lethal dose of energy.

This attitude may be developed throughout Season Three, after Desmond returns to the castaways' camp a changed man. The Hatch's implosion may have triggered spiritual changes in Desmond, as well as the "superpower" that Hurley believes the returned "savior" may possess.

SYMBOLS OF THE CHURCH

The symbols surrounding the Catholic Church are powerful, as Mr. Eko and Charlie know, and abusing icons and imagery associated with Catholicism carries more weight for these characters. Eko (mis)uses the priest's collar and black suit as a disguise for his illicit drug activities. Long before Eko washes ashore, the plane carrying his dying/dead brother and heroin shipment crashed on the island. Boone and Locke discover the body of a dead "priest" in the jungle—a Nigerian drug smuggler in disguise ("Deus Ex Machina," 1.19). They don't know that unlike the drug runners, Yemi, Eko's brother, truly is a priest who accidentally becomes a passenger. Boone discovers that the broken Virgin Mary statues conceal bags of heroin. Days later, when Sayid and Charlie take a breather on their search for baby Aaron, they pause by the wreckage. Sayid shows Charlie where Boone died and explains the drug operation ("Exodus," 1.24). Eko manipulates important symbols of the Church to mislead authorities and so protect himself and his drug trade. These symbols take on even greater significance for Charlie.

Heroin introduces temptation once more into Charlie's life, and symbols within the storyline indicate the potential dangers if he takes this path. The priest's body hanging from a tree mirrors Charlie's near-death by hanging ("All the Best Cowboys Have Daddy Issues," 1.11); Charlie already has cheated death at least once and may not be so lucky again. The broken vessels themselves point to Charlie as a young man—a religious vessel himself—whose purpose is later defiled by drugs. Like the Madonnas, he is broken—spiritually.

One of Charlie's first acts early in Season Two is to take a Madonna away from Claire after she discovers it in his backpack. Charlie is playing with Aaron when Claire asks Charlie about the statue. When she comments that she didn't know that he was so religious, he quickly replies that he isn't, but nonetheless immediately trades the baby for the statue. Charlie keeps a careful eye on what he views as "insurance" in case something bad happens ("Adrift," 2.2). Karl Marx once insisted that religion is an "opiate," but Charlie's opiate-filled Madonna statue fails to protect him and leads him to further emotional and physical crises.

Among the many conscious or unconscious reasons Charlie is attracted to Claire is because she is his real-life version of a Madonna. Although Aaron's conception is hardly virginal, young mother-to-be and later mother Claire initially seems sweet and innocent in Charlie's eyes. She bears a child in difficult circumstances and places him in the rough-hewn cradle that Locke has built ("Numbers," 1.18). Although the baby is not his, Charlie longs to protect Claire and her child. His protective streak becomes almost obsessive during Season Two, when he questions Claire's ability to care for the child and asserts what he feels is his rightful place with the baby. The Madonna and child image is further strengthened when Locke demonstrates how to swaddle Aaron; the newborn becomes a babe wrapped in swaddling cloths ("Abandoned," 2.6). For Charlie, this most Christian of images must resonate with his ideal of motherhood and parental love.

When Charlie has dreams of Aaron in danger, he envisions his mother and Claire as angels, urging him to "save" the baby. After Charlie discusses his dream with Mr. Eko, the surrogate father becomes convinced that Aaron must be baptized. Convincing Claire, however, is difficult, because she recently has learned about the heroin-filled statue and sent Charlie away ("The 23rd Psalm," 2.10). Charlie's erratic behavior prompts her to want spiritual insurance herself, and Claire asks Eko to baptize her and her child.

The episode's title, "Fire + Water" (2.12), offers several symbolic meanings, but baptism is perhaps the most important one. Charlie faces baptism by fire, not only a blaze close to camp but an angry confrontation with other castaways after he abducts the baby. Aaron's baptism is more traditional, with water blessed by a priest. Charlie is left outcast, in an emotional and possibly spiritual crisis now that his personal Madonna and child are unreachable, but he fulfills his mission to save Aaron, at least spiritually.

By the end of the second season, Charlie sees the Madonna statues and Claire differently. His experiences after Claire ostracizes him force him to face himself and to look at both his—and her—shortcomings. As Charlie continues to build the church he and Eko started together, he becomes agitated when the dog Vincent drops a Virgin Mary statue at his feet, as if daring him to keep it—or worse. Charlie tracks down the remaining statues and throws them into the ocean. Perhaps Charlie isn't as interested in what's on the outside as what's within; his outer persona for a long time sheltered the drug addict within. By throwing away the statues of the Blessed Mother, Charlie ironically draws nearer to the religion of his youth.

As well, Charlie likely sees Claire in a new light, too. His Madonna isn't perfect, and she likely will irritate him again as she learns how to be a good mother to Aaron. She no longer is on a pedestal as the ideal mother. However, because Charlie now can see Claire as a real person instead of an icon or ideal, and as she allows him once more to be close to her, the couple stands a better chance of having a good relationship. Charlie's life is on the right track when he trades his false god for the real thing and looks past the veneer to see what's real.

Images, such as the Madonna statue, are only one form of religious symbol. Scriptures also play a prominent role in Christianity, and they remind Eko in particular of what should be important to him. He often carves scriptures on his "Jesus stick" and repeats the 23rd Psalm. One scripture gains prominence in

Season Three: "Lift up your eyes and look north." Claimed to be from the "Book of John (3:05),"[1] this scripture provides John Locke directions for his next mission.

Words from the Bible have special significance to Eko, although Charlie also is quick to recognize the 23rd Psalm when Eko repeats it ("The 23rd Psalm," 2.10). Locke's interpretation is more pragmatic; the words become a way for the island to speak to him ("I Do," 3.6).

Each character finds and interprets the symbols that mean the most to him or her. Whereas tangible objects (the Virgin Mary statues) hold special significance for Charlie, Locke takes the more intangible words of scripture quite literally as his next sign. *Lost* provides a variety of symbolic objects, images, and words so that every spiritual character finds at least one special symbol that resonates with his or her past. Spiritual symbols are the most powerful, because they tap into long-held emotions and beliefs. When *Lost* introduces such symbols into the story, the characters and we in the audience ascribe special meanings to them that enhance their importance.

ISLAM

Other religions play a role on *Lost*, though not as prominently as Christianity. The modest attire worn by Muslim women, in particular Sayid's friend Nadia, indicates Islamic belief in modesty ("Solitary," 1.9). However, when Nadia makes a brief appearance in California during a Locke backstory, she is dressed like a modern Western woman ("Lockdown," 2.17). The contrast between her former and current life signals a shift in her expression of spirituality as well as her adoption of Westernized ideas.

Sayid stays in Sydney to claim the body of his former roommate and provide a proper burial, a choice that puts him on Oceanic 815 ("The Greater Good," 1.21). Islam makes one of Sayid's comments to Jack in an early episode more understandable. When Jack insists that the crash victims' bodies be burned,

Sayid wants to wait to determine the religious backgrounds of those who died, for cremation is not acceptable to Islam. Sayid seems appalled at the wholesale cremation ("Walkabout," 1.4). We may not understand why at first, but once we hear Sayid's comment in "The Greater Good" (1.21) that cremation is wrong, we understand why Sayid responds so forcefully to Jack's pragmatic treatment of the dead.

When Sayid buries Shannon ("What Kate Did," 2.9), he works the prayer beads as he attempts a eulogy for his lover. For all the ways that Sayid seems far removed from his religion during much of the second season as he relishes his renewed role as soldier and interrogator, by the Season Two finale he again reveals a more spiritual side. As Jin and Sun pilot Desmond's sailboat so that Sayid can rendezvous with Jack's band on the other side of the island, he bows toward Mecca and chants prayers. He seems again a devout Muslim ("Live Together, Die Alone," 2.24).

Although Sayid doesn't use religion as a crutch, he seems to return to spiritual practices more diligently during times of duress. When Sayid needs guidance or looks for a sign, he finds it; he accepts as a given that his actions will be directed so that he can fulfill his destiny.

PAGANISM, NATURE, AND NEW AGE

Even pagan cultures receive a nod in *Lost* during the first season. As soon as Charlie dubs Claire's baby "Turnip Head" ("The Greater Good," 1.21), fans on the Internet speculated on the nickname's hidden meaning. Why would Charlie choose that particular name? In Celtic cultures throughout what is now the United Kingdom (Charlie's homeland), people carved lanterns out of turnips for Samhain, more commonly known as Halloween among nonpagans. The frightening lanterns kept away evil spirits. Oceanic 815's flight date is listed on ABC-TV's Oceanic-air website as September 22[2] (which is on or near a pagan equinox holiday). If that is the true crash date, and if the first season encompasses the castaways' first forty days (also a Christian biblical number), then Turnip Head's birth is on or close to Halloween.

Fans also speculated that Claire may be a modern Rosemary from *Rosemary's Baby*, and the series's creators admit that Roman Polanski's 1968 film influenced a scene in "Homecoming" (1.15) in which pregnant Claire nervously waits for Ethan to come for her.[3] Coupled with the interest in Turnip Head, officially named Aaron ("Exodus," 1.24), fans further speculated that Claire's baby is somehow demonic. In the larger struggle between good and evil—not confined to any one religion—can there be something inherently evil in such an innocent looking child? During Season Two and early Season Three, Aaron seems to be a remarkably normal baby. However, fans still question whether Aaron may have a larger role in the castaways' future. The Others certainly want the baby ("Maternity Leave," 2.15), but then they also seem inclined to take all children. Seeing whether Aaron lives up to his biblical name or his early pagan moniker may yet be seasons away.

During Season One, pagans and other nature enthusiasts were dismayed that Locke is viewed by many fans (and characters) as a shady, slightly creepy man who knows more about the island than he should. Even when he becomes less "island friendly" in Season Two, Locke's motives still are questioned. People who are or have been closer to nature than civilization often seem suspect to those who prefer urban life.

In early episodes, the island is Locke's religion. Locke frequently sits or stands in the rain, arms outstretched, as if being blessed by Mother Nature ("Pilot," 1.2). He knows nature so well that he accurately predicts when the sudden downbursts will occur ("All the Best Cowboys Have Daddy Issues," 1.11; eerily "repeated" in a backstory scene during "Further Instructions," 3.3). He takes what he needs from the island to make weapons and tools. He understands which animal parts or plants are necessary to make items ranging from glue ("Numbers," 1.18) to

medicinal salve ("Hearts and Minds," 1.13). He walks purposeful-
ly throughout the jungle and never seems to lose his way. Locke
is "one" with the island. He understands and reveres it in what we
perceive as mysterious ways.

However, when Locke moves into the Hatch, he largely abandons his island worshipping, and *Lost* loses any pagan connection
for the remainder of Season Two. When Locke seeks guidance
from the island via a vision quest and soon receives what he
believes are supernatural signs ("Further Instructions," 3.3), he
again attains an aura of mysticism.

Unlike Charlie's or Eko's dreams, which carry distinctly
Christian symbols, Locke's Season One visions take place while
he is awake. He also helps other characters in what amount to
vision quests (known in Australia as "Walkabouts," the title of
a Season One episode). In "White Rabbit" (1.5) Jack already
believes he is hallucinating when he meets Locke in the jungle.
Locke guides him toward leadership of the group by pointing
out that, in many ways, Jack already has taken control of situations and seems respected by others. Locke further helps Jack
accept the vision/hallucination of his father; in Locke's eyes
Jack isn't crazy but in need of a sign. When Jack accepts that
what he sees may be real, even if logically he cannot understand
it, he is able to follow his father's apparition to the caves. His
discovery not only helps him deal with his father's death but
provides the castaways with a much-needed water source and
new shelter.

In another episode, Boone seems hopelessly bound to Shannon
and tells Locke he cannot keep secrets from his sister. Locke not
only knocks Boone unconscious to help him get started on his
vision quest, but provides what might be a hallucination-inducing
balm for Boone's head wound. Although Locke later denies his
concoction is anything more than a healing salve, and indeed
Boone might have had a mild concussion that causes him to see a
horrific vision, there is still a hint of the mystical, and Locke alone

seems to understand it ("Hearts and Minds," 1.13). He tells Boone that the dream symbolizes his overreliance on Shannon, not a premonition of her death.

Locke also serves as a counselor or an advisor who mysteriously shows up just when someone needs guidance. He motivates Charlie with music, first to give up heroin ("The Moth," 1.7) and later to become a button pusher in the Hatch ("Everybody Hates Hugo," 2.4). He tells Sawyer a strange story about animals embodying the spirits of dead people, which causes him to question the human qualities of the boar he tracks ("Outlaws," 1.16). Turning up just in time to watch Sun destroy her garden in frustration (". . . And Found," 2.5), he understands her anger but, more importantly, tells her to stop looking for what she has lost (such as her wedding ring), because then she will find it. He helps Claire swaddle a cranky Aaron just at the time when she questions whether she wants Charlie's help ("What Kate Did," 2.9). Locke has an uncanny ability to know when and where he needs to offer advice.

More than any of the castaways, Locke seeks redemption and salvation, not only healing and the culmination of his destiny, through belief in the island. If the island has sinister motives rather than a predestined providence for the survivors, what does that say about Locke's character? During "Further Instructions" (3.3), Locke's friend Eddie, who turns out to be a police officer infiltrating the commune where Locke lives, tells the older man that he was selected to become Eddie's mentor because of Locke's psychological profile. Locke seems easily coerced, and thus the police force believes he can be turned from his friends in the commune. On the island, Locke's belief is a cornerstone to his effectiveness; when he trusts the island, he agrees to do anything it asks. The island—or whoever controls what's happening there—might easily manipulate Locke because of his faith.

This Season Three episode also shows Locke's multiple spiritual practices that span more than one traditional religion. When Locke realizes that his final actions in the Hatch result not only in its destruction and endangerment of himself, Desmond, and Eko, he comes to terms with the idea that he's made yet another mess in his life, a fact that spirit-guide Boone delights in reminding him later ("Further Instructions," 3.3).

Locke's first action is to build a sweat lodge where he can purify his body while his spirit awaits guidance and perhaps forgiveness. With a reluctant Charlie's help, Locke builds the lodge and sets a guard outside. This might not seem strange to anyone who has participated in such a ritual, and Locke does indeed seem to know what he's doing. What might seem odd is that this spiritual practice is much more common among aboriginal peoples in North America, and although appearances might be deceiving, Locke doesn't appear to be Native American. His practice might be more New Age and adaptive rather than a precise ritual in the Native American religious tradition.

Locke also brings this non-Christian practice right into the center of the church that Charlie and Eko have been building. The framework for a Christian church is completed; Locke fills in this frame with his sweat lodge, which becomes the first ritual or service within the structure. Locke's actions show his appreciation for holy ground of whatever faith and the need to be sanctified before he can continue his life. The type of religion doesn't matter to Locke—only the recognition of sacred space and sincere spiritual expression are important.

Locke's actions in the sweat lodge show he's participated in this ritual many times before; his backstory confirms that he's visited a sweat lodge earlier in his life. Charlie notes the irony that Locke, whom he now despises for beating him just because he thought Charlie was taking heroin again, openly prepares a hallucinogenic paste for the ritual. To Locke, drugs outside of ritual may be wrong for a whole host of reasons, but to gain spiritual enlightenment, the use of a certain natural drug within the context of a ritual is not only acceptable but a requirement. Locke's practice resembles descriptions of the use of peyote in certain

Native American rituals; although this practice is highly controlled and frowned upon by many, peyote has been used to help the faithful gain spiritual insights as part of their religion.

Locke's vision surprises him. Boone guides him, a reversal of their earlier roles as follower and mentor, and easily forgives Locke. He even recognizes his status as a sacrifice required by the island, a reference to Locke's interpretation soon after his death ("Do No Harm," 1.20). Locke then sees the Sydney Airport, where Boone points out his friends preparing to board a flight, although the roles are very different from reality. Hurley is an Oceanic Airlines employee; Claire, Charlie, and Aaron are a happy family (Charlie wearing a velvet suit and ruffled shirt in a parody of a successful rocker's outfit); Sawyer playfully swipes Kate's passport, another parody of Kate's theft of Joanna's passport and her botched attempt to gain passage on the raft. This vision, no matter how modern, seems an acceptable sweat lodge vision aided by Locke's spirit guide.

In the vision's final moments, Locke is forced to abase himself by dragging himself up an escalator; he literally must pull himself up to a higher plane of existence to understand the meaning of the vision. He picks up a broken half of Eko's Jesus stick, covered in blood. (Not coincidentally, in the real world, Locke nearly is clubbed on the head with the broken fragment as it falls from the sky after the Hatch's implosion; it seems that Locke has to be hit over the head spiritually before he understands what he must do.) As Locke holds the stick and looks at the scripture, Boone tells him he must save Eko. Boone's bloody countenance might simply indicate his fatal injuries, but they may also be interpreted as reflections of Eko's wounds.

Locke receives his next instruction when he sits with an unconscious Eko, waiting for Charlie to retrieve water from a nearby stream. Locke "confesses" to the "priest," asking forgiveness and recounting his recent sins. Eko tells him to save Kate, Jack, and Sawyer. When Charlie returns a moment later, Eko is still unconscious. Again, Locke's "message" may be interpreted in multiple ways:

- He may still feel the aftereffects of the drug-laced paste and hallucinate the message.
- He may be under some form of mind control as part of an island experiment.
- He may want a sign so badly that he thinks he receives one.
- He truly hears Eko speak to him.

Locke, however, believes the message is yet another gift from the island. With signs that seem, at least to Locke, to be from a supernatural source, his faith is confirmed yet again. Once more he is ready to do what the island asks of him.

Although Locke returns to faith, his religious expression bridges more than just one religion and may be an amalgam of several religions in which he has participated at some point in his life. He's pulled together spiritual concepts and practices that make sense to him, and they provide him with the guidance and support he needs to live a meaningful life.

Although "New Age" doesn't equal "pagan," many New Age believers also are proponents of a simpler, back-to-nature lifestyle. Some people labeled New Age are pagan, but the broader concept of New Age beliefs often is expanded in popular consciousness to include everything from acceptance of extraterrestrial life forms to extrasensory perception. For our purposes, "New Age" means belief in extrasensory information for guidance. Dreams, visions, communication with the dead, and precognition can fit into this belief system.

Lost explores both sides of the question whether such New Age spirituality is real or merely faked by charlatans out to make a buck. Spiritual messages can't be scientifically proven, and New Age beliefs, because they find less mainstream acceptance, often draw skeptics' attention. On *Lost*, the Malkin family illustrates a gamut of spiritual beliefs, some reflecting New Age concepts.

Self-proclaimed psychic Richard Malkin tells Claire she must raise her baby herself, a premonition that seems to come true

("Raised by Another," 1.10). Malkin's persistence—and his refusal to keep Claire's money for the initial reading—add weight to his claim. However, when Eko acts as the representative for the Vatican in assessing the possibility of Charlotte Malkin's miracle resurrection, her father tells the priest that his wife is merely a religious zealot out to embarrass him, because he's a fraud. His supposed psychic powers, he explains, rely on research about his clients and his ability to tell people what they want to hear ("?" 2.21). But that certainly wasn't the case with Claire; she wanted Malkin to stop pestering her.

Is Malkin telling the truth to Eko, or does he really have a precognitive ability? Has Malkin been hired by someone else to make sure that Claire gets on Oceanic 815?

Joyce Malkin insists that her daughter has come back from the dead. She contacts local religious authorities to verify what she knows is true—Charlotte drowned and only a miracle brought her back to life. Her traditional religious beliefs no doubt play a role in wanting to expose her husband's sin of cheating clients.

Charlotte is the "happy medium" in this family, a bad pun that rings true. The teenager may display her father's psychic gift, if indeed he has one; she claims that Yemi speaks to her in a dream and confronts Eko at the Sydney airport to deliver Yemi's message: Eko is a good man, she insists, and Yemi will see him soon. It seems like Yemi makes good on this promise, because Eko later receives what he believes to be divine guidance delivered by his brother. Based on this experience, Eko's final encounter with dream-Yemi leads to his death at the hand of the Monster ("The Cost of Living," 3.5).

Are these dream-given messages true, as Charlotte and Eko come to believe? Is someone other than God manipulating their dreams? Are the messages merely wish fulfillment, or, in Charlotte's case, the result of effective research? The veracity of this psychic information becomes subject to our—and the recipients'—interpretation.

Perhaps because most viewers would question the veracity of New Age or pagan practices more than they would other religions, *Lost* also raises more questions about this type of spiritual expression. By illustrating less mainstream spiritual practices, however, *Lost* shows that all forms of spirituality may be valid and connected in more ways than we may realize. What matters is that each character who feels spiritually lost can find a life path that makes sense to him or her.

Lost doesn't cover every major religion, but through references within the series (e.g., *dharma*) and illustrations of characters' spiritual practices, it presents a much wider view of spirituality than any other television series, past or present.

Notes to Chapter Five, "Formal Religion as a Way to Unlock Meaning"

1. In fact, John 3:5 reads, "Jesus answered, 'Truly, truly, I say to you, unless one is born of water and the Spirit, he cannot enter the kingdom of God'" (Revised Standard Version). The only place in the Bible where one is directed to lift up one's eyes and look northward is Ezekiel 8:5.

2. *Oceanic Air.* Retrieved November 25, 2005, from www.oceanic-air.com.

3. *Lost,* The Complete First Season DVD.

CHAPTER SIX

LARGER SPIRITUAL CONCEPTS

Like the castaways, viewers of *Lost* must learn to live with fear and loss as well as joy. The stakes on the island are high, just as in real life. The characters have as many different ways of dealing with uncertainty as we do. However, *Lost* also illustrates larger concepts that most people consider or confront during their lives. Hope, faith, redemption, rebirth, fate, destiny, and love transcend a single religion and express the universality of spiritual and philosophical beliefs. *Dharma* is another concept specific to some religions, including Buddhism and Hinduism, that can be understood in terms of spiritual development even by non-Buddhists and non-Hindus. *Lost* presents multiple interpretations of these themes and leaves it up to characters and us to determine how important any one of these concepts will be in our lives.

Series creator Damon Lindelof calls the episodes of *Lost* "redemptive stories. We show character flaws in the past, and explore ways these people can evolve on the island and redeem themselves."[1] The series' themes force characters to change as they struggle to find their way in their new environment, develop a society, and work closely with people from diverse backgrounds, representing diverse worldviews.

No matter how great or small a role spirituality plays in our and the characters' lives, some concepts are widely recognized and valued. Hope, faith, love, fate, and destiny are important to our understanding of humanity as well as of *Lost*. Redemption and rebirth, key components of many religions, become major themes within *Lost*'s overarching story. Even a concept closely associated with a few religions, such as dharma, attains special significance when *Lost*'s creators show how such a benevolent idea can be subverted for an organization's personal gain. These keywords illustrate more than spiritual concepts common to many religions; they emphasize important themes within *Lost* and individual characters' responses to larger life issues.

HOPE

Hope is one of the concepts, like faith, fate, and destiny, that are repeated in many episodes by different characters:

- Sayid mentions that hope is dangerous to lose ("Tabula Rasa," 1.3).
- Christian Shephard suggests Jack give hope, even false hope, to his patients ("Do No Harm," 1.20).
- Kate refuses to move to the caves because to do so would be to give up hope that help will arrive ("House of the Rising Sun," 1.6).
- Locke believes hope is at the bottom of the Hatch ("Exodus," 1.23).
- Sawyer lies to Kate so that she might maintain hope that they can escape from the Others ("I Do," 3.6).

Hope is on shakier spiritual ground than faith, because hope is unsubstantiated. The cliché is that people cling to hope as a last resort, an undying response to a dire situation. More vague than faith, it is sustaining nevertheless and is considered such an important life concept that, according to myth, it alone brings balm to the world's hurts after Pandora opens that famous box. (See Chapter 4 for a longer discussion of the Hatch as Pandora's Box.)

Despite its fewer references in episodes, the characters seem most afraid of losing hope; they don't want to believe that their situation is literally hopeless. To maintain their hope in a better future, if not ultimately for rescue from the island, they often rely on faith, which receives much more emphasis on *Lost*.

FAITH

Faith, a certainty that something as yet scientifically unproven exists or is true, usually has a spiritual connotation. Characters such as Rose express strong religious faith. However, this strong belief doesn't always imply a religious context. Jack, for example, places his faith in science and technology but sometimes loses faith in himself, especially during his first days as the group's leader and again after Boone's death. In *Lost*, faith frequently takes two forms: spiritual faith (e.g., expressed by Rose, Locke, and Mr. Eko) and secular faith in oneself (e.g., illustrated by Jack and Sawyer).

LOCKE'S FAITH

Locke maintains the strongest faith in the island. Of course, he, like Rose, has ample reason to believe in the island's power and to trust its beneficence. For Locke, the island offers not only the experience he has sought in an Australian walkabout but the healing that traditional medicine could not provide.

During the second season, Locke faces a crisis of faith but later reconciles his doubt. However, when Locke acts secure in his faith in the island—which should be perceived as a positive— his complete confidence in a "being" that others distrust makes him seem eerie and more than a little frightening to the other survivors. They, and we, have difficulty knowing whether Locke always has the best interest of others at heart.

Even the series's cast and crew question whether Locke is good. In a March 2005 gathering at the William Paley Festival,

J. J. Abrams and several actors from *Lost* discussed Locke's character. Abrams asked who thought Locke was a good guy. Ironically, only Ian Somerhalder (Boone) raised his hand.[2] Is Locke just human, with good and bad qualities like any other character, or is there something sinister going on? Should the castaways—should we?—be concerned that Locke is dubbed the "man of faith"? Should such faithful leaders be suspected or followed? Even "faith" becomes a debatable topic as we unlock *Lost's* secrets.

Whatever his morality, Locke is both a mystical and symbolic character. He knows how to find his way without a compass; in Season One and again by the finale of Season Two, he knows where he is going and feels comfortable navigating his life on the island, even with its spiritual minefields. When Locke gives Sayid the compass the older man declares he no longer needs, Sayid discovers that north is not where it is supposed to be on the device ("Hearts and Minds," 1.13). If Locke's moral compass is indeed off kilter, it could help explain why he feels at home on the mysterious island or why he seems most solidly faithful when he follows a divine calling outside the norm.

As a mentor, Locke embodies tough love along with his faith in others, even when they lose faith in themselves. Charlie initially exchanges his drugs for Locke's information about the location of his guitar. Locke, however, gives Charlie three chances to ask for the drugs; on the third request, they will be returned. Each time Charlie begs for them, Locke expresses his faith in the addict's ability to give them up. In response to the last request, Locke hands over the bag, which Charlie tosses into the campfire. Locke restates his faith in the shaky young man ("The Moth," 1.7).

Yet Locke's early faith in Charlie later is undermined by the younger man's growing closeness to Claire and his bizarre behavior toward Aaron. Locke doesn't approve of Charlie's "holier than Claire" attitude when Aaron's surrogate father criticizes Claire's parenting. He notes the irony of an addict criticizing someone else's behavior ("Collision," 2.8). When Charlie's attempt to baptize Aaron frightens Claire and endangers the baby, Locke is the first to confront him as soon as he returns the child. Locke soundly beats Charlie and seems to take a perverse pleasure in "correcting" his one-time pupil ("Fire + Water," 2.12). Charlie further breaks their bond by baiting Locke when Desmond sails back to the island ("Live Together, Die Alone," 2.23) and again when Locke needs his help during a vision quest ("Further Instructions," 3.3). Locke's spiritual and secular faith hinges on his latest experience or information. When Charlie's behavior no longer justifies Locke's faith, the latter cuts him loose.

At least Charlie fares better than Boone, another Locke protégé. In "Hearts and Minds" (1.13), Locke knocks Boone unconscious, then smears on a salve that seems to promote a gruesome hallucination, in which Boone believes the Monster mutilates Shannon. Tormented by the vision, he attacks Locke, who shows him that the vision is not real but can motivate him to start a new life. Locke feels confident in dispensing wisdom, even in painful ways. In his own strange way, he shows his faith in others' ability to make the right decision.

Before the final episode of the first season ("Exodus," 1.24), only one character sees the Monster—Locke. Early in the first season, in "Walkabout" (1.4), Locke comes face to face with it, but it does not harm him. He later tells Jack that he has looked into the island's eye, and it is "beautiful." When Locke is attuned to the natural world, with its healing grace as well as horrific dangers, he is empowered by that which frightens others.

This is evident in a Season Three Eko backstory, "The Cost of Living" (3.5). Locke briefly sees the Black Smoke Monster disappear from behind Eko when the latter bends in the stream for a drink. Appropriately, Eko and Locke face off across the stream, a symbolic foreshadowing of their separation across the river delineating life from death (e.g., the River Jordan, the River Styx). As soon as they have a private moment, Locke asks Eko what he saw and shares his own positive experience. Eko warns that his experience wasn't as beautiful, a revelation soon illustrated as the Monster kills him during their next encounter. Locke knows what killed Eko, although he's hesitant to share that information with the other castaways who discover his body. Instead of fearing the island and its monsters following Eko's death, Locke instead finds a sign on the remnant of the Jesus stick being used as a grave marker. "Lift up your eyes and look north" gives Locke the information he needs for his next journey—to rescue Jack and company.

On *Lost*, faith requires confidence that one's actions are necessary and right, because they are firmly grounded in one's belief system. Jack and Locke, the survivors' most frequent leaders, place their faith in very different ideals. With Locke barely surviving the Hatch's destruction and Jack a captive of the Others, the castaways may have difficulty deciding in whom to place their faith in Season Three. By the 2006 fall finale, Locke seems to have comfortably taken Jack's place, and his renewed purpose makes him a more formidable presence.

Eko's Faith

One of the most spiritual characters in the series, Mr. Eko seems an unlikely "man of faith." As a former drug lord and reluctant "fake" priest, Eko would be more likely to abandon his childhood religion in favor of a more pragmatic, church-free lifestyle. Although his backstory is featured in only two episodes, they prominently feature Mr. Eko's faith, or lack thereof: "The 23rd Psalm" (2.10) and "The Cost of Living" (3.5). The 23rd Psalm, a pivotal scripture, unites Eko and Charlie not only in their religion but in a rededication of their lives. On *Lost*, however, nothing is a simple as repeating a verse well known and commonly memorized by Christians. Both Eko and Charlie misquote a passage: "Yea, though I walk through the *shadow* of the *valley* of death" ("The 23rd Psalm," 2.10) instead of "Yea, though I walk through the *valley* of the *shadow* of death" as they pray simultaneously. Although the change in wording might be a writer's error, the resulting alteration to the scripture invites questions about Eko's (and Charlie's) spirituality. Is their faith equally off track, despite their confidence in what they're saying? Or is this rephrasing merely an update that reflects their most recent experience? Their inaccurate recitation makes the characters seem to be on the same wavelength or to share the same thoughts.

Quite literally Eko has just walked through the shadow—the Black Smoke Monster—in the valley of death. Encounters with the Monster, of whatever type, seem to result in immediate death, yet Eko, like Locke before him, initially faces the Black Smoke Monster and lives. (Charlie doesn't yet face his "monsters"—his usual method is to run away and hide from them rather than confront them directly. While Eko faces the Black Smoke Monster, Charlie witnesses the face-off from his hiding place up a tree.)

Eko doesn't fare that well upon another encounter with the Monster. Perhaps "The Cost of Living" (3.5) shows that Eko's deepest love is for his brother Yemi, not God. Further flashbacks to the boys' past show that Eko spent his boyhood looking out for Yemi—stealing food and protecting him from the harsh nun who catches them. Eko is a protector and parental figure, not so different from Michael, who also would someday go to extremes to protect Walt. Just like Eko defied the nuns of his childhood faith, he tells the Monster-posing-as-Yemi that he's proud of his often violently achieved accomplishments—through his sacrifice, the real Yemi was able to grow up to become a priest. Perhaps Eko's version of heaven is a reunion with Yemi and the return of his brother's adoration, as when they were boys. A final scene shows young Eko and Yemi walking together into the sunset. This scene might also be interpreted as God's ultimate forgiveness of Eko; God's judgment is kinder than the Monster's and even greater than Eko might have believed possible.

Eko's behavior follows two very different axioms, one secular

(Teddy Roosevelt's "Walk softly but carry a big stick") and one spiritual (Proverbs 16:18: "Pride goeth before destruction, and a haughty spirit before a fall"). He struggles between following a spiritual and following a secular path; between listening to God (or one of God's representatives) and deciding for himself what he should do. Eko usually got his way either by softly but convincingly explaining his argument, or if that didn't work, knocking some sense into (or knocking the stuffing out of) people who stood in his way. Eko's self-determined purpose in life seems good: protect Yemi and, later, keep his work alive. No matter how proud he was of his methods, however, Eko sometimes relied just a bit too much on that big stick.

Characters who can honestly look at themselves and their past actions should survive their encounters with monsters from the past. These characters may not be the most moral people, but if they accept who they are and face what they've done, they can live. If they sincerely are trying to live a good life, so much the better. But they have to look the Monster in the eye steadfastly and without any excuses.

Eko does that on his first encounter with the Monster ("The 23rd Psalm," 2.10); so does Locke, who may see a reflection of his awe and gratitude at his renewal on the island ("Walkabout," 1.4). Eko doesn't see something beautiful (as he reveals to Locke in "The Cost of Living," 3.5), but he accepts what appear to be replayed scenes from his past and is well on his way to leading a more spiritual life. By recalling his past actions and, soon after, finding Yemi's body in the plane, Eko decides to take yet another chance for a more spiritual life. He repays Yemi by building a new church; he follows Yemi's dream-given command to push the button. He carves even more scriptures on the Jesus stick to remind him of his renewed faith; he wears a cross around his neck.

Eko's rejection of this spiritual path and his return to self rather than divine direction for his life is illustrated with his loss of spiritual "talismans." The Jesus stick breaks under the blast door ("Live

Together, Die Alone," 2.24), but a fragment almost smacks Locke in the head as he walks in the jungle following the implosion ("Further Instructions," 3.3). In this way Locke gains an important symbol of Eko's spirituality. Locke also finds Eko's cross; when he picks it up, the transfer of "spiritual" leadership is complete. Eko's role as priest becomes diminished—and soon ends in death ("The Cost of Living," 3.5); newly reaffirmed man of faith Locke asserts his role as one of the most spiritual characters as well as a likely spiritual and political leader of the castaways living on the beach. He even looks more priestlike by hearing Eko's final words ("The Cost of Living," 3.5), then tending his body and taking care of the burial ("I Do," 3.6).

Eko's mistake on the most recent Judgment Day is to reveal his pride, whether to the image of Yemi or to a massive smoky fist. Eko is inordinately proud of surviving many conflicts throughout his life, and even the prized Jesus stick retains the blood of the Others he killed during their attempt to abduct him. He rationalizes his bloody past; he certainly lacks humility when he confronts the Monster/Yemi. In his last moments, however, Eko doubts whether Yemi can forgive all he's done and perhaps believes that the monsters from his past have a right to come get him. Even Eko's belated and fearful recitation of the 23rd Psalm abruptly ends when he falls into the Monster's clutches ("The Cost of Living," 3.5).

Monsters preying upon fears or doubts can take any shape and literally strip characters bare or squeeze the life out of them. Ironically, Eko's death confirms the story he tells worried murderer Michael: one must be sincere in the desire to repent before sin can be forgiven ("Three Minutes," 2.22). Although Eko takes on the role of priest more than once in his life, either he never truly asks forgiveness for his violent past or he never believes that he truly can be forgiven. His final words ("The Cost of Living," 3.5), most likely, "You're next," instead of the Locke-interpreted, "We're next," indicate that everyone will need to look the Monster in the eye before long.

The most spiritual characters wrestle with their faith and often question whether it is wiser to be people of faith or people of science. Their struggles fuel character development and illustrate the difficulty many people have today in reconciling their faith with what they see going on around them.

REDEMPTION

Like faith, redemption is one of the most important themes of the series. Being saved from their past lives—whether characters consider them particularly sinful or just not as fulfilling as they wanted—has been an issue from the earliest episodes. Redemption is not just a matter of personal decision to live a better (i.e., more spiritual or moral) life in the series' stories but is significant in the stories that the castaways tell each other. On *Lost*, Locke and Eko share stories, either ones they've heard or ones that come from their experience and that borrow from the Christian canon, especially Christ's parables.

In "The Moth" (1.7), Locke tells Charlie the parable of this less beautiful but hardier insect to help him realize his strength (and potential for redemption). He explains that moths are stronger and more valuable because they spin silk. If the cocoon is opened prematurely, the moth will be too weak to survive. But the moth that struggles out of the cocoon on its own is able to survive in the world. Locke clearly believes Charlie is a moth and slowly convinces him he is much stronger than he believes. Although Locke never discusses religion, his use of a natural metaphor reflects his source of spiritual strength.

During "Outlaws" (1.16), Locke describes a dog who wandered into his boyhood home soon after his sister died. The dog became a companion for Locke's grieving foster mother, but the animal's strange arrival and uncanny knowledge of the dead girl's room led the woman to believe her daughter had returned. Locke's story may be one reason why Sawyer, who hears whispers in the jungle, fails to shoot the bothersome boar he hunts.

Eko takes the role of storyteller/religious counselor during Season Two. Michael vaguely asks about the possibility of God's forgiveness and the reality of hell for the unforgiven. In reply, Eko describes a confession he heard from a boy who killed the dog who mauled his sister. The boy wondered if he would be punished for killing the animal. Eko believes that if the boy is truly repentant, God forgives him, but if the boy only fears meeting the dog in hell and uses that fear to motivate his penitence, that won't count. However, the priest suspects that fear of retribution really motivates the boy—as well as Michael ("Three Minutes," 2.22).

Eko himself might wonder if he's good enough to become a "real" priest, even after impersonating one for so long. In a dream, Eko's brother assures him, "What is done is done" ("?" 2.21); the future is more important.

However, Monster/Yemi refuses to accept Eko's pride in his violent past ("The Cost of Living," 3.5). Eko kneels in front of the image of his brother—although this Yemi wears ash-stained clothes and seems far less of a divine apparition than his previous incarnation. Echoing the image of Christ on the cross shown in the previous backstory scene, Eko stretches his arms in supplication. Although he retains the proper pose, his words belie a sincere desire to be forgiven for his sins. In fact, he justifies his past actions as necessary in order to survive; he's proud of his survival and the way he protected Yemi. This response disgusts the "fake" Yemi, who turns away from Eko while asking, "Why do you speak to me as if you were talking with your brother?" Monster/Yemi is not nearly as forgiving as Priest Yemi, who would condemn the sin, not the sinner.

Although any character might be ripe for redemption, some characters seek redemption more than others. Their arrival on the island and subsequent relationships with other survivors force them to look at themselves and change. As Damon Lindelof told *Entertainment Weekly* in April 2005, *Lost* is like other well-done character-driven shows in that it is about individuals "searching for redemption in the face of their flaws and struggles."[3]

In Season Two in particular, Charlie and Hurley become the poster boys for the ups and downs of the redemptive process. Hurley also understands the ongoing problem of temptation that Charlie faces. Both characters have addictive personalities: Charlie to heroin, Hurley to food.

Hurley thought he'd be safe from overeating on an island where fruits and fish are more common than candy and carbs. He even tightens his belt a few notches ("Confidence Man," 1.8; "Dave," 2.18). But then Locke opens the Hatch, which contains a well-stocked pantry. To make matters worse, Jack puts Hurley in charge of inventory and food distribution ("Everybody Hates Hugo," 2.4). Hurley seems to give away all the goodies, but, like Charlie ("The Long Con," 2.13), he actually stashes some "insurance" in the jungle ("Dave," 2.18).

Libby finally convinces Hurley to destroy his stash. He does so ("Dave," 2.18), upending jars of peanut butter and ranch dressing, just as Charlie also proves he doesn't need heroin by smashing a Virgin Mary statue in front of Claire and then scattering granules of heroin in the sand ("The 23rd Psalm," 2.10). Perhaps both young men find strength to battle their temptations while they're standing before their potential girlfriends.

Unfortunately, temptation shows up again. No sooner does Hurley free himself from unlimited, largely unhealthy food than several of his friends rush past him on the way to a rumored cache dropped from the sky. It's a humorous scene— Hurley looks ready to bash his head against the nearest tree in frustration—but it points out an important point about temptation and redemption. People can't retreat even to a remote tropical island in order to avoid facing their problems; those serious about changing their lives have to confront their "monsters," not run away from them. Hurley, like Charlie, finds out the hard way that temptation keeps returning, and it takes willpower (and many fans will also list spiritual support) to deal with it.

The way that *Lost* typically operates, in Season Three we might find the Others cultivating a poppy plantation or opening a Mr. Cluck franchise on the other side of the island. *Lost* characters have to accept that living a good life for its own sake is motivation and reward enough to keep them from succumbing to what tempts them.

THE PERILS OF REDEMPTION

The theme of "second chances" also comes up in conversation frequently, especially during the first season. Locke tells both Boone and Shannon, individually, that they can have second chances at a new life. In reality, that means that they don't need to be co-dependent. Sun and Jin are at the breaking point in their marriage. Sun already plans to leave Jin at the airport but changes her mind at the last minute. Neither partner is happy within the marriage, and each shares in the problems. Lack of communication is one big problem, and the couple needs to learn to trust each other. But those who take their second chance aren't guaranteed a happy ending.

That characters should be careful of being "redeemed" or they would immediately die became a running joke in Season Two. Although they begin a romantic relationship, Shannon still needs Sayid to believe in her unconditionally, to accept that she sees Walt in the jungle, even when it seems impossible for him to be there ("Collision," 2.8). When Sayid convinces Shannon that he loves her for herself and believes in her, she believes in herself. She has a redemptive moment, albeit one that isn't religious. She accepts that she is a lovable person in her own right, not because of her beauty or her apparent wealth. Shannon's life is brief, but she realizes her worth and is "redeemed" by being able to let go of the past and lead a new life. Unfortunately, her new life is cut short almost immediately, but Shannon still has that moment of grace when she knows she is loved for herself.

Ana Lucia's first important act upon encountering additional survivors from Oceanic 815 is to imprison and interrogate them ("Adrift," 2.2). Later, she accidentally kills Shannon as the Tailies approach the other castaways' camp ("Collision," 2.8). We've also seen the manslaughter of the "Other" Goodwin by her hand ("The Other 48 Days," 2.7) and, in a backstory, Ana Lucia takes the life of the man who shot her and inadvertently killed her unborn child. Her role in the castaways' new society isn't much different from her pre-crash occupation. Ana Lucia agrees to play "good cop" to Sayid's "bad cop" as they interrogate Henry Gale ("The Whole Truth," 2.16). She has a long history of doling out justice as she sees fit, and thus she expects other people to be unable to forgive her for Shannon's death. But then Ana Lucia has an epiphany.

She tells Michael that she can't torture or kill Henry Gale, who earlier in the episode nearly strangles her; she is no longer that type of person ("Two for the Road," 2.20). Whereas when she first arrives in camp she confesses to Sayid that she is emotionally dead ("What Kate Did," 2.9), after a few weeks there, Ana Lucia gradually becomes part of the group. When she gains acceptance from other castaways and begins to fit in, she also realizes that her new life doesn't have to be like her old one. She doesn't have to be so tough or hurt others. With that acceptance, or redemptive moment, Ana Lucia takes her second chance to break old habits and refuse to be the person she doesn't want to be. Again, unfortunately, after a redemptive moment, a character dies. Ana Lucia is murdered. Taking a second chance obviously doesn't ensure a long life, but it does offer characters the chance to change their ways and to recognize their self-worth.

Kate's inability to make the most of her second chance stems from the belief that she is inherently flawed. Her gene pool is bad. The man she grows up thinking is her abusive, drunken stepfather is really her biological father. The stalwart military man who loves Kate as his own child is really her stepfather. When Kate learns the truth, she hates herself as much as her biological father. Her later actions—such as torching the home where her father is passed out—not only separate her from her mother and the man she thinks of as her "real" father but from herself. Sam

Austen tells Kate that she has "murder in her heart," and although saddened by events, he knows that Kate is capable of killing. The best he can do is give her a few hours to get away before he calls the authorities ("What Kate Did," 2.9).

Kate's life as a fugitive involves the wounding of Marshal Edward Mars, the death of Kate's love Tom Brennan, the shooting of Kate's accomplices in a bank robbery, and other similar crimes ("Whatever the Case May Be," 1.12; "Born to Run," 1.22; "What Kate Did," 2.9). Her love for husband Kevin leads her to realize she'll ruin his life when he learns that wife Monica is fugitive Kate. Her decision to drug and abandon him is motivated by love ("I Do," 3.6). On the island, Kate is involved with the poisoning of another castaway and a botched attempt to steal another woman's identity and buy a way onto the escape raft ("Born to Run," 1.22). However, for all Kate's many flaws, she is likable and a natural leader. She takes on difficult jobs, everything from boar hunting ("Walkabout," 1.4), to tracking Ethan Rom ("All the Best Cowboys Have Daddy Issues," 1.11), to nursing Sawyer back to health ("Outlaws," 1.16). She volunteers to carry dynamite from the *Black Rock* ("Exodus," 1.23) and is the first to shimmy down a cable into the Hatch ("Man of Science, Man of Faith," 2.1).

If Kate could see that she is a valuable person and believe that anyone can be saved—no one is too bad to be redeemed—then maybe she could use her second chance to live the kind of life she now believes is out of reach.

Kate's beliefs make us question our definition of who is good and who is bad, who is redeemable or not. The Others draw up a list of those who are "good" people to be retrieved and added to their group ("The Other 48 Days," 2.7; "Three Minutes," 2.22). They specifically request Kate and Sawyer, as well as Jack and Hurley, to be brought to their camp—these are the "good" people they want in their group.

Kate acts as though biology, or nature, alone can determine who is good enough to be redeemed. She approaches life without a spiritual foundation, as if she is too far removed from God ever to be saved, either from the island or within her life. Even her good actions don't seem to be enough to equal her previous bad deeds, as least in Kate's estimation. This approach to life can be an excuse for future bad acts or harm against other people. After all, if Kate really is too bad ever to be redeemed, what's the point of her trying to lead a good life? She struggles to do the right thing. When life becomes difficult, or when Kate doubts herself because she is fearful or only self-interested, she blames her resulting actions on her bad genes. As long as she does that, she'll never realize her true potential.

New lives require dedication and nurturing. Change is difficult to sustain, and even the best intentions are tough to maintain when people are stressed, overworked, and challenged. As these characters illustrate, redemption is an ongoing process that requires a daily desire to change for the better.

LOVE

Redemption often is motivated by love—whether secular or spiritual. *Lost* illustrates many types of love: agape, romantic, and parental. This emotion becomes a motivating force, but again, because this is *Lost*, love may not take a positive direction. Characters choose how love will guide them, and possessive or obsessive love sometimes leads to dangerous conclusions.

AGAPE

Agape is the purest form of love for others, love that is given with no expectation of anything in return. In spiritual terms, agape involves unconditional love of everyone. In practical terms, it frequently requires self-denial or self-sacrifice for others.

Desmond demonstrates agape when he offers to sacrifice himself to save the world as he knows it. He believes that Locke saved his life by pounding on the Hatch window and distracting him from committing suicide. Desmond later believes that his life has been spared so that he can save others' lives by operating the fail-safe and restoring the electromagnetic balance to the island ("Live Together, Die Alone," 2.24).

Why does Desmond make this decision? He reads a letter from his love, Penny Widmore, in which she tells him that all he needs—all anyone needs—is one person who believes in him and loves him unconditionally. Penny loves Desmond unconditionally, and so he feels compelled to help (and thus love) others.

Agape is just this type of all-encompassing, compassionate love for others—whether strangers or friends. It prompts selfless actions; other people become more important than oneself. Perhaps one reason for Desmond's act is this type of love.

ROMANTIC LOVE

Of course, Desmond also loves Penny romantically, and a good part of his motivation to operate the fail-safe must be attributed to the physical and emotional love they share. Before his around-the-world race, Desmond declares to benefactor Libby, "I shall win this race for love" ("Live Together, Die Alone," 2.23). This force primarily motivates him, and although he fails to finish the race sponsored by Charles Widmore, Desmond still may succeed in the "race" to win Penny Widmore as a spouse.

If Desmond is going to survive to see Penny again, he must save the island. The odds aren't great for his survival in either situation, but he at least can gain more control of his life by attempting to balance the forces about to pull apart the island. Love, whether secular or spiritual, moves people to act in courageous ways.

Jin would understand Desmond's self-sacrifice. He, too, would do anything to save Sun, the love of his life. Sun's and Jin's relationship, especially in Season Two, has been called a great romance. But it isn't always that way. Jin at first is a controlling husband who has just found out that his plans to start a new life in the United States with his wife will be thwarted by his father-in-law, who is also his employer. Jin realizes that he forever will be an "enforcer" in the family business, even though his work and its toll on him emotionally also doom his marriage. Sun secretly learns English and plans to run away from her husband, leaving no trace ("House of the Rising Sun," 1.6; "...In Translation," 1.17).

These plans end when Oceanic 815 crashes, but the couple's marital problems don't stop with the crash. Jin still is a controlling husband who tells Sun that she only needs to rely on him and not talk with the other castaways ("Pilot," 1.1). Sun later shames Jin by revealing that she speaks English—he was unaware of her knowledge and ends the marriage ("...In Translation," 1.17).

Still, Jin comes to realize that his actions hurt Sun; he's been a less than ideal husband. As he watches Sun blossom with her new independence, he realizes just how much he's limited his wife. Jin vows to save Sun from being exiled on the island; he blames himself for her predicament.

After Sun learns that the raft has been destroyed, she only wants her husband's safe return. When Jin arrives back in camp, the couple rediscover their love for each other ("Collision," 2.8).

But love alone isn't enough. They also work on better communication. When Sun tells Jin that he's not going into the jungle to search for Michael—and in front of someone else—he later tells her that he doesn't like her tone and doesn't like to be told what to do. "I didn't like that for five years," she tells him. Jin considers this statement. "I expect that you didn't," he admits ("The Whole Truth," 2.16).

The couple's marital ups and downs undoubtedly haven't ended, but Sun and Jin seem more committed to their marriage. With the surprise revelation that Sun is pregnant, when the couple believed that they couldn't have children, their bond may be strengthened, as well as tested, with the addition of a child. In Season Three we learn that Jin may not be the baby's father ("The Glass Ballerina," 3.2). We also learn that both Sun and Jin are capable of violent acts and continuing deceptions; in this episode Sun sides with Sayid against her husband and lies to Jin, but he now knows enough English to catch her in this lie. Although their bond is still strong, recent backstories show that they are both strong personalities who are capable of great deceit as well as great love.

Love is the redeeming force for this couple, but it doesn't come automatically. It requires a great deal of work and efforts to communicate with each other. Sun and Jin remember that they love each other, but they may not always agree with each other. Now they seem more likely to discuss their differences of opinion and to work out a solution together. In essence, their marriage seems to be saved, which in turn, "saves" each partner.

Love is often more painful than romantic on *Lost*. Although the writers kept their promise that Kate would choose either Sawyer or Jack as her lover before the 2006 fall finale, the Kate–Sawyer tryst may not signal eternal devotion. Part of Kate's torture at the hands of the Others comes from being forced to break her tough girl façade to reveal her deepest feelings. Convinced that her love is cursed and brings only misery for the one she loves (e.g., Tom, Kevin), she then must watch while Sawyer is tortured or threatened with death.

Kate's love for Sawyer raises questions. Is their love tainted and doomed to end tragically? Can these characters know what love is? When Kate previously trusted Sawyer, she found herself used, either to get a kiss ("Solitary," 1.9) or to persuade Jack to do what Sawyer wanted ("The Long Con," 2.13). Even in "The Glass Ballerina" (3.2), Sawyer's sudden liplock only takes place so that he can goad the guards into attacking him, thus testing their strength and ability to fight. Kate really has no basis for trusting Sawyer beyond his short-sighted momentary need. The fall finale in 2006 poises the couple at a crossroads that likely will separate them and test whether there's truly is a long-term romantic love.

PARENTAL LOVE

Parental love can be another "redeeming" emotion, as Michael discovers when he's finally able to rescue his son from the Others. But his devotion to Walt, only realized after they crash-land on the island, raises a disturbing question: How far will a parent go to save his or her child? Loving parents would say without hesitation that they would do anything for their children, but how extreme? *Lost* forces Michael and us to contemplate just what might be required; in Michael's case, he ends up killing two castaways who are supposed to be his friends ("Two for the Road," 2.20). Although he might have found other ways to regain Walt, Michael's love for his son makes all other relationships moot and any action justifiable. Even abandoning such friends as Jack, Sawyer, Kate, and Hurley can be justified as he seeks a way to get Walt back to civilization. Off the island, possibly back home in New York, Michael might someday question just how far "love" pushed him to act, and whether what he felt was truly "love" for Walt or a darker emotion. Walt, too, might wonder just what his father did to ensure their passage home, and Michael's actions may ultimately cause further estrangement from his son.

Even Charlie realizes the power of "parental" love, although it may not always end well. Claire's baby stirs protective feelings in Charlie, to the point that he obsessively monitors Aaron. The baby becomes almost a substitute drug to the former addict. Even so, Charlie isn't above using the baby to get what he wants. "You wouldn't lie to the baby, would you?" Charlie badgers Hurley to tell him what is in the Hatch ("Everybody Hates Hugo," 2.4). Aaron serves as a convincing prop when Charlie holds him up in Hurley's line of sight. But Charlie's misguided parental love at its worst is still nothing compared to Michael's "crazy" love for his son. After Walt's abduction, Michael runs into the jungle to search for his child, and he doesn't reappear for several weeks. He turns against his friends and leads them into captivity to win Walt's release. He becomes so fixated on being the one to rescue Walt his way that he doesn't consider any alternative plan of action.

But not all examples of parental love are negative. Claire struggles to regain her missing memory so that she can better care for Aaron, who suffers from a rash. Although Jack assures her that this is a typical baby ailment, Claire recalls fragments of Ethan Rom's explanation that the baby needs injections in order to remain healthy on the island. When she remembers enough to be able to return to the "medical hatch" where Ethan treats her, she also remembers more about her captivity ("Maternity Leave," 2.15).

Claire's willingness to put herself in physical and emotional danger to return to the site of her captivity is only made possible by her overriding love for her son. When Charlie brings her vaccine from the Hatch, Claire is wary of injecting herself or Aaron, although she still thinks that such injections may protect the baby from island-borne diseases. Charlie assures her that he's tested the drug on himself a few times first, to make sure there are no side effects. This selfless action not only makes Claire think a bit more fondly of Charlie, but it also satisfies her need to protect her child ("?" 2.21).

Love takes many forms, but its power shouldn't be underestimated. In its purest, most selfless forms, it embodies the best of what people value about spirituality. When characters are able to love each other selflessly and unconditionally, they are "reborn" into a new life that is focused on others instead of themselves. They have given up their previous self-interested way of looking at the world and what others can do for them to see how they can help others.

REBIRTH

Each survivor of Oceanic 815 symbolically dies in the crash and is reborn on the island. Scenes of death and rebirth are sprinkled throughout the first season's episodes, perhaps most blatantly in "The Moth" (1.7). Butterflies are often used as a metaphor for rebirth, but in this episode, Locke, in his role as Charlie's temporary spiritual advisor, prefers moths to symbolize rebirth.

When entombed with Jack during a cave-in, Charlie sees a moth flying toward the top of the cave. He follows it and pushes his way through the earth into the sunlight. The camera focuses on Charlie's forearm struggling through the soil until it pushes free, looking very much like a horror movie shot of the undead rising from a fresh grave. The heavy-handed symbolism illustrates Charlie's growing faith in himself without drugs; he is able to save himself and Jack by finding another way out of the caves. Charlie the addict "dies," and a drug-free man struggles to be reborn.

Charlie also is the focus of another death/rebirth scenario in "Raised by Another" (1.10). Jack and Kate find Charlie hanging, apparently left for dead by Ethan. Jack desperately performs CPR for so long and with such violence that Kate begs Jack to stop. Charlie appears long dead, and Kate sobs not only for his loss but for Jack's inability to let go. With a final effort, Jack pounds life into the young man, whose loud gasp again suggests the undead coming back to life.

CPR also brings other characters back to life. In the pilot episode (1.1), Jack corrects Boone's CPR technique. Rose also seems beyond help, but through Jack's persistent efforts comes back to life and suffers no permanent damage from her brush with death. In Season Two, Sawyer is the catalyst for rebirth. When Michael nearly drowns, Sawyer performs CPR and mouth-to-mouth resuscitation until Michael comes back to life ("Adrift," 2.2).

Locke's faith may have a deeper spiritual underpinning, at least symbolically. In Western funereal practices, people are buried without shoes. In the pilot episode, Locke is shown shoeless until his "rebirth" with the ability to walk again. Then he ties on his shoes and gets to work helping others. An interesting detail in "Man of Science, Man of Faith" (2.1) is the camera's, and Jack's, lingering look at a pair of shoes neatly placed outside the entrance to Desmond's underground living/working quarters. If this were not a significant detail, why would the camera pause long enough for Jack—and us—to notice the shoes? Jack soon hears Locke's voice and realizes that he is being held prisoner; seeing the nondescript shoes is really not a clue about the identity of the person who owns them. The following episode shows Locke without his shoes—he removes them before he encounters Desmond ("Adrift," 2.2). Is he walking on "holy ground," the Mecca where his pilgrimage has led him? Or does being shoeless mean that inside the Hatch, Locke himself is "dead" again? He does seem to stray from his spiritual roots once he becomes a Hatch dweller.

Eko also removes his shoes before entering the Hatch ("Live Together, Die Alone," 2.23). A few scenes later, electromagnetic forces pull it apart. In such a cliffhanger, does the removal of shoes signal impending death or merely respect for a sacred place? Eko does survive into the third season, but he doesn't last long.

Even the death of the first main character parallels a birth. Boone's death scene is intercut with scenes of the birth of Claire's baby. As Jack cries over Boone's body, Claire's face shines with tears of joy ("Do No Harm," 1.20). The cycle of life continues, with birth and death being closely related.

The Christian concept of being born again, or "saved," even affects characters who don't seek redemption and, most likely, doubt that they are spiritually saved. When self-proclaimed sinner Sawyer awakens from delirium caused by a nearly fatal infection, he finds himself in a bunk bed inside the Hatch. The veneer of "civilization" makes him believe that the castaways have been rescued. Kate assures him that they are still on the island and finally takes him outside the Hatch to prove it. "We're not saved?" Sawyer mournfully asks. "Not yet," Kate replies ("Outlaws," 1.16). Although the two "outlaws" have not yet sought redemption, *Lost*'s writers imply that spiritual rebirth— being saved—is possible even for those who so far have not embraced their second chance for a new life.

In yet another irony, we might expect self-proclaimed "good" people to have some sort of spiritual belief. On most U.S. TV programs the heroes or "good guys" may struggle with their beliefs, but they usually express belief in God, or at least the Divine in their religion. Yet Henry Gale, a self-proclaimed "good guy," forces Locke to question the existence of God. In "The Whole Truth" (2.16), when Locke quips, "God knows where we are," Gale immediately replies, "Not even God knows where this island is." His comment begs the question whether there is any place removed from divine sight. Gale's demeanor even makes Locke pause, possibly wondering whether Gale is stating a fact or merely trying to make him question what to believe.

In Season Three, Gale, now known as Ben Linus, asks Jack whether he believes in God. With a reversal of his attitude during the discussion with Locke, Ben states that he realized he had a spinal tumor and a short time to live; a few days later a spinal surgeon landed right next door ("The Cost of Living," 3.5). With Ben Linus/Henry Gale, it's difficult to know when he's revealing the truth as he sees it and when he's merely playing a convincing role to manipulate someone else. Perhaps Ben sometimes feels forsaken by the outside world and its God; although he says that he chooses to stay on his island home, we have to wonder why he wouldn't leave for an off-island hospital if he so desperately needs surgery. Jack's fortuitous arrival might inspire Ben's faith.

Ben tries to play God as he calls forth, judges, and metes out punishment to Kate, Sawyer, and Jack. He determines what happens to them and sets impossible tasks that test their morality and basic humanity. The reward for not only surviving this punishment but becoming "good" people is the possibility to return home—in effect, to start a new life in a familiar location. Once the castaways experience life on the island, they are forever changed and thus "reborn" to whatever life, blessed or tortured, awaits them in the future.

Early in Season Three, one more castaway becomes reborn in a surprising way. Shipwreck survivor Desmond also survives the Hatch's implosion ("Further Instructions," 3.3). He arrives in the jungle naked—a very symbolic "rebirth," almost like Adam in the Garden, although this "Adam" is very knowing. In fact, part of Desmond's rebirth makes him more than a survivor; he has been changed by the experience.

Desmond inexplicably knows what Locke thinks and says about his new mission to save his friends from the Others, although Locke hasn't yet made this declaration. There seems no logical explanation for Desmond's new clairvoyance, unless he, as Hurley teasingly suggests, has turned into "the Hulk." Although Desmond may lack superhero abilities, the aftermath of the implosion may have fundamentally changed him—giving him a spiritual rebirth.

Cinematography in the episode's last shot of Desmond emphasizes his change in status, especially in Hurley's eyes. Hurley reverently watches Desmond, clad only in one of Hurley's oversized tie-dyed T-shirts, throw stones into the ocean. He stands alone, and the setting sun halos his head in golden light. As one TV critic and fan remarked on the day after "Further Instructions" aired, Desmond looks like "Jesus-as-happy-hippie"[4] from *Godspell.* Interestingly enough, Henry Ian Cusick, who plays Desmond, starred as Jesus in *The Visual Bible: Gospel of John.* Desmond may be just the reborn clairvoyant to help lead the castaways on the beach into a better life on the island.

Rebirth indicates personal choice to live a different type of life, one more responsive to helping others than helping oneself. On *Lost,* characters who feel "reborn" take responsibility for acting differently (i.e., kinder, more helpfully) toward others; they take the opportunity for a second chance at a new life.

FATE AND DESTINY

Fate and destiny, on the other hand, seem to offer very little personal choice in how characters respond to challenges, yet these, too, are important themes on *Lost.* How much independence do humans have in their actions? How much is determined by fate?

Does each person have a destiny only he or she can fulfill? In some religions, fate and destiny are key components, although these concepts are more abstract to most Westerners. Jin, Sun, and Sayid, however, find such questions particularly important to their growth, and Jin and Sun especially wrestle with these spiritual concepts as the couple part.

In Sun's and Jin's backstories—"...In Translation" (1.17) and "House of the Rising Sun" (1.6)—we see the couple lose their way in an increasingly tense marriage. Both commit acts they come to regret.

Sun wonders whether the survivors are being punished for past actions or secrets. After all, she has kept secrets from Jin— such as her plan to abandon him once she learned English and start a new life in a new land. She knows he is shamed when she reveals her language skills. Once Jin sails on the raft and Sun is left behind, she asks Shannon whether fate could be punishing them. Claire responds that fate does not have any bearing on their situation, but Sun and Shannon look far less certain ("Exodus," 1.24). Fate, in Sun's estimation, could be the great equalizer to balance past misdeeds with current punishment. Only when fate is satisfied can the survivors truly start a new life free from their pasts.

As alluded to in the series, fate is also part of devout Muslim belief. When Sayid infiltrates a terrorist cell in Sydney, his friend, a member of the cell, tells the others that Sayid was a communications officer and has valuable skills they can use. The group's leader declares that Sayid's reunion with his college roommate is no coincidence; fate intervenes to provide the terrorists with just the new member they need ("The Greater Good," 1.21). This scene sets up two very different possible interpretations, depending on one's belief in the power of fate. Those who do not believe fate is a controlling force can interpret the terrorist's comment as naïve; Australian and American intelligence agencies have provided Sayid with his friend's whereabouts and coerced him to spy on the group. Those who accept that fate plays an important role in human interaction realize the intelligence agents merely provide Sayid with the opportunity to fulfill fate's mission. Part of *Lost*'s successful storytelling is its ability to layer meanings into simple dialogue; the words can take on different meanings for different members of its audience.

When Sayid is later held prisoner by Ana Lucia, she asks him whether she should let him go. She believes that if Sayid is truly a good man, she should not kill him. He explains that he has done terrible deeds in the past and suggests that perhaps Ana Lucia is meant to kill him ("Collision," 2.8). Ana Lucia's belief system holds that good people should be saved. Sayid believes that whatever is meant to happen will happen.

The arrival of Desmond's sailboat off the castaways' beach also may be interpreted as fateful. Sayid suggests to Jack that they wait to determine how to handle the rescue expedition to retrieve Walt. Sayid believes that the best approach will become evident, although they currently don't know what to do. When the sailboat arrives off shore, Sayid tells Jack that "fate has given us our answer" ("Live Together, Die Alone," 2.23). The sailboat then becomes an integral part of their plan.

Those with a Christian spiritual orientation might believe that God sent the sailboat to help the castaways; Muslims may attribute the boat's arrival to Allah's will; agnostics might explain the timing as coincidence. This event, like so many others, can provide spiritual meaning for fans and characters with widely divergent religious beliefs, but it doesn't *have* to mean anything spiritual. There isn't one "correct" interpretation, but the way the scene is written allows Fate to be just as much a possibility as any other reason.

Even Mr. Eko seems to value fate. Locke marvels at the coincidence that Eko would find the missing segment of the Dharma Initiative's orientation film, bring it with him to the other side of the island, see the film, and be able to splice the missing segment back into the film. Mr. Eko cautions Locke not to confuse coincidence with fate ("What Kate Did," 2.9). During "The Cost of Living" (3.5), Locke echoes this line as he speaks to Desmond. Locke seems to know the difference between fate and coincidence now that he's regained faith in the island.

The significance of character names hints at further predestined connections among the survivors. Although Thomas is a common Western name, its repetition probably is not coincidental: Kate's love, Tom; Charlie's dealer, Tommy; Claire's lover, Thomas; Christian Shepherd's Australian alias, Tom; the Other, Tom, also known as Mr. Friendly. (See Appendix C for more similar names.)

Familiar faces also show up in different episodes, sometimes as different characters. The actor who plays Charlie's parish priest ("The Moth," 1.7) rides the scooter Hurley buys at the Sydney airport ("Exodus," 1.24). One of Sawyer's girlfriends ("Confidence Man," 1.8) and Hurley's "lotto girl" ("Numbers," 1.18) are played by the same actress, Brittany Robinson Perrineau, who is Harold (Michael) Perrineau's wife.

The survivors' lives are "intertwined before they all got on that plane," Damon Lindelof told *TV Guide* in October 2004.[5] Hurley appears on the Korean television program seen in the house where Jin threatens his boss's wayward client ("House of the Rising Sun," 1.6). A handcuffed Sawyer is led through the Sydney police station where Boone talks with an officer ("Hearts and Minds," 1.13). Sawyer walks into the car door being opened by Christian Shephard as he ends a conversation with Ana Lucia ("Two for the Road," 2.20). Libby sits at a table near Hurley in a mental institution ("Dave," 2.18). (See Appendix B for more common experiences and unlikely connections among characters.)

The first-season finale also indicates that "destiny" might be another word for "curse," at least in Hurley's case. The mystical Numbers pop up throughout the scenes of Hurley rushing to the airport. His car breaks down, the speedometer falling from one lottery number to the next. He goes to the wrong terminal and must run to the international area, passing a soccer team clad in jerseys bearing the lottery numbers. When he finally makes it to the correct gate—twenty-three, of course—the door is closed. Hurley's plaintive insistence on getting on this flight compels an attendant to ensure that he is allowed on the plane. Destiny in these scenes is humorous, an entertaining way for us to learn about the characters' interconnectedness.

Locke, however, takes destiny much more seriously. Although Sun perceives fate as a punishing force and likely fears destiny, Locke sees fate as beneficent and destiny a powerful force for good. He believes that each survivor is "chosen" for an important purpose on the island. Locke explains to Jack that everything—all messages from the island, all visions, all events, including Boone's death—has led to the opening of the Hatch ("Exodus," 1.24). Jack refuses to believe in destiny and tells Locke as much. "That's just becomes you don't know it yet," Locke assures him, confident that destiny is the operative force. Even death-by-Monster doesn't shake Locke, who tells Sayid that Eko's death had a purpose ("I Do," 3.6). Sayid, a believer in fate, no doubt would agree, even if neither he nor Locke understands exactly what that purpose might be.

Fate and destiny may be the most difficult concepts for many Western audiences to accept, but for that reason, if no other, they are important to understand in terms of *Lost*'s storytelling. They require looking at life from a different perspective and take many viewers outside their comfort zone in order to understand the characters for whom fate and destiny are readily accepted tenets of life.

DHARMA AND **DHARMA**

During Season Two, *dharma* ("Orientation," 2.3) becomes a key term, although far removed from its origins. Dharma is a Buddhist or Hindu spiritual concept[6]; DHARMA, as in the Dharma Initiative, is a secular acronym for Department of Heuristics And Research on Material Applications.[7] (Fans who watch only the TV episodes may not know the acronym; it is revealed as part of The *Lost* Experience game, played through multiple media during mid-2006 during the hiatus between *Lost*'s second and third seasons.) Even this juxtaposition of sacred and secular can further illustrate the battle between faith and reason/science.

Dharma, in both Hindu and Buddhist beliefs, refers to a life plan in harmony with the greater good. Only when people are in harmony with the universal power—living in balance with nature, spirit, and other people—can true happiness be realized. Those who do not spiritually follow dharma must live life on earth again, being reincarnated into a new life to learn more about following the true path. Perhaps Desmond's comment about the next life symbolically matches this aspect of dharma.

Dharma also means protection along one's spiritual path. The quarantine on the outside world indicates the Dharma Initiative means to protect what is stored in or who lives down the Hatch. However, little spiritual development can take place for those who are forever sheltered from the outside world.

In some religions, including Hinduism and Buddhism, dharma forms the basis of moral and judicial law; human practices must be based on universal spiritual law. In Jainism, human virtue is derived from the universal life force. Although the specific definition of dharma varies among religions, it combines a powerful spiritual force—the way the universe operates—with human action. People must act in accordance with this benevolent life force to attain perfection; when people become aligned with dharma, they live in harmony with everything, and the universe itself is in harmony.

Although this spiritual perfection may seem impossible to attain on earth, the Dharma Initiative's mission statement indicates that it sincerely meant to try. Its funded experiments were devised to help advance the human race. For many spiritually minded castaways or viewers, spirituality serves the same purpose, although people most likely do not want to be considered guinea pigs in an ongoing experiment.[8]

The Dharma Initiative may have started as Karen and Gerald DeGroots' pet project to help humanity. However, between the early 1970s and the 2000s, intervening forces, such as the Hanso Foundation and Widmore Corporation, may have subverted their research to help humanity. The Dharma Initiative on the island offers different types of technology, depending on where the island-dwellers live and work. (See Chapter 2 for a further discussion of technology.) Its employees are packaged like other commodities; Desmond and Kelvin wear coveralls with the familiar Dharma logo ("Live Together, Die Alone," 2.23–24). The men are labeled just like the boxes of corn flakes on the Hatch's pantry shelf. Science and technology are clearly important to the Dharma Initiative, although individuals may be viewed as only part of a global product.

The appropriation of a word with spiritual connotations by a non- or for-profit organization isn't new. Project HOPE (Health Opportunities for People Everywhere) and, in the U.S., Jerry Lewis' Muscular Dystrophy Association's "Love network" of TV stations participating in telethons rely on the emotional attachment people have to hope and love; people are more likely to volunteer or donate to organizations when they are emotionally attached to their message, and words like "hope" and "love" increase that likelihood. FATE is popular as an acronym; it represents more than a dozen organizations ranging from Future Aircraft Technology Enhancement to Florida Association of Theatre Education to Foundation Aiding The Elderly.[9] According to a press release from the Institute for Science Learning at the University of North Carolina at Chapel Hill, DESTINY stands for Delivering Edge cutting Science, Technology, and INternet for Years to come.[10]

Whether DHARMA turns out to be a sinister organization or an agency aiding the global population, the choice of name illustrates a common marketing principle used by real-world philanthropies and businesses such as those listed in the preceding paragraph. *Lost's* writers recognize the way that any organization—good or not so—often plays upon people's emotional connection to words representing important life or spiritual themes. The emotional connection to projects or missions that involve science and technology, as the majority of these examples do, is an effective way to make something often perceived as "cold," such as technological advancements or scientific research, more personable and humanistic. Linking science/technology with words loaded with spiritual or emotional personal meaning is a good marketing strategy. The Dharma Initiative, and those who probably subvert it, likely realize the effectiveness of choosing dharma as their acronym.

* * *

The castaways undoubtedly will find their beliefs tested as they continue to seek redemption or enjoy the possibilities of a new life. *Lost* illustrates the range of good and bad associations that can be made with even the most spiritual concepts, such as love, hope, and faith. Life, not only on *Lost's* island, requires people to make choices based on what they believe. Those who believe love should be possessive or jealous act in ways that ultimately prove harmful to themselves or others. So it is with each of these spiritual concepts. *Lost* excels in showing the pitfalls and pinnacles of the castaways' lives as they struggle with each of these life themes.

NOTES TO CHAPTER SIX, "LARGER SPIRITUAL CONCEPTS"

1. Dinah Eng, "'Lost' World Created by Diverse Writing Staff," Gannett News Service, November 26, 2005. Retrieved February 16, 2007, from http://www.azcentral.com/ent/tv/articles/1126lostwriters.html.

2. Hercules (screen name), "Moonshine Has Seen the Museum of Radio & Television *Lost* Event!! Garcia & Holloway Steal Show!!" *Ain't It Cool News*. March 14, 2005. Retrieved February 16, 2007, from http://www.aintitcool.com/node/19645.

3. Jensen, "The Beach Boys," 22.

4. Fenno, "Sweating the Big Stuff." *Entertainment Weekly*, October 19, 2006. Retrieved October 19, 2006, from http://www.ew.com/ew/article/commentary/0,6115,1547985 _3_0_,00.html.

5. Malcolm, "Secrets of *Lost*," 28.

6. Several online sites provide an introduction to the concept of *dharma:* For example, "In Hinduism, the consciousness of forming part of an ordered universe, and hence the moral duty of accepting one's station in life" ("Dharma," retrieved October 1, 2005, from http://www.tiscali.co.uk/reference/encyclopaedia/hutchinson/m00 19389.html) resonates with life on the island—not only the survivors' attempt to make sense out of the island, but their acceptance of life there; "station" is also an interesting choice, given that the Dharma Initiative requires the castaways to push the button in Station 3: The Swan. Other hatches, or stations, also required people to stay at their job without question for long periods of time. Other sites with information about dharma include these: "Essential Elements and Doctrines," retrieved October 1, 2005, from http://www.hindunet.org/quickintro/hindudharma; "Living *dharma*," retrieved October1, 2005, from http://www.livingdharma.org.

7. Wikipedia, The Free Encyclopedia, *DHARMA Initiative*. Retrieved September 7, 2006, from http://en.wikipedia.org/wiki/ DHARMA_Initiative.

8. *Lost*'s site for the Dharma Initiative provided the film shown in "Orientation." (*TheDharmaInitiative.org*, retrieved November 1, 2005, from http://thedharmainitiative.org). The Hanso Foundation also had a separate site with further information pertinent to *Lost* (*The Hanso Foundation*, retrieved November 1, 2005, from http://thehansofoundation.org/dharma.html). On the site in late 2005, the Dharma Initiative was listed as an "active project" dealing with human development to advance the human race. With the violence and paranoia typical of Seasons Two and Three, we might question the project's success if the castaways are indeed subjects in this experiment. As the *Lost* Experience progressed between May and September 2006, the Hanso Foundation site changed several times, and its manipulative nature became revealed to game-players. Characters, including Rachel Blake, fought to bring down the Foundation and to reveal how its mission had become subverted. Information from the *Lost* Experience may be slowly integrated with storylines in regular episodes, so that the *Lost* viewing audience may know as much about the Hanso Foundation as do those who followed the interactive *Lost* Experience. As of February 2007, the Hanso Foundation site contained only a message from Alvar Hanso, and the Dharma Initiative domain had reverted to a general-purpose web portal.

9. "Acronyms," *The Free Dictionary*. Retrieved September 7, 2006, from http://acronyms.thefreedictionary.com/FATE.

10. Jannette Pippin, "College Students Face DESTINY," *The Institute for Science Learning at the University of North Carolina at Chapel Hill*. April 14, 2005. Retrieved September 7, 2006, from http://www.isl.unc.edu/about_us/press_room/4_14_05.html.

PART FOUR

THE *LOST* FANDOM

CHAPTER SEVEN

CULT(IVATING) A *LOST* AUDIENCE: THE PARTICIPATORY FAN CULTURE OF *LOST*

Lost fans are like Talmudic scholars. They have creat-ed a body of scholarship about every episode.
—JAVIER GRILLO-MARXUACH

EARLY *LOST* FANDOM

Every new pilot on network television must overcome similar obstacles and navigate the same stepping stones in order to succeed: gaining widespread support from programming executives, generating interest from a potential viewing audience through well-placed marketing and advertising, and securing a viewer-friendly timeslot. But no challenge is as precarious as the formation of a solid, appointment-viewing fan base.

Creating a series with lasting power in the ratings market is challenge enough, and *Lost* has apparently accomplished that feat, but it has also inspired the buying and promotional power of viewers who not only engage in regular watching but actively engage with the text of the series. *Lost's* creators and writers have given fans an inter-active environment that draws on multiple levels of audience partic-ipation, enticing viewers to decipher the hidden clues and secret meanings that might lend insight into a complicated mythology.

In doing so, *Lost* has redefined the concept of the "cult" audi-ence. *Lost* fans are neither small in number nor remotely obscure: They are a community of tens of thousands of like-minded indi-viduals—a network of engaged, active viewers who invest time, money, and effort into a series they love for its innovation, capac-ity for game play, and broad appeal. In addition, the diverse cast offers at least one character every viewer can identify with, there-by securing a diverse, international viewership.

In (cult)ivating its audience and fandom, *Lost* faced several challenges. The original concept (plane crashes on island; *Survivor* meets *Lord of the Flies*) was questionable, the price tag on the pilot was hefty, and the timeframe between greenlight, casting, production, and broadcast was drastically short, even by television standards. Series creators J. J. Abrams and Damon Lindelof shared in the network's skepticism about the concept before penning a script that offered much more than just a group of survivors on a desert island—working together to craft a mythology that offered fear and suspense in a mystery/action/adventure that could easily hook an audience and acti-vate a fan base. Casting and auditions, as we learn from the Bonus Features on the *Lost: The Complete First Season* DVDs, inspired an influx of creative ideas, and original characters mutated while others were added, eventually expanding the number of series regulars to sixteen. From early on, the cre-ators' ever-evolving, ever-innovative vision of *Lost*, backed by a small band of vigilant supporters at ABC, drove a series that would, within less than a year, be declared a major primetime success in the United States and an international hit as well.

Following casting in spring 2004, news of the series, cast, and concept filtered out on the Internet. Zap2it.com, *Hollywood Reporter*, and *Variety* reported on signing cast members, including Dominic Monaghan, Matthew Fox, and Terry O'Quinn. Monaghan's participation may have been the first catalyst for fan activity. Best known for his involvement in the *Lord of the Rings* film trilogy as the hobbit Merry, the actor already had a solid fan following. Our summer 2005 survey of 117 *Lost* fans reflected that 73 percent of respondents reported Monaghan's participation influenced their initial viewing. A visit to MTV in May 2004 by Monaghan added more fuel to *Lost*'s fire, as he revealed on *Total Request Live* that the pilot was one of the most, if not the most, expensive in television history. His appearance coincided with a spoiler that circulated on the Internet that a polar bear would appear in the first episode, which began the trend of fan speculation that would later become trademark.

By May 2004, fans had become convinced the series had potential for early (and possibly preemptive) cancellation. In response, they organized a pledge drive in support of the series and publicized a letter writing campaign to ABC and Touchstone. The campaign originated on one of the earliest fan sites, *Lost-TV.com*, and sixty-nine potential fans had signed up as supporters by the time the pilot was screened by test audiences. At the same time, a variety of Internet news sites reported that the pilot had randomly aired on cable television networks, including the Game Show Network (GSN). These impromptu screenings, aired commercial free, increased the buzz surrounding *Lost*. Soon after the encouraging test runs, ABC officially picked up the pilot plus eleven episodes, toying with the idea of the series serving as a midseason replacement for *Alias*. Clips from the pilot airing on Entertainment News Network and several media outlets either testified to ABC's creativity or condemned the series to an early death as a result of its expense and genre limitation. After a month of consistently positive feedback, however, ABC officially assigned an 8 (Eastern and Pacific)/7 p.m. (Central) timeslot on Wednesdays.

The early formation of the fandom as a network of interconnected individuals planning to become regular viewers piqued by the premise, cast, or teaser ads for the series gave a preliminary indication of future trends in the intensity of activity and engagement. Such promotional efforts influenced ABC-initiated fan base development markedly. Fans cited the promotional materials based on the premise as a significant (35 percent) influence on their viewership, and word of mouth also played a role: Seventeen percent of fans responded that they initially viewed the series based on the recommendation of a friend or family member or through a third party Internet source.

E-Online's entertainment gossip series Watch with Kristin continually promoted the series throughout June 2004, as the popular host gushed that the series was one of the most anticipated of the fall premieres. This weekly Internet talk show airs exclusive interviews with actors and series creators, holds interactive chats, and provides spoiler information on a host of shows with heavy Internet fandom activity (*Gilmore Girls, Smallville, Alias*). *Watch with Kristin*'s promotion of the show as having a mythology grounded in science fiction and fantasy, along with frequent mention of series creators Abrams's and Lindelof's involvement, aided in a cross-pollination effect that occurred across several interrelated fandoms.

In June 2004, trade magazines announced David Fury's plans to join the creative team as writer and co-producer. Fury had previously written for Joss Whedon's *Buffy the Vampire Slayer* and *Angel*, both series with active fan bases. The addition to *Lost*'s creative team of Javier Grillo-Marxuach, who had been involved in *Jake 2.0* and *Pretender* and had an adoring (if small) fan base, inspired additional interest. Intentional or not, the addition of writers with existing fan bases further secured active initial support for the series.

Early visibility continued to generate popular interest after cast and creators attended the Comic Con convention in San Diego (July 2004), which featured posters depicting characters with "Help me—I'm *Lost*" beneath grainy black-and-white "Wanted"-style photos. During Labor Day weekend, only weeks before *Lost*'s television debut, ABC placed a thousand message-in-a-bottle advertisements for the series along popular coastlines, a creative marketing campaign that hoped to entice beachgoers to get *Lost*.

The *Lost*-TV site was still collecting petitions and drumming up interest for the freshman series throughout the summer as official marketing efforts continued. The site secured a telephone interview with Lindelof to discuss the way the show had evolved from premise to reality and the creator's feelings regarding the importance of listening to a fan base. This interview cemented the value ascribed to the fan base by the series' creators and the commitment of the marketing and creative team that fans were already important to them, even if still relatively small in number. Lindelof self-identified both as a fan of his collaborator Abrams and *Alias*, and as a former student of sociology and psychology. His comments in the interview, which focus on the nature of forming fan bases and the psychology of viewing, indicated that Lindelof was acutely aware of the significance of fandom support.

In July 2004, DavidFury.net interviewed Fury about his involvement with *Lost*. The interviewer (referencing his writing for *Buffy* and *Angel*) asked whether Fury planned to "terrorize the *Lost* net fandom," and he jokingly responded that he hoped to create a "*Lost* fan Fight Club"—a broad ambition for a series three weeks before its premiere. Fury understood the value of his fans as potential viewers, and a promise to engage his present fan base in a new environment was a motivation for some of his more skeptical fans to tune in to the ABC drama.

The key players of *Lost*'s creative team had experienced both the positive and negative influence of fandom: The *Alias* fan base,

Abrams was well aware, had helped to keep the ratings-struggling series afloat in the third and fourth seasons, and writers Fury and Drew Goddard realized the influence of fandom from working with Joss Whedon on Nielsen bottom-feeders *Buffy* and *Angel*. Fans can help make or break a series, and the writers, creators, and actors of *Lost* were acutely aware of the precarious nature of consciously attempting to construct a fan base. Cultivating—and maintaining—a positive relationship with the fans was especially important to Abrams, who had experienced fan backlash resulting from the plot and lack of character-driven storylines in the third year of *Alias*. He admitted in a May 2005 interview that "The Internet has really changed the way we watch TV. Instantaneously, thousands of people are reacting and creating a consensus on what they like and don't like. The scrutiny is mind-blowing, and you'd be moronic not to listen to the fans."

The first season of *Lost* premiered with some of the highest ratings of any ABC debut, earning ninth place in the ratings overall for the week. Following the premiere, *Lost*-TV's webmaster, Xander, e-mailed a congratulatory message, and Lindelof was quick to respond with: "We're obviously in shock over how well the show did . . . but what REALLY thrills us is the fan response. Thank you SO much for your continued dedication to LOST— we'll keep doing our best to earn the love. . . . Hugs, Damon." The focus of the e-mail is not on the ratings the premiere achieved but on the viewers and fans themselves, and the language cements the relevance of that relationship—the affectionate, "hugs, Damon" exudes familiarity. What's more, Lindelof has not forgotten the role *Lost*-TV played in development of the fan base: He sent a thank-you card from all the writers and creators of the series on the one-year anniversary of the site in March 2005.

Listening to—and understanding—the fan base fell on the shoulders of the creative and marketing teams working together in order to create a distinctly unique experience for the *Lost* viewer. Interactivity continues to play a critical role in the sustained development of the fandom. Actual online gaming environments and hidden clues and "Easter eggs" distributed within the episodes of the series have fueled development of the fan base. In the week of the premiere, for example, Internet-savvy fans were granted access to the hide-and-seek game I-am-*Lost*. The Flash-based game allowed players to scavenge through virtual plane wreckage and tropical undergrowth for clues about their favorite cast members—clues that included Kate's handcuffs, Jack's medicine, and a blinking red light marking the location of the plane's transceiver—that linked the game to the ABC website for the show. (Tie-in games and websites were not new for an Abrams series: the first year of Alias saw the launch of a dummy website for the fictional "Credit Dauphine," where Sydney Bristow worked as a double agent; later seasons brought an interactive online game acting as a precursor for a live-action gaming console release.) In October 2004, *Lost* message boards were abuzz with news of the game which acted as a gateway for series information: each week, the content of the game coincided with the show's narrative development and clues for upcoming episodes.

I-am-lost.com set an important precedent for the level of textual involvement by *Lost* fans. The game became more and more complex each week, with new stages and items to explore without posted rules or guidelines. The lack of official information about how to play the game created a need for discussion on the Internet with other fans. Bouncing off ideas about new developments the game and the series might take initiated fans who might not have otherwise been interested in engaging with a community of online *Lost* enthusiasts. The Internet worked to fuel the speculation of fans, as more and more people tuned in each week to get *Lost*. Fans also took their water cooler discussions about the series to the Internet, which opened up additional new avenues for speculation and community building. More and more Websites devoted to the series, its actors, fan fiction, and art populated the Internet throughout the first year of the series. Fans, it seemed, could not get enough of the mysterious island and even more mysterious castaways.

The online game was not the only interactive element of the series. Beginning with the first episode, *Lost*'s multiple, creepy enigmas teased viewers. What is the monster? "Where are we?" (Charlie's panicked question at the end of the pilot). But the biggest game of the season had hardly begun. Questions about Jack's visions of his dead father and Locke's mysterious recovery from paralysis dominated the first half of Season One until the mysterious numbers were introduced: 4, 8, 15, 16, 23, and 42 would soon prove to be more than just Hurley's accursed lottery winners; they became inscrutable signifiers that somehow held the key to *Lost*. The successful integration of the numbers stemmed from the initial concept of interweaving characters into flashback scenes, sometimes for foreshadowing (Hurley's cameo on television as the Mega Lotto winner during "House of the Rising Sun"[1.6]), or continuity (Sawyer's arrest in the background during Boone's visit to the police station during "Hearts and Minds" [1.13]), or foreshadowing (Claire's baby's father, Thomas, an artist, has a mural painted in their apartment during "Raised by Another" [1.10] that reappears in the Hatch during Seasons 2 and 3). Such moments marked the start of the intertextual "Easter eggs" of the show. In the video game industry, Easter eggs are secret items, hidden in the game's architecture, that are unessential to the overall success or comprehension of the game as a whole, but are a bonus adding to the player's overall enjoyment. The Easter eggs in *Lost* work in similar fashion: they enhance viewer enjoyment—if the viewer is so inclined to explore in deeper detail.

The numbers clued a large number of viewers in that there was more than meets the eye to the text of *Lost*. The first tip-off was the flight number: Oceanic 815 contained two of Hurley's numbers in succession, and supported the theory that the numbers were cursed—the plane had crashed after all. But the introduction of the numbers in episode eighteen piqued the interest of enough fans who were interested in seeing whether the numbers had made an appearance in earlier episodes. They had. A fury of interactivity began as information about the numbers spread across the Internet and has continued to grow more complex. The numbers continue to play a crucial role, either in combination or alone. Near the end of "Exodus," Part 2 (1.24), Hurley realizes that the outer door of the Hatch has been stamped with the sequence, and in Season Two they are discovered to be the code that must be input into the computer within the Hatch every 108 minutes—or 4+8+15+16+23+42.

Knowing the numbers proved essential during the break between the first and second season and the introduction of the Oceanic Air Website, which, for the first month of operation, required that visitors enter them, in proper succession, in order to navigate an Easter egg–laden web address that included a hidden link to the theory and speculation boards of OceanicFlight815.com.

LOST FAN SITES

Complex discussion has always been at the heart of the *Lost* fandom. LiveJournals and blogs dedicated to theory and speculation only augmented the intense conversations already under way on message boards across the Web. The "official" ABC boards for the show quickly grew in membership numbers and traffic, and as fans sought new information, they stumbled upon already existing or newly created Websites that seemed designed for their particular fan discourse. Premier fan site *Lost*-Media.com launched in September 2004 with a small collection of links to other fan sites, and by the close of the year it had an active and engaging message board community. Other message boards flourished as well, as people joined to discuss their own concepts and theories about the show. Attuned to this trend, the Abrams-supported message board website The Fuselage appeared, an innovative community where fans are invited to ask the creative team (including the creators and executive producers) and actors questions, as well as discuss theories, speculations, and spoiler content. Part of the continued efforts of *Lost*'s makers, The Fuselage indicates that the powers-that-be behind the show were actively interested in what fans think and feel about the series and the direction it is taking.

A popular fan site that features discussion of myths and rumors even more than news (a staple of *Lost*-Media.com) or the extremely broad-based discussion on the many threads of The Fuselage is TheTailSection.com, hosted by the popular Doc Arzt. The success of this site led to the second Doc Arzt–created *Lost* site: The*Lost*Experience.com. There fans posted their experiences and solutions to clues as they played the game. It quickly proved to be one of the most important fan-based sites during the summer of 2006.

The advent of fan sites exploded during the second and third seasons of *Lost*, with fans providing more comprehensive indices of source-text materials. The fan-updated *Lost*pedia (a Wikipedia-type encyclopedia devoted exclusively to *Lost* content, including fan theories, episode and character guides, music from the series, and promotional and marketing materials) launched during the second half of Season Two. The success of the site prompted ABC to create their own fan "wiki" on the official *Lost* website following the first six episodes of Season Three, during the thirteen-week hiatus. The subsite, *Lost* Wiki, invites visitors to "Help build the definitive fan guide to *Lost*." The official *Lost* Wiki caters to a variety of fan interests—not only does it allow visitors to update encyclopedic information, but during the third-season hiatus it included a section catering to more creative fan interests, including prompts to "Give Writing for *Lost* a Try," to share experiences related to *Lost*, and even to write *Lost* haiku.

In similar vein, the *Lost* Wikia, a fan-driven website that focuses on discussion about series characters and episodes, launched in

December 2005. Collaborative editing from visitors (in the same format of the popular Wikipedia and *Lost* Wiki) produced articles and analyses conducted by experts (including author Lynnette Porter) on subjects such as spirituality and relationships, as well as detailed, introspective examinations of character motivations, common motifs, and themes. At the time of writing, the site hosted over 1200 articles.

THE WHISPERS

Fan activity extends beyond official game play or theory and speculation. Websites devoted to the translation of conversations between Korean-speaking Jin and Sun and the French distress transmission picked up by Sayid's transceiver circulated on the Internet. Fans calculated the exact number of years the message had been broadcast, challenging the sixteen-year calculation put forward in the pilot. Screenshots of Rousseau's maps made their way online as fans speculated as to what, and where, the "Black Rock" was. As the first season neared a winter break, fans began to converse about the mysterious "whispers" heard in several episodes. The first documented discussion of whispers followed the Sayid backstory episode, "Solitary" (1.9), in which the former Iraqi soldier is captured by Rousseau during his trek in the jungle. A transcript of the whispers from *Lost* Links detailed what fans heard after repeated careful listening:

> MAN'S VOICE: Just get him out of here
> MAN'S VOICE 2: He's seen too much already
> MAN'S VOICE: What if he tells?
> WOMAN'S VOICE: . . . Could just speak to him
> MAN'S VOICE: No

An intense discussion began among fans about the validity of the whispers and the accurate transcription of the voices. Those who could hear the whispers began to speculate about the existence of underground tunnels and other experiments on the island, while other fans claimed the whispers were simply auditory hallucinations. When the whispers reappeared during "Outlaws" (1.16)—heard this time by Sawyer, fans claimed to detect the following dialogue (also from *Lost* Links):

> WOMAN'S VOICE: Maybe we should just talk to him
> MAN'S VOICE: No, if he sees us it will ruin everything
> MAN'S VOICE: What did he see?
> WOMAN'S VOICE: They could help us
> MAN'S VOICE: Can't trust Come back around

In the episode, Sawyer pauses, causing the audience to question whether he can hear the whispers.

> MAN'S VOICE: What did he see?
> MAN'S VOICE: Nothing, he was following it
> WOMAN'S VOICE: Speak
> MAN'S VOICE: Nothing

For several months following the first airing of these episodes, the validity of the whispers generated a great deal of contention among fans. On The Fuselage, fans banded together and formed the group W.H.I.S.P.E.R.—an acronym that stood for "We Hear Interesting Sounds Per Episode Replay" (new members had to testify to hearing, and believing in, the whispers)—which garnered a great deal of negative response from "non-believers." The most interesting aspect of this development within the theory and speculation fandom was not whether the whispers actually did exist but the way supporters organized themselves.

"Whisper" believers set up camp in the relationships area of The Fuselage message boards and began to recruit those whom they termed as "converts." The existence of "shippers" (or "relationshippers") within fandom has dated back at least to *Star Trek* Kirk and

Spock enthusiasts who wished to see the two men engaged in something more than a professional relationship. The use of the term "shipper" is well documented within *X-Files* fandom (shippers longed for a romantic relationship between Fox Mulder and Dana Scully). From the start of fandom, the dynamic of romance and relationships has been a distinctive, even dominant, element of fan behavior. *Lost*, too, has its traditional relationship-centered fans, but the whisper-centric segment of the fandom has created something new: a highly specialized "ship" of their own.

In the *Lost* survey many enthusiasts explained their involvement in the pursuit of whispers as a direct response to the lack of updates in the I-am-*Lost* game and their need to help fuel their obsession. This led, in turn, to the repeated watching of previously aired episodes, in the hope that "clues" could be found that included whispers. The listening trend has continued, and the investigative nature of *Lost* fans has been pushed to new limits: In the premiere episode of the second season, "Man of Science, Man of Faith," Shannon encounters a spectral Walt, who whispers incoherently. When played backward, Walt seems to be saying either "Don't push the button, No, the button's bad," or "Push the Button, No Button's Bad." Each has decidedly different implications, and message board fans have been in an uproar arguing over the articulation. Like many other discussions in *Lost* fandom, this one lost importance once the implosive result of the button not being pushed aired (in the Season Two cliffhanger finale and early Season Three episodes).

FAN ACTIVITIES

Although this particular level of interactivity—with fans recording sound clips and digitally reversing them—is initially accessible only to the digerati, the fandom can become engaged on any level and as consciously as they want. They can research the origins of the characters' names—theorizing the significance of "Rousseau" and "Locke," count the recurrences (and combinations) of the numbers and speculate on their significance (when the episode "Numbers" aired in March 2005, within hours a fan registered *4815162342.com* to host a message board site for number theory speculation, while others have played the fateful numbers— unsuccessfully—in state lotteries), plot the possible geographic location of the *Lost* island, analyze the images of the mural found in the Hatch, catalogue all of *Lost*'s many intertexts and references, create transcripts of episodes, or explore the origins of backgammon.

The audience is welcome to take from the series what it wants. Fans who want only to watch the series and enjoy the pleasure of a continuing serial each week can do that, yet those who revel in hours spent plumbing the show's hidden mysteries will not be disappointed. *Lost* does not prescribe in advance levels of access or forms of enjoyment.

But like all major fandoms, *Lost*'s devotees do more than surf the web. A variety of fan gatherings and conventions have also enticed and inspired fans. On March 12, 2005, for example, the series became the subject of a panel at the William S. Paley festival, which honors breakthrough television shows. One of the first Paley events to sell out, it featured a majority of the cast and creative team: Abrams, Naveen Andrews, Bryan Burk, Carlton Cuse, Emilie de Ravin, Matthew Fox, Jorge Garcia, Maggie Grace, Josh Holloway, Malcolm David Kelley, Daniel Dae Kim, Yunjin Kim, Evangeline Lilly, Dominic Monaghan, Terry O'Quinn, Harold Perrineau, and Ian Somerhalder all attended. Cuse asked the attendees and audiences whether they thought Locke was good or evil, received a mixed response, and opened the floor to questions and answers. Notable responses included Andrews' comment that the show didn't insult the intelligence of its viewers and Abrams' confirmation that one of the series regulars would die in Season One.

Following the success of the Paley festival, fans themselves organized a fundraising event convention titled, "Destination: L.A. A Party for *Lost* Fans," organized by E.M.A. Fan Geek

Productions. ("M" [Maya] and "A" [Allyson] were both grassroots fan-supportive organizers who had hosted several "Save Our Show" and fundraising silent auctions in the past.) Organizers auctioned a lunch with supervising producer Javier Grillo-Marxuach, various autographed *Alias* and *Lost* scripts, autographed *TV Guide* covers featuring the cast, and an exclusive memento from Grillo-Marxuach: his first script, "House of the Rising Sun." The entire cast and creative team were invited, and Kim, Abrams, Perrineau, and Greg Grunberg, among others, made appearances. (The Destination: L.A. fan events have continued, with the third event being hosted in spring 2007.)

Touchstone Television and ABC would hire Creation Entertainment, well known within sci-fi fandoms for their fan conventions for such shows as *Xena*, *The X-Files*, and *Star Trek*, to host a series of *Lost* conventions, the first in June 2004 in Burbank, California. In a press release announcing the event, Bruce Gersh, senior vice president of Business Development for ABC entertainment, explained that "*Lost* has a tremendous fan following, and it is time we gave back to the fans." At the convention, an upcoming bimonthly glossy fan magazine and fan club were announced, and the event sold a variety of merchandise, including clothing (T-shirts and $130 *Lost* jackets), character banners, and signed photographs. Three lucky winners enjoyed lunch with de Ravin and Terry. Creation Entertainment continues to host the Official *Lost* Fan Club, complete with membership packs and online publications, and *Lost*'s actors occasionally make appearances at conventions.

The convention craze isn't limited to fans living in the United States. In late 2006, word circulated on the Internet that a *Lost* convention in the London area would take place in mid-2007. Celeb Events set up a website for Oceanic, a convention specifically for *Lost* fans. Former *Lost* cast members can be found at other U.S. and U.K. conventions, such as FX (Orlando, Florida) and Collectormania events throughout the United Kingdom.

At the 2007 annual International Consumer Electronics Show (C.E.S), which hosted 140 exhibits in categories from robotics to electronic gaming, Walt Disney CEO Robert Iger delivered the keynote address. Evangeline Lilly and Matthew Fox joined Iger at the Las Vegas convention, which focused a great deal on *Lost*'s success, which Iger described as heavily reliant on both technology and the support of fans: "It has become the most successful multi-platform show ever. ABC.com has been overrun with fans coming to watch podcasts, discuss the show, or view full length episodes."

Evangeline Lilly elaborated on the important role of fans, stating, "We are really at the mercy of the fans. Producers go online to look at what is being said, and they react to that." Lilly's and Fox's appearance confirm that not only producers are impacted by fan responses—the show runners and actors are aware of the importance of making such conference appearances, as they are responsible for the core audience of the most devoted of *Lost* fans: the technophiles.

Expanding *Lost*'s "reality" through technology has been a constant within the *Lost* fandom. Early in the first season, two fans created a DriveShaft website (www.driveshaftband.com) mourning the missing Charlie Pace and providing a history of the band (complete with a cohesive backstory, discography, and concert history), critical reviews of their albums, and transcribed articles detailing the "tragedy" of Oceanic 815. The well-designed site led a majority of the fandom to assume it had been created by ABC and Touchstone and was so successful the ABC website offered a DriveShaft video for "You All Everybody" and suggested the possibility of a DriveShaft CD.

The second season of *Lost* encouraged a proliferation of fan-created websites such as the DriveShaft site that appeared to offer official, ABC/Bad Robot–sanctioned content, especially following the introduction of the Hanso Foundation. These websites utilized the images and ideas used on the series or on official, series-supported websites to mimic official sites, often including false information to fans. One of the best-done and most elaborate fan fabrications was the illegitimate Dharma Initiative Classification Video, which outlined the different areas of study and featured several look-alikes to the Degroots and Alvar Hanso as seen in the original "Orientation" filmstrip.

The MPEG "Classifications" Video hit the Internet in October 2005, with a post originating on The Fuselage by a Samuel DeGroot. The authenticity of the video was eventually disproven by *Lost* writer Javier Grillo-Marxuach on The Fuselage.

The majority of fabricated content comes from the creation of websites that enhance the continuity of the series while adding to theory and speculation. When asked on The Fuselage about the websites, Marxuach offered: "There are things on the Web that are ours and others that are not. . . . There are a lot of great fan-sites that take a speculative approach to the mythology—and I think that is a cool thing, but overall, I'd rather neither confirm nor deny!" This aspect of fan engagement possibly influenced the creators of the Alternate Reality Game (ARG) The *Lost* Experience, which ran from May until September 2006.

Our *Lost* survey offers insight into the amount of time and dedication fans commit to the series. While a modest 35 percent stated that they spent between one and two hours per week, the average amount of time spent on *Lost* activity was eleven hours. The largest reported amount was seventy-five hours per week, and 16 percent devoted twenty-five hours or more. Fan activities included visiting fan and speculation sites, participating in message boards, writing and reading blogs, and writing and reading fan fiction. In addition, 60 percent indicated that they spent a majority of their time developing theories to explain the complicated mythology of the show, and 66 percent admitted to seeking out storyline spoilers.

While the creative team repeatedly asserts (and even has a disclaimer on The Fuselage) that they are prohibited from reading fan fiction while working on the series, they do support it. In an interview with PopGurls.com, once supervising producer and writer Grillo-Marxuach confessed to being a "big fan" of fan fiction, and that "I'm a big supporter and admirer of fanfic. . . . I encourage everybody to write it at all times." *Lost* fanfic writers face challenges not known by those who sought to tell their own *X-Files* or *Buffy*verse stories. "Fanfic seems to be difficult, with the way the plot twists every episode," one *Lost* fan, vampiresetsuna, reflects. "It seems the prevalent activities in this fandom are icon-making, theory-speculating, and analyzing screen captures for relationshipping quality."

The writing of critiques or essays, made popular within the *Buffy, Angel,* and other fandoms, seems a prevalent fan activity for *Lost.* Entire websites are devoted to academic-toned essays that evaluate the series with scholarly rigor. Episode reviews are also a popular practice, with most of the reviews appearing on blogs and LiveJournals. Most of these contain humorous or insightful anecdotes from the characters in the show.

The behavior of *Lost* fans is not, of course, wholly unique: All fandoms, at some level, actively engage with the source text of their fandom. What makes *Lost* fans different is that they have formed a discourse community or knowledge network—a group of individuals devoting time and effort into discussing, analyzing, and investigating their favorite series as though it were a distinct discipline of study. Their behaviors mesh well with Matt Hills' theory of the fan-scholar—a fan who studies the object of his or her fandom in discursive fashion. In some large-scale fandoms, the creation of derivative works, from fan fiction to art, is the most prevalent activity; the *Lost* fandom, however, is more likely to be engaged in discussion, research, and synthesis of ideas presented within the series. Seventy-seven percent of fans reported spending time discussing the series on message boards, and 65 percent regularly visited blogs that focus on the show. Forty-two percent self-published their thoughts on their own blogs, and 17 percent wrote essays, critiques, or reviews of the series. These

CULT(IVATING) A *LOST* AUDIENCE   257

numbers are interesting when compared to the derivative activities of the fandom: Thirty percent wrote fan fiction, 34 percent created art, and 18 percent created or watched videos.

LOST IN ACADEMIA

Serious fan engagement requires a level of commitment to the series far beyond casual appointment viewing. The establishment of the Society for the Study of *Lost*—a website that houses scholarly essays on the series and publishes a peer-reviewed internet journal—further illustrates the dedication and commitment of fan-scholars to explore the series in full detail. The website also hosts archived message board posts from *Lost*-TV.com by category ("literary allusions," "psychology 101," "astronomy," and "physics").

Professors, television critics, and more "traditional" scholars who also happen to be *Lost* fans analyze the series at academic conferences, too. Since 2005, when *Lost* morphed into the show to watch for scholarly as well as entertainment reasons, panels have discussed the series, its development, fandoms, and just about every other aspect of its creativity and marketability. Conferences held by the Popular Culture Association, at the regional and national levels, and the Hawaiian International Conference on the Arts and Humanities, for example, feature scholars' research and analysis of the series and its popularity. *Lost* is becoming acceptable subject matter for televisionary studies even as it continues to evolve as a series.

WHY IS *LOST* SUCH A PHENOMENON?

What inspires such an incredibly active community? When asked to evaluate the appealing elements of the series, 88 percent of fans indicated aspects directly related to the writing and narrative of the series—from the premise of a plane crashing on an island, to the interconnected backstories and flashbacks, characterization, mythology, and mystery. Characters and characterizations were continually represented favorably. As one fan explains:

"Because the show's main group of characters reflect such a large panel of people, beliefs, and backgrounds, it makes their situation actually possible to identify with. Every one of them is a full-fledged three-dimensional character with a rich backstory, and that's the kind of writing that appeals to me."

The highly speculative elements of *Lost*—those that lend to theorizing, reading spoilers, and analyzing data (60 percent of responding fans regularly engage in such)— appear to be key factors in the continued interest of fans in the series and is often the object of fan scholarship. Hidden "Easter eggs" on official websites, within the series, and on the Seasons One and Two DVDs provide additional thrills for secret-seeking viewers. These "Easter eggs" have been the platform in developing the multiple games created in conjunction with the series. Each episode reveals new and different mysteries, and the devotion of fans to rewatch episodes fuels the fire. The two-part Season One finale, "Exodus," revealed on careful examination a link to the Oceanic Airlines website, and the fan-detectives found a plethora of goodies involving the ill-fated airline. Oceanic-Air.com not only provided fans with material to discuss in relation to the series' unique mythology but also fostered a sense of continued community investment.

The second season's *Lost* Experience game was introduced to fans through a commercial (during the broadcast itself) for the Hanso Foundation that flashed a 1-800 number and a link to the website. Engaging fans in interactive game play is a key component to the long term success of the series.

CONSPIRING WITH A *LOST* AUDIENCE

Keep in mind that at root the word "conspire" means to "breathe together." *Lost* "conspiracy" theories are distinctive ways of thinking about the show's many puzzles that bring together not only numerous individual mysteries but like-minded fans smitten, at least temporarily, with particular theories that help make sense of what they are watching, and ready to share them—at the water cooler, on discussion boards, and on websites.

Lost conspiracy nuts have engaged in a wide variety of suppositions. In our first edition, we discussed some of the lesser-known theories, including string theory, the theory of two planes, alternate universes, and the debunked (both by the series and by the series' creators Lindelof and Cuse) 2009 theory. As the series has progressed, several new theories have been introduced.

While there are many sites to access to read *Lost* theories, The Fuselage offers visitors the most updated and ever-evolving *Lost* theories. Some of the more interesting theories and the people who fuel the fire of theoretical posturing that occurs in the *Lost* fandom are detailed in the following paragraphs, giving a portrait of the people behind the most engaging and interesting of theories about *Lost*, the *Lost* island, and the Others.

One of the more active theory groups is undoubtedly The Fuselage's journey for the "QU.E.S.T.": The acronym QU.E.S.T. stands for "QUesting for Every Single Theory" and uses riddles posted by the cryptic "Tiberius." Tiberius's cryptic riddles feature clues about biblical verses, saints, Greek mythology, science, and philosophy, to name a few. Tiberius began posting his riddles during the first season of the series. The riddles are a way of spawning new theories and often run concurrently with upcoming series information (in effect, the theories sometimes act as spoilers). Group members refer to themselves as "The Gathering."

THE CRASH WAS PLANNED THEORY

There are many variations on the "planned" crash scenario, and this theory has existed since the first season. The information given about the others at the beginning of Season Three ("A Tale of Two Cities," [3.1]) has encouraged speculation about Oceanic Flight 815, with proponents of the theory citing the fact that Ben's group of the Others appeared less than surprised about the crash. More interestingly, fans cite that Juliet's movie, made for Jack, where she uses poster board to give him information about Ben, was filmed at her home, and possibly on the same day of the crash—as she is wearing the same clothes and hairstyle as she wore the day of the book club meeting.

The Collective Consciousness/Big Brother/Implanted Memories Theory:

Another theory that has seen many evolutions, the "implanted memory" theory uses a variety of platforms for its explanation, yet hinges on the interconnected memories shared by the survivors of Oceanic 815. Add in repetitious themes (and near identical phrases, even, at times) uttered by the survivors and the Others' uncanny knowledge about the survivors, including the most intimate of details, and it is easy to see how theories are spun. One Fuselage poster in particular, Lucidity, has come up with a derivation of this theory of particular interest—one entitled, "The Soul Catcher Hypothesis." Lucidity postulates that the survivors all have tiny computer chips implanted in their eyes, an idea borrowed from in-development technology by British Telecom for a chip that records all manners of information, from what is viewed by the user as well as detailed sensory input. Lucidity's theory explains a great deal of the island's goings-on, including the fixation on eyes and eyes opening, mirror-image representations (as the chip would record information in mirror image format), and the reason behind the use of flashbacks. Perhaps most interestingly, this recorded information might explain why the smoke monster was able to show Eko images from his past—perhaps because Eko's chip had been accessed. Like most of the theories floating around on the web, Lucidity's theory has many holes and generates unanswered questions—but these questions are what continue to encourage *Lost* fans to continue their quests for answers to the ultimate of questions: What, exactly, is going on?

The opening of the Hatch, of course, hatched a multitude of theories. Now that we have watched the Dharma Initiative's (dis)orientation film, eaten Apollo bars, looked at the mural (painted by director Jack Bender during the first season of the series), found a man (Desmond) Jack met in L.A. trapped in the Hatch, met the Tailies, learned that the Others kidnap only "good" people, seen the Dharma logo on a shark (and, retrospectively, on Oceanic 815), seen a horse (from Iowa) loose on the island, conspiracy theories seem to be completely legitimate, entirely essential, weapons in our ever-challenging engagement with *Lost's* narrative power.

The "Orientation" video, first viewed during the Season Two episode with the same title (2.3), briefly discusses the role of the Dharma Initiative. Filmstrip host Dr. Marvin Candle—a mysterious, white-coated scientist with a prosthetic hand—briefly outlines the work of the initiative, which includes research in meteorology, psychology, parapsychology, zoology, electromagnetism, and utopian societies. In a heavily spliced video, the survivors of Flight 815 learn what Desmond had tried to explain: that a code must be entered into the central terminal of the computer every 108 minutes—or else. Without any other explanation, the video concludes with Locke's bewildered, "We'll have to watch that again"—a recommendation taken to heart by TiVo, DVR, VCR, and Web users worldwide when the filmstrip appeared on the *Hansofoundation.org* website.

The Dharma Initiative videos did not stop there. When the survivors of Oceanic 815 find another hatch, the Pearl, they are offered another video, this time hosted by a Marvin Candle lookalike, Mark Wickmund. More pieces of Dharma Initiative videos were released during the *Lost* Experience online. The "Psychology Test Video," with a repeated sequence of 115 photograph frames, offers a variety of images, including explosions, swans, and polar bears. In the Sri-Lanka video, Hanso Foundation creator Alvar Hanso explains the significance of the numbers, revealing that the accursed sequence is actually an equation, formulated by mathematician Enzo Valenzetti, predicting the end of humanity.

Although weekly developments in watched and rewatched broadcast episodes serve as the main conspiracy generators, official websites and the "Easter eggs" planted there have certainly aided and abetted conspiracy theorists. Oceanic-Airlines.com launched immediately following the Season One finale with embedded messages (a script page, for example) and hidden message-in-a-bottle-style letters, presumably from the Flight 815 survivors. From May through mid-July 2005, the site featured a banner that proclaimed, "Taking you places you never imagined," with an island shot of a perfect blue sky and clear, unoccupied water. In July, the banner was replaced with an image depicting a ship that resembled the Black Rock and a swirling column of smoke that seemed unremarkable, until compared to another interesting switch. The original site invited visitors to "Visit Mysterious Australia," a banner switched in July to "Visit Ancient Australia."

The layer-embedded Flash seating chart on the site offered "Easter eggs" such as Danielle's maps and Kate's arrest information (dated 7/17/2004). Late July, visitors who entered "The" and "Boy" on the flight tracker information screen were treated to pencil drawings of New York, the Statue of Liberty, and World Trade Center towers in plain sight, and the self-portrait Michael drew during his recovery (dated 2003). Appearing on an official site, each of these items took on, at least potentially, extra significance and fueled fan speculation.

Another official web location, the Disney-owned Hanso Foundation website, offered additional portentous goodies, including the "Orientation" film originally viewed in the eponymous episode. The first incarnation of the website (launched in fall 2005) offered visitors abbreviated information: They were given a brief biography of Alvar Hanso, the foundation financial backer, who has an aversion to showing a full view of his facial features. We also learned the mission statement: "The Hanso

Foundation: a commitment to encouraging excellence in science and technology and furthering the cause of human development." This development includes the Hanso life extension project, electromagnetic research, the quest for extraterrestrial life forces, mathematical forecasting, cryogenic development, juxtapositional eugenics, and accelerated remote viewing. While most of the website links for the first Hanso Foundation proved dead ends, some revealed a series of memos that alluded to the work—and progress—of the foundation.

Dated September 21, 2005, a memo celebrating the eugenics experiments of the foundation appears under the life extension project link and cites the longevity of a chimp named Joop (he was 105). Clicking at the bottom of the memo reveals a password-protected backdoor site that, with entry of the word "Copenhagen," gives access to a letter from the GHO (Global Health Organization) ordering a cease and desist for activities occurring at the Hanso Foundation's offshore facility near Zanzibar, dated two days before the triumphant accounts of Joop's lifespan. The letter references an outbreak of a mengioccoccal-type disease in the region of Tanzania.

Alvar Hanso's biographical information on the website—we learn that he delivered munitions in World War II and served as "the leading purveyor of high-technology armaments to NATO"—adds complexity to an already mysterious individual. Linking from his biography photo—shadowy, as always—a mouseover effect reveals that the picture is more than meets the eye. A hidden computer message—mimicking the scene from "What Kate Did" in which Michael seemingly makes contact with the outside world—identifies the person at the terminal as simply "mole." From there, another letter appears from the GHO thanking the foundation for their generous donation and encouraging the continuation of "important work" at the Zanzibar facility.

The second incarnation of the Hanso Foundation, corresponding with the launch of The *Lost* Experience ARG, featured a completely revised interface. This time, visitors were treated to videos and job advertisements, and could even look at a webcam of the celebrated Joop only mentioned in memos before. The website lasted as long as the ARG and was continually updated throughout the game. As of February 2007, the site provides only a heartfelt message from Alvar Hanso, with promises to revitalize and restructure the Hanso Foundation.

For those who seek them out, such "paratexts" (as media scholars call them) feed back into *Lost* proper and become, at least for that segment of the audience engaged in active interpretation of the "text," important elements in their deeper understanding.

SUPPORTING THE *LOST* FANDOM

Midway through the first season, ABC aired a "catch-up" episode for *Lost* for the unenlightened few who were not tuning in to the hit series. The basic premise was recounted, characters were introduced, and a brief summation of the action up to the present point in the March hiatus were disclosed. What the catch-up episode did not offer was all of the hidden subtexts, creepy sub-plots, and continuing mysteries that true fans already knew intimately. Similar episodes were shown in January 2006 and February 2007 before new episodes aired after a long hiatus. They, too, offered only the highlights of plots and character development but failed to reveal any carefully gathered information from months of previous online interaction.

The conscious exclusion of the more subtle elements of the show served a dual purpose. It allowed the interested viewer to enter the show with a surface accumulation of knowledge while granting them the opportunity to become enchanted later by the subtleties. And the catch-up episodes preserved as well the status of the "true" fan in relation to the show: None of the information fans had worked so hard to recover through repeated viewings, discussion board marathon sessions, or LiveJournal posts had been disclosed to the "outside" audience. Fans maintained the level of access the creators have repeatedly praised and supported. Entrée to the *Lost* fandom was through initiation only.

ABC's sponsorship of the already-mentioned Oceanic-Air.com site following the Season One finale likewise fed fan hunger and kept them busy. Visitors could find a host of clues and a second-season trailer—if they knew the numbers, and discovered, too, that the website creators, celebrating the investigative nature of the fandom, had embedded hidden messages in the source code and even a page from a "secret" script. The site launched at the close of May, and although news spread across the Internet about its existence, fans had to decipher the clues on their own. Entering the numbers in specific order allowed access to a seating chart for Oceanic flight 815, along with embedded Flash components that generated further speculation. And, in typical *Lost* fandom fashion, intrepid fans were allowed access to a new message board dedicated solely to theory and speculation. Traffic on the Oceanic-Air Website increased as the link circulated on the Internet, and an article appeared in *Newsweek* on June 10, 2005. "With this show, everything happens for a reason, and it's the same with this site," Mike Benson, senior vice president of marketing at ABC disclosed in the interview.

Oceanic-Air was, however, only the tip of the iceberg: The *Lost* Experience developed a multiplatform fan experience that required a true amount of dedication from fans to follow the material and content contained within. The ARG was announced by Lindelof and Cuse during their weekly podcast in spring 2006. A *New York Times* article described the game as "a multimedia treasure hunt that makes use of e-mail messages, phone calls, commercials, billboards and fake websites that are made to seem real."

Selling *Lost*: Merchandising and Fans

Merchandise sales are often affected positively by strong fan bases; fans, after all, are likely to buy products—"commodity intertexts" as media scholars call them—related to a product they endorse in order to both support and advertise their fan status, and this is no different in the *Lost* fandom. "Official" *Lost* merchandise offers diverse products for the most discerning fan, from t-shirts and mugs to trading cards, magazines, and conventions. The Season One and Two DVD box sets have held steady in the top ten DVD sales at Amazon.com since their release. An extensive selection of tie-in products, from five novelizations and a companion book *Bad Twin* by fictional author Gary Troup, to a glossy wall calendar, which had sold tens of thousands of copies prior to its October 2005 release date, boosted the overall profitability of the series. Sixty-seven percent of participants in the fan survey on *Lost* indicated that they had or planned to buy merchandise for the show, 58 percent had preordered the Season One DVDs, and 21 percent indicated future plans to attend upcoming conferences or special events.

From the start, marketing and advertising of *Lost* almost always utilized the unique font and lettering of the series title and now includes other trademarks on official merchandise as well: the Oceanic Airlines logo appears on tote bags and hooded sweatshirts, and the accursed numbers are featured on several mugs and t-shirts (one travel mug comes with a compass). Fans can download episodes from iTunes for $2.99 each, join the fan club, buy action figures, buy a *Lost* "Dharma Composition Book" ($15.99 for a notebook with the Dharma Initiative logo on it), collectible cards featuring autographs and costume snippets, action figures, the official board game, a variety of jigsaw puzzles, the same silver Halliburton attaché case carried by the Marshal, and the official television soundtracks for Seasons One and Two (featuring "Monsters Are Such Interesting People" and "Run Away! Run Away!" but not "You. All. Everybody" by DriveShaft).

In January 2007 a mobile telephone game, created by Gameloft, features Jack as he interacts with a variety of series characters including Kate, Sawyer, and Hurley. The game focuses on reenactments of pivotal series events, from discovering the Hatch to meeting the Others. The mobile game is supported in a variety of formats and languages, including English, French, German, Spanish, and Portuguese. Ubisoft planned to release an interactive video game in May 2007, to be offered on home consoles as well as PC platforms. Ubisoft's Montreal studios were working with Executive Producer Brian Burk to develop the game. Bruce Gersh, senior vice president of business development for ABC and Touchstone, conveyed his excitement about the forthcoming game in a press release from October 2006: "We are excited to work together with Ubisoft to create a gaming experience that will allow fans to further immerse themselves into the mysteries and intrigues of the series." Burk's enthusiasm for working on the game, entitled "*Lost*: The Transcendent Videogame," is apparent: "With the ability to tell new interactive stories within the *Lost* universe, we're giddy to be developing a game that, once completed, will be as engaging and fun to play as it is to create."

If fans are not enthused about official merchandise or games, a plethora of fan-designed gear available on the Internet should satisfy any merchandise craving. "The Hatch" fansite sells a variety of fan-designed gear, and the popular *Lost* Links.net Website's "Black Rock Shop" sells coffee mugs emblazoned with "I Survived Flight 815" for $14.95. The marketing doesn't stop there: Tie-in marketing has also proved highly profitable. The *Lost* Experience Game included commercials for products including Verizon Wireless, Sprite, Jeep, and Honda.

Fans who wish to research *Lost* ancestor texts have been ready to spend as well. When Abrams mentioned the copy of Stephen King's *The Stand* in the writer's room, fans went out to buy copies to see just why the text was so important. Early on in Season One, Sawyer is seen reading Madeleine L'Engle's *A Wrinkle in Time* and Richard Adams' *Watership Down*—novels fans just had to have. Flann O'Brien's *The Third Policeman*'s cameo appearance in

"Orientation" (2.3), a book that had sold 15,000 copies in two earlier printings, became a top-200 best selling book on Amazon.com at the start of October. (By comparison, O'Brien's first novel, *The Poor Mouth*, was in the 860,000th rank.)

Elements of community discourse, referral, speculation and scholarship within an extremely large fan base are reflective of the cultural significance of the series to an international audience. Abrams once said that the fans were a thousand times smarter than the writers, and playing into—and with—that intellect is a key challenge for the continued success of the series and cultivation of the *Lost* fandom.

THE *LOST* CULT?

While labeled by the network and media news as a "cult," the *Lost* fandom extends beyond the traditional label of the term, which often carries a negative connotation. Cult fans usually operate in small circles of reference and often must act as anchors and advocates for a rating-challenged program's continuation. With an average viewership for a new episode between fifteen and twenty million in the United States alone, the *Lost* fandom is anything but small. Perhaps we should think of *Lost* not as a "cult" program but as a "mythology" show. Like *The X-Files*, *Buffy the Vampire Slayer*, and *Twin Peaks*, cousins in the mythology genre, *Lost* has attracted a devoted following of "cultish" fans.

Lost fans are hardly the typical small minority group of outsiders typical of cult fandom. Puzzling *Lost*'s deep mysteries has become mainstream as millions upon millions of viewers— *Lost*ies, *Lost*aways, *Lost* fanatics—tune in worldwide to create a unique phenomenon. Yet no one concrete label captures the *Lost* fan, and the variety of engagement within the fandom poses a unique question: How do you define a cult audience that has extended beyond the typical definition of the term? A majority of the media articles published during the first season of *Lost* centered on trying to either define the show or create parallels to other series, generally those in the "mythology" bracket.

A *Boston Globe* article in October 2004 categorizes mythology shows as those that attract a "lively, game audience"; mythology shows make their "viewers into cosmic Sherlocks. . . . Mythology writers expect rigorous, un-couch-potato-like viewing—and they get it."

While the third season has seen a decrease in the number of viewers in the United States, and fans were less than satisfied with the six-episode "mini-series" arc in the fall of 2006, the truest of *Lost* fans—those who engage in the alternate reality games, record and decipher audio clips, and create theories—don't seem to be going anywhere. Fans continue to view episodes from the free *ABC.com* online viewer, purchase downloads from iTunes (in fact, at the time of writing, *Lost* remained in the top twenty downloads for all six of the miniseries arc episodes that launched Season Three). Internet sites for or about the series continue to proliferate on the web. The fandom, in the United States, is still going strong. Outside North America, *Lost* has been sold to 210 territories worldwide—the second most popular series in the world (next to the long-running crime investigation drama *CSI: Miami*).

As long as the series gains worldwide popularity, and as long as fans download episodes and official and unofficial podcasts, purchase licensed merchandise, and rewatch their DVDs, *Lost* will continue to thrive.

EPILOGUE

LOST IN THE FUTURE

After we finished the first edition, the end of *Lost*'s second season, as expected, provided the conclusion to some castaways' stories but led other characters in exciting and sometimes frightening new directions. Michael's and Walt's story seems to end with their reunion and apparent exodus from the island. However, in true *Lost* style, we don't see what happens to the little boat once the father and son motor off screen. Perhaps they return home but never tell their tale, but—more likely, and also in true *Lost* fashion—they remain spiritually if not geographically lost for some time to come. Michael, at least, someday must deal with the ramifications of murdering two people, even if he currently feels that the sacrifice of his friends is necessary for Walt to be freed from the Others' camp. At some point, *Lost* likely will deal with this loose end, alluding to or even showing what happened to two of the original castaways. Although the actors may change, Michael and Walt are still part of the *Lost* story, if on their own hiatus during Season Three.

Also as expected, the first six episodes of Season Three and the early episodes after another long hiatus ended in February 2007 feature the Others. Although many fans wish that the story would be focused only on the remaining original castaways, or even newly introduced Paolo and Niki plus now-regular character Desmond, the series' creators still have quite a bit of the Others' story to tell. Henry Gale/Ben Linus, Juliet, and their comrades are an interesting, if often disturbing addition to the *Lost* family. And, as with all

272 UNLOCKING THE MEANING OF LOST

dysfunctional families, we doubt that their interpersonal problems and sociopolitical machinations will end any time soon.

What keeps us returning to this series, despite long hiatuses, the death of favorite characters such as Mr. Eko, and the loud buzz of unhappy fans who want "their" (defined in as many ways as there are fans) *Lost* right *now*, is the depth and difficulty of the story. Sure, the creators and writers haven't answered most of our questions and have some pretty big threads hanging loose within the weave of the plot, but the story hasn't unraveled yet. *Lost* requires us to think about the many story lines and to keep our own hope alive, even in the darkest plots. In many ways we're like the castaways. We didn't realize just what we were getting into back in September 2004, but we're here for the long haul. Like Locke, we may have lapses of faith, but deep down we're true believers.

Where is *Lost* headed? In terms of story, we're probably about halfway there, and as actors and writers come and go, we'll likely see many more changes. Season Three is a pivotal point in the story and in *Lost*'s television life. *Lost* is unique among television series today in that it tells one long story over a span of years, unlike *24* or *Desperate Housewives*, which can begin and end one complete story during the course of a season, even if the serial premise can run many years. *Lost* takes us to dark corners of the psyche and then lets us bask on the beach; it dares to go places other series wouldn't, and it likely will be able to maintain this momentum until the entire story is told within four or five years. Audiences are used to instant gratification and quickly give up on series that have only begun to tell their tale before their fate is decided; watching a complex story that requires years to reach its resolution is unheard of, frustrating, and compelling, all at the same time.

During a *Lost* convention in June 2005, Lindelof told fans that story arcs had been projected for three seasons and five seasons; the series wouldn't go longer than five years to tell the complete story, which could be told basically within three years. (However, in late January 2006, original cast members received a hefty per-episode raise, with the caveat that they also sign a contract for an additional year. Obviously, the producers and ABC are banking on *Lost*'s continued success, which could prolong the original estimated storyline.) Although Lindelof admitted that some aspects of the story (such as the Numbers) take on a life of their own, which then requires reworking the primary arcs to accommodate new details and sidestories, the series' basic concept had been outlined. He promised that there would be no "reunion" shows or spin-offs.

Season Three is underway at the time of our writing, and the time frame for the story's ending is changing. Hints throughout fandom suggest that in Season Four, ABC may follow Season Three's schedule of six new episodes in the fall, another long hiatus, and then the remaining number of episodes arriving in time for February sweeps and ending during the all-critical May sweeps period. This schedule helps alleviate the huge time gap between U.S. first-run airings and global distribution and keeps the problem of Internet spoilers to a minimum for those watching outside the U.S. In addition, Lindelof and Cuse also have hinted that a movie may follow the series' television ending, bringing the *Lost* story to a glorious big-screen finale.

Strange as it seems, *Lost* isn't the hot new kid on the block any more, but it still generates more than its share of watercooler comment. Fans can and do "get *Lost*" from multiple sources; they may be acutely tuned to the series' happenings without necessarily being tuned in on Wednesday nights. The series continues to break new ground by offering "television" in non-TV venues and by telling its story in atypical ways. *Lost* is performance art as well as pure entertainment; it may look like a TV series and act like a TV series, but it still defies easy definition. Like the ephemeral Monster, *Lost* is a shapeshifter that still is hard to pin down but is fascinating to watch, whatever it does.

Lost's marketing machine continues to roll out new products and, better yet, interactive experiences. It involves fans in activities far beyond passive viewing and tries to tap into every segment of consumers. A series of traditional cardboard puzzles launched in late 2006 and continuing in 2007 provide clues to upcoming episodes; a board game requires players to develop a survival strategy. The collectibles market includes not only the ever-popular costume and autograph cards but several series of action figures posed within *Lost* scenes and speaking characters' lines. Interactive games such as The Lost Experience and the mixing of media to blur the lines between reality and fantasy attract online game players and Internet-savvy fans. As with storytelling, *Lost*'s marketing continues to evolve in a variety of directions that show other television series just how to capture consumers' imaginations.

In 2007, it still seems safe to say that many of us will find ourselves watching *Lost* for the foreseeable future, and hardcore fans likely will spend a great deal of time analyzing details, reading background materials featured in episodes, and participating in such activities as The Lost Experience. The show continues to provoke discussion, pique our curiosity, and promote itself in innovative ways. So far, the series hasn't *Lost* its way, although we might wonder at times whether Abrams, Lindelof, Cuse, and company are following Locke's wayward compass. *Lost* is a once-in-a-lifetime trip, and we're glad to be along for the ride.

APPENDIX A

CHARACTER SKETCHES

KATE AUSTEN

Interests—Steering clear of the authorities; getting and keeping Tom's model airplane. **Home Base (Approximately)**—Originally Iowa, most recently Australia. **Family**—Mother, Diane Jensen (possibly deceased); legal stepfather, but also biological father, Wayne Jensen (deceased); legally recognized "biological" father, Sam Austen; ex-husband Kevin. **Former Job(s)/Career**—Ranch worker, bank robber, homemaker. **Closest Friend(s) on the Island**—Jack, Sawyer; but Kate is friendly to just about everyone and never completely trusts anyone. Sawyer becomes Kate's lover in Season Three. **Key Moments on the Island**—Helping Sayid transmit a distress signal; volunteering for every dangerous mission into the jungle; kissing Sawyer, more than once; trying to take a dead castaway's identity and escape on the raft; being the first to enter the Hatch; going after Walt; being captured and surviving incarceration by the Others; making love with Sawyer. **Greatest Personal Challenge on the Island**—Trusting others; not revealing her deepest emotions, when being held captive by the Others. **Greatest Personal Achievement on the Island**—Retrieving the model airplane from the marshal's briefcase; developing a relationship with Sawyer. **Backstory Episodes**—"Whatever the Case May Be" (Season 1); "Born to Run" (Season 1); "What Kate Did" (Season 2); "I Do" (Season 3).

Boone Carlyle

Interests—Shannon, mother's business. **Home Base (Approximately)**—California, formerly lived in New York. **Family**—Mother Sabrina; father (deceased); stepsister Shannon; stepfather Adam Rutherford (deceased). **Former Job(s)/ Career**—Manager of a division of his mother's wedding business. **Closest Friend(s) on the Island**—Shannon, Locke. **Key Moments on the Island**—Joining forces with Locke; uncovering the Hatch; sending a distress signal from the Beechcraft; dying as a result of injuries from a second plane crash; becoming Locke's spirit guide during a vision quest. **Greatest Personal Challenge on the Island**—Living his own life, separate from Shannon. **Greatest Personal Achievement on the Island**— Working with Locke. **Backstory Episodes**—"Hearts and Minds" (Season 1); "Abandoned" (Season 2).

Ana Lucia Cortez

Interests—Unknown. **Home Base (Approximately)**—Los Angeles, California. **Family**—Mother: Captain Teresa Cortez. **Former Job(s)/Career**—Police officer; airport screener. **Closest Friend(s) on the Island**—Mr. Eko, at first; Jack. **Key Moments on the Island**—Leading the Tailies; killing Shannon; finding Henry Gale's balloon; dying. **Greatest Personal Challenge on the Island**—Keeping her group of survivors safe from the Others; joining the other castaways after killing Shannon. **Greatest Personal Achievement on the Island**— Maintaining control of the Tailies, as well as keeping them safe; refusing to kill Henry Gale. **Backstory Episodes**—"The Other 48 Days" (Season 2); "Two for the Road" (Season 2)

Michael Dawson

Interests—Art; son Walt. **Home Base (Approximately)**—New York City. **Family**—Son: Walt; unnamed mother (to whom he speaks on the phone in the Sydney airport; "Exodus"). **Former**

Job(s)/Career—Construction worker, artist. **Closest Friend(s) on the Island**—Early attraction to Sun; surprising friendship with Jin. **Key Moments on the Island**—Engineering a way to rescue Jack from a cave-in; rescuing Walt from a polar bear; building and sailing the raft; killing two castaways; retrieving Walt from the Others; leaving the island after betraying his friends. **Greatest Personal Challenge on the Island**—Building a positive relationship with Walt; finding Walt after his abduction. **Greatest Personal Achievement on the Island**—Gaining Walt's love; being reunited with Walt; leaving the island. **Backstory Episodes**—"Special" (Season 1); "Adrift" (Season 2); "Three Minutes" (Season 2).

JAMES (SAWYER) FORD

Interests—Women, reading, running cons, reading. **Home Base (Approximately)**—Not known: he travels throughout the U.S. South as he runs cons; as a child, lived in Tennessee. **Family**—Parents deceased; possibly a daughter, Clementine Phillips (with one-time lover and mark Cassidy). **Former Job(s)/Career**—Confidence man. **Closest Friend(s) on the Island**—Surprisingly, late in Season Two, Jack; Kate, who becomes his lover in Season Three; a fragile friendship with Michael and Jin. **Key Moments on the Island**—Kissing Kate, more than once; hoarding luxuries gathered from the plane and survivors' belongings; sailing on the raft; surviving a bullet wound inflicted by the Others; having sex with Ana Lucia; surviving incarceration by the Others; making love with Kate. **Greatest Personal Challenge on the Island**—Dealing with his grudge toward everyone; escaping from the Others. **Greatest Personal Achievement on the Island**—Telling Jack about Christian's feelings toward his son; trying to protect Kate from further injury by the Others. **Backstory Episodes**—"Confidence Man" (Season 1); "Outlaws" (Season 1); "The Long Con" (Season 2); "Every Man for Himself" (Season 3).

MR. EKO

Interests—Religion. **Home Base (Approximately)**—Nigeria. **Family**—Brother: Yemi (deceased). **Former Job(s)/Career**— Drug lord/self-appointed priest. **Closest Friend(s) on the Island**—Ana Lucia Cortez, although he shares interest in the Hatch with Locke and begins to build a church with Charlie. **Key Moments on the Island**—Killing the Others who attack him; serving as tracker and guide as the Tailies travel to the other side of the island; facing the Monster; finding the Pearl station; dedicating himself to becoming a priest; dying during another encounter with the Monster. **Greatest Personal Challenge on the Island**—Overcoming remorse from killing others, even in self-defense; returning to his religious roots. **Greatest Personal Achievement on the Island**—Finding his brother's body in the Beechcraft and gaining closure about this death; bringing a missing segment of the orientation film to the Hatch and helping Locke splice the film; finding spiritual purpose in pushing the button. **Backstory Episodes**—"The 23rd Psalm" (Season 2); "?" (Season 2); "The Cost of Living" (Season 3).

DESMOND DAVID HUME

Interests—Books by Charles Dickens; sailing; Penelope Widmore. **Home Base (Approximately)**—Scotland. **Family**— Unknown (mother to appear in a backstory in Season 3) **Former Job(s)/Career**—Dishonorably discharged as a lance corporal from the army. **Closest Friend(s) on the Island**—Kelvin (when there wasn't anyone else around). **Key Moments on the Island**—Pushing the button; unlocking the Hatch's fail-safe; surviving the Hatch's implosion; saving Claire and Aaron from lightning. **Greatest Personal Challenge on the Island**—Trying to get back to Penny. **Greatest Personal Achievement on the Island**—Developing his ability to see the future. **Backstory Episodes**—"Live Together, Die Alone" (Season 2).

SAYID JARRAH

Interests—Electronics and occasionally romance (with Shannon). **Home Base (Approximately)**—Tikrit, Iraq (although he left home several years ago and had been searching for his friend Nadia) **Family**—Unknown; an overprotective mother was mentioned in "Solitary". **Former Job(s)/Career**—Communications officer in the Republican Guard. **Closest Friend(s) on the Island**—Shannon, as a love interest; Jack, as an ally. **Key Moments on the Island**—Triangulating the source of the Frenchwoman's distress call; torturing Sawyer; being tortured by Rousseau; fixing Desmond's computer; falling in love with Shannon; torturing Henry Gale; leading a rendezvous party to the other side of the island. **Greatest Personal Challenge on the Island**—Overcoming his shame for his role during Sawyer's interrogation; overcoming his grief and rage after Shannon's death. **Greatest Personal Achievement on the Island**—Getting Shannon to believe in herself. **Backstory Episodes**—"Solitary" (Season 1); "The Greater Good" (Season 1); "One of Them" (Season 2).

JIN-SOO KWON

Interests—Being a successful businessman; taking care of his wife. **Home Base (Approximately)**—Seoul, South Korea. **Family**—Fisherman father; father-in-law Mr. Paik; mother-in-law; wife Sun. **Former Job(s)/Career**—Employee of Mr. Paik (generally his "enforcer"); formerly a waiter and doorman. **Closest Friend(s) on the Island**—Michael, although he is sometimes solicitous of Sawyer; Sun, once they are reunited in Season Two. **Key Moments on the Island**—Attacking Michael for "stealing" his watch; ending, for a time, his relationship with Sun; building and sailing the raft with Michael; being reunited with Sun (Season 2); sailing the boat toward a rendezvous on the other side of the island. **Greatest Personal Challenge on the Island**—Becoming a better husband; protecting Sun's unborn child. **Greatest Personal Achievement on the Island—** Becoming a part of the group, instead of staying apart from the castaways; becoming a prospective father. **Backstory Episodes—** ". . . In Translation" (Season 1); "House of the Rising Sun," in Sun's backstory (Season 1); ". . . And Found" (Season 2); "The Whole Truth," in Sun's backstory (Season 2); "The Glass Ballerina," in Sun's backstory (Season 3)

SUN-HWA KWON

Interests—Art; her dog Popo; gardening; healing methods; her marriage (at times); her love affair with Jae. **Home Base (Approximately)**—Seoul, South Korea. **Family**—Wealthy but overbearing parents in Seoul; husband Jin. **Former Job(s)/Career**—Graduate with an art history degree; wife. **Closest Friend(s) on the Island**—Kate and, for a time Michael; Jin, once they are reunited. **Key Moments on the Island—** Revealing that she speaks English; rebuilding a relationship with Jin; finding herbal remedies to ease Shannon's asthma and to assist in Boone's surgery; planting a garden and an orchard; discovering that she is pregnant; helping to sail the boat toward a rendezvous point on the other side of the island; shooting and killing an Other. **Greatest Personal Challenge on the Island—** Rebuilding her marriage with Jin; becoming a mother. **Greatest Personal Achievement on the Island**—Becoming a more independent woman. **Backstory Episodes**—"House of the Rising Sun" (Season 1); ". . . In Translation," in Jin's backstory (Season 1); ". . . And Found," in Jin's backstory (Season 2); "The Whole Truth" (Season 2); "The Glass Ballerina" (Season 3).

CLAIRE LITTLETON

Interests—Baby; astrology. **Home Base (Approximately)—** Sydney, Australia. **Family**—Estranged mother; Thomas, former lover and father to her baby; son Aaron; (speculation) father, Christian Shephard; half-brother, Jack Shephard. **Former**

Job(s)/Career—Fast-food employee at Fish 'n' Fry. **Closest Friend(s) on the Island.** Charlie (although their relationship is on and off); Locke (at times, when he steps in as a protector). **Key Moments on the Island**—Being kidnapped by Ethan; giving birth to Aaron; having Aaron kidnapped by Rousseau and later by Charlie; recovering memories about her abduction. **Greatest Personal Challenge on the Island**—Being a good mother. **Greatest Personal Achievement on the Island**—Being a good mother. **Backstory Episodes**—"Raised by Another" (Season 1); "Maternity Leave" (Season 2).

WALTER (WALT) LLOYD
Interests—Comic books, dog Vincent, backgammon. **Home Base (Approximately)**—Sydney, Australia, most recently, although he has lived in New York, Amsterdam, and Rome. **Family**—Mother Susan Lloyd (deceased); stepfather Brian Porter, who adopted Walt; father Michael Dawson. **Former Job(s)/Career**—Student. **Closest Friend(s) on the Island**—Vincent. **Key Moments on the Island**—Learning to throw a knife; burning the raft; giving Vincent to Shannon; being kidnapped by the Others; sending messages while abducted. **Greatest Personal Challenge on the Island**—Getting to know his father; surviving the Others. **Greatest Personal Achievement on the Island**—Rebuilding the raft with his father and learning more about him in the process; being reunited with his father; leaving the island. **Backstory Episodes**—"Special" (Season 1); "Adrift" (Season 2—featured as a baby and toddler).

JOHN LOCKE
Interests—Games of all types. **Home Base (Approximately)**—Tustin, California. **Family**—Biological father Anthony Cooper, biological mother Emily Annabeth Locke, foster mother (deceased), foster sister (deceased). **Former Job(s)/Career**—Regional collections manager for a box company; once a toy store

employee and a home inspector; worked and lived in a commune. **Closest Friend(s) on the Island**—The island itself. **Key Moments on the Island**—Hunting boar; finding, helping to open, and exploring the Hatch; accidentally luring Boone to his death; serving as a counselor/advisor to characters who are having an emotional crisis; organizing a system for inputting the code into the Hatch's computer; having a spiritual crisis about pushing the button; regaining his faith in the island; surviving the Hatch's implosion; following instructions given via a vision quest. **Greatest Personal Challenge on the Island**—Determining and then doing what the island wants him to do. **Greatest Personal Achievement on the Island**—Becoming "found;" regaining the ability to walk. **Backstory Episodes**—"Walkabout" (Season 1); "Deus Ex Machina" (Season 1); "Orientation" (Season 2); "Lockdown," (Season 2); "Further Instructions" (Season 3)

CHARLIE PACE

Interests—Music (playing professionally, composing). **Home Base (Approximately)**—Manchester, later London, England. **Family**—Brother, Liam; sister-in-law, Karen; niece; mother (possibly deceased). **Former Job(s)/Career**—Bassist for DriveShaft, sometime grifter. **Closest Friend(s) on the Island**—Claire (although they have an on and off relationship), Hurley. **Key Moments on the Island**—Saving Jack during the cave-in; shooting Ethan; bringing back Claire's baby; giving up heroin, later finding a stash on the island, and finally destroying it; having dreams that convince him to baptize Aaron; trying to save Eko from death in the Hatch. **Greatest Personal Challenge on the Island**—Staying away from heroin; regaining Claire's trust. **Greatest Personal Achievement on the Island**—Looking after Claire and Aaron. **Backstory Episodes**—"The Moth" (Season 1); "Homecoming" (Season 1); "Fire + Water" (Season 2).

HUGO (HURLEY) REYES

Interests—Popular culture (at least he knows about a lot of movies); music, including CDs and concerts; backgammon. **Home Base (Approximately)**—California, possibly Santa Clara. **Family**—Mother, Carmen; brother, Diego; former sister-in-law; grandfather, Tito (deceased). **Former Job(s)/Career**—Counter man at Mr. Cluck's Chicken Shack, lottery winner, wealthy investor. **Closest Friend(s) on the Island**—Charlie, sometimes Jack (but he is more of an authority figure), Libby (until her death), Desmond (as a possible role model). **Key Moments on the Island**—Building a golf course; getting a battery (and information) from Rousseau; distributing food (twice—most recently from the Hatch) to the castaways; dating Libby; being abducted and then released by the Others. **Greatest Personal Challenge on the Island**—Stepping on a sea urchin; overcoming Libby's death; overcoming food addiction. **Greatest Personal Achievement on the Island**—Keeping in everyone's favor, even when he is in charge of something; dating Libby. **Backstory Episodes**—"Numbers" (Season 1); "Everybody Hates Hugo" (Season 2); "Dave" (Season 2).

SHANNON RUTHERFORD

Interests—Tanning, ballet. **Home Base (Approximately)**—California originally, most recently Sydney, Australia. **Family**—Father, Adam Rutherford (deceased); mother (deceased); stepbrother Boone (deceased); stepmother Sabrina Carlyle. **Former Job(s)/Career**—Student, dance teacher. **Closest Friend(s) on the Island**—Sayid. **Key Moments on the Island**—Wearing an orange bikini while others established a camp; translating the Frenchwoman's notes; attempting to kill Locke for his role in Boone's death; searching for Walt; making love with Sayid; being shot and killed by Ana Lucia. **Greatest Personal Challenge(s) on the Island**—Overcoming grief at Boone's death; believing in her self-worth. **Greatest Personal Achievement on the**

Island—Finding someone who loves her unconditionally.
Backstory Episodes—"Hearts and Minds" (Season 1);
"Abandoned" (Season 2).

JACK SHEPHARD

Interests
Mostly work related, but perhaps wilder in the past—he sports
several tattoos and took flying lessons; possibly running. **Home
Base (Approximately)**—Los Angeles, California. **Family**—
Mother, Margo; father, Christian (deceased); ex-wife, Sarah;
(speculation) half sister, Claire Littleton. **Former Job(s)/
Career**—Spinal surgeon at St. Sebastian's Hospital. **Closest
Friend(s) on the Island**—Kate. **Key Moments on the Island**—
Accepting leadership of the castaways; treating castaways' injuries
(e.g., giving CPR to Rose and Charlie, treating Sawyer's stab
wound, transfusing his own blood into Boone); confronting
Desmond—and part of his past; planning revenge on the Others;
surviving incarceration by the Others. **Greatest Personal
Challenge on the Island**—Being able to let go of situations he
cannot control. **Greatest Personal Achievement on the
Island**—Keeping as many people alive as possible. **Backstory
Episodes**—"White Rabbit" (Season 1); "All the Best Cowboys
Have Daddy Issues" (Season 1); "Do No Harm" (Season 1);
"Man of Science, Man of Faith" (Season 2); "The Hunting Party"
(Season 2); "A Tale of Two Cities" (Season 3).

APPENDIX B

CHARACTER CONNECTIONS

During the complete first season and first half of the second, the characters share not only space on the island, but facts from their histories or actions on the island that mirror each other's. The connections do not include every task that characters have done together; only events and traits that are mirrored between characters are included. The following list provides an indication of the links between and among characters that help us make meaning from *Lost* and help the characters begin to understand themselves and each other.

Character	And	Connection
Ana Lucia	Charlie	shoot and kill their attackers, who once left them for dead
	Claire	become pregnant and later are abandoned by the baby's father
	Hurley	live and work in Los Angeles
	Jack	share a drink in a bar at the Sydney airport; live and work in Los Angeles; follow a parent into the "family business"

CHARACTER	AND	CONNECTION
Ana Lucia (cont)	Kate	flirt with Jack; are called Ann or a variation of that name during part of their lives
	Locke	live in California
	Sayid	feel dead inside because they have lost loved ones
Boone	Hurley	have lots of money; live in California
	Rose	live in New York City for a time
	Shannon	share past history as stepsiblings and lovers; die on the island
Charlie	Ana Lucia	shoot and kill their attackers, who once left them for dead
	Claire	are kidnapped and traumatized by Ethan
	Desmond	come from the UK; are Catholic
	Hurley	have listened to DriveShaft and like music; stay in the same hotel the night before they take Oceanic 815; are Catholic; are comforted by Rose during an emotional crisis
	Jack	have tattoos; save each other's life on the island
	Jin	believe that a real man takes care of his wife/girl friend, sometimes to the point of being obsessive or jealous toward others
	Locke	enjoy DriveShaft's music

CHARACTER	AND	CONNECTION
Claire	Ana Lucia	become pregnant and later are abandoned by the baby's father
	Charlie	are kidnapped and traumatized by Ethan
	Cindy	are Australian
	Danielle (Rousseau)	give birth on the island; have a child kidnapped
	Hurley	work at a fast food restaurant
	Michael	go through the process of giving up a child for adoption; are the single parent of a child on the island; have a child kidnapped
Danielle (Rousseau)	Ana Lucia	capture and tie up Sayid for interrogation
	Claire	give birth on the island; have a child kidnapped
	Hurley	understand the significance of the "cursed" Numbers
	Michael	have a child kidnapped by the Others
	Sayid	know how to interrogate and torture others
	Shannon	speak French
Desmond	Charlie	come from the UK; are Catholic
	Hurley	are Catholic

CHARACTER	AND	CONNECTION
Desmond (cont)	Jack	like running; talk briefly in Los Angeles
Hurley		
	Boone	have lots of money; live in California
	Charlie	have listened to DriveShaft and like music; stay in the same hotel the night before they take Oceanic 815; are Catholic; are comforted by Rose during an emotional crisis
	Claire	work at a fast food restaurant
	Desmond	are Catholic
	Danielle (Rousseau)	understand the significance of the "cursed" Numbers
	Jack	live in California
	Jin	quit a job after being reprimanded by the boss; as boys, fish with their fathers; Hurley may have been seen by Jin on Korean television after Hurley won the lottery
	Locke	have Randy as a boss; are connected to the box company (Locke works there; Hurley owns the company)
	Sun	have fond memories of owning a special dog
	Walt	read the same comic book; are known in their youth as playing backgammon well

CHARACTER	AND	CONNECTION
Jack	Ana Lucia	share a drink in a bar at the Sydney airport; live and work in Los Angeles; follow a parent into the "family business"
	Boone	Jack fails to save Boone's stepfather after an accident brings Adam Rutherford into the emergency room where Jack is working; live in California
	Charlie	have tattoos; save each other's life on the island
	Desmond	like running; talk briefly in Los Angeles
	Hurley	live in California
	Libby	treat a man's leg injury immediately after the crash
	Sawyer	have talked with Christian Shephard; perform CPR on a castaway to save a life; flirt with Kate
	Shannon	Jack walks past Shannon when she learns of her father's death; Jack fails to save Shannon's father after an accident brings Adam Rutherford into the emergency room where Jack is working; grow up in California
	Sun	share an interest in healing; lose a wedding ring
	Walt	have difficulties understanding their respective fathers
Jin	Bernard	are separated from their wives for a time on the island

CHARACTER	AND	CONNECTION
Jin	Charlie	believe that a real man takes care of his wife/girl-friend, sometimes to the point of being obsessive or jealous toward others
	Hurley	quit a job after being reprimanded by the boss; as boys, fish with their fathers; Jin may have seen Hurley on Korean television after Hurley won the lottery
	Rose	are separated for a time from a spouse on the island
	Sun	share a history as spouses; speak Korean
Kate	Ana Lucia	flirt with Jack; are called Ann or a variation of that name during part of their lives
	Libby	say they have "trust issues"
	Locke	are good trackers
	Mr. Eko	are good trackers
	Sawyer	are forced to leave Australia because of a criminal past; use different names to conceal their true identities
Libby	Jack	treat a man's leg injury immediately after the crash
Locke	Ana Lucia	live in California
	Boone	live in California
	Charlie	enjoy DriveShaft's music

CHARACTER	AND	CONNECTION
Locke (cont)	Hurley	have Randy as a boss; are connected to the box company (Locke works there; Hurley owns the company); live in California
	Jack	live in California
	Kate	are good trackers
	Mr. Eko	are good trackers
	Michael	Locke rolls past Michael in the Sydney airport
Mr. Eko	Kate	are good trackers
	Locke	are good trackers
	Rose	actively profess their religion and pray for survivors
Michael	Boone	live in New York City for a time
	Claire	go through the process of giving up a child for adoption; are the single parent of a child on the island; have a child kidnapped
	Rose	live in New York City
	Danielle (Rousseau)	have a child kidnapped by the Others
	Sun	share a love of art, she with an art history major, he as an artist

CHARACTER	AND	CONNECTION
Rose	Boone	live in New York City for a time
	Jin	are separated for a time from a spouse on the island
	Mr. Eko	actively profess their religion and pray for survivors
	Michael	live in New York City
	Sun	are separated from her husband on the island, for a while
Sawyer	Jack	have talked with Christian Shephard; perform CPR on a castaway to save a life; flirt with Kate
	Kate	are forced to leave Australia because of a criminal past; use different names to conceal their true identities
Sayid	Danielle (Rousseau)	know how to interrogate and torture others
	Shannon	talk to each other in the Sydney airport; are lovers on the island
Shannon	Boone	share past history as stepsiblings and lovers; die on the island
	Jack	Jack walks past Shannon when she learns of her father's death; Jack fails to save Shannon's father after an accident brings Adam Rutherford into the emergency room where Jack is working; grow up in California

CHARACTER	AND	CONNECTION
Shannon (cont)	Danielle (Rousseau)	speak French
	Sayid	talk to each other in the Sydney airport; are lovers on the island
	Walt	lose a close family member and grieve on the island; take care of Vincent
Sun	Jack	share an interest in healing; lose a wedding ring
	Hurley	have fond memories of owning a special dog
	Jin	share a history as spouses; speak Korean
	Michael	share a love of art, she with an art history major, he as an artist
	Rose	are separated from their husbands on the island, for a while
Walt	Hurley	read the same comic book; are known in their youth as playing backgammon well
	Jack	have difficulty understanding their respective fathers
	Shannon	lose a close family member and grieve on the island; take care of Vincent

SIMILAR NAMES

Names are another way to make meaning in *Lost*. Several characters, major and minor, have similar names, either by name origin, root, translation, or similar sounds (e.g., close-sounding names in English, rhyming names). The following table indicates some connections among characters or perhaps some interesting coincidences among character names.

NAME	DESCRIPTION OF CHARACTER	EPISODE(S) OR RECURRING CHARACTER
Adam	Dubbed Adam and Eve as the "first people" on the island; bones found in the caves.	"House of the Rising Sun"
Adam Rutherford	Accident victim who dies in the emergency room before Jack can treat him; Shannon's father	"Man of Science, Man of Faith"
Annie	Kate uses this name during her stay on a farm in Australia	Recurring character (Kate); Annie only in "Tabula Rasa"

Emily Annabeth Locke	John Locke's biological mother, who helps Locke's biological father, Anthony Cooper, trick John into donating a kidney to his father	"Deus Ex Machina"
Ana Lucia Cortez/Ann	Survivor from Oceanic 815's tail section; brutal leader of the Tailies	Introduced in "Exodus"; recurring character in the second season
Ann	Ana Lucia is called Ann by her police partner	"Collision"
Brian Porter	Walt's stepfather, Walt's mother's husband who adopted the boy but later gave him up to Michael	"Special"
Bryan	Shannon's boyfriend in Sydney, Australia, who takes money from Boone and abandons Shannon	"Hearts and Minds"
Christian Shephard	Jack's father; former chief of surgery at St. Sebastian's Hospital in Los Angeles	"White Rabbit"; "All the Best Cowboys Have Daddy Issues"; "Do No Harm"; "Man of Science, Man of Faith"

Chrissy	Oceanic representative who tells Jack that his father's body cannot travel on flight 815	"Exodus"
Kristen	Newlywed who, with husband Steve, dies in the crash of Oceanic 815	"Walkabout"
Danielle Rousseau	Frenchwoman whose daughter was kidnapped by Others years before	Recurring character introduced in "Solitary"
Danny	Ana Lucia's partner, who leaves her	"Collision"
Danny Pickett	One of the Others who takes out his anger over his wife's death on Sawyer	"Every Man for Himself"
Daniel	Altar boy at Yemi's church	"The Cost of Living"
Dave	Hurley's imaginary friend	"Dave"
David	Libby's husband	"Live Together, Die Alone"
David	Jessica's husband, whom Sawyer is trying to con	"Confidence Man"
Desmond David Hume	Inhabitant of the Hatch who explains to Locke the need to push the button	"Live Together, Die Alone" (when Desmond's full name is revealed)

Eddie	Gatekeeper at Anthony Cooper's estate	"Deus Ex Machina"
Eddie	Uncover police officer who infiltrates the commune where Locke lives	"Further Instructions"
Elizabeth	Name of Libby's and David's boat; Libby's real first name	"Live Together, Die Alone"
Libby	Nickname for Elizabeth	
Emily Annabeth Locke	John Locke's biological mother	"Deus Ex Machina"
Emma	Child kidnapped by the Others shortly after the crash	"The Other 48 Days"
Ethan Rom (similar in structure to Nathan, also the characters seem to mirror each other's behavior in much of their individual story arcs)	Reportedly one of the Others	Recurring character, "Whatever the Case May Be"; "All the Best Cowboys Have Daddy Issues"; "Homecoming"
Nathan (similar in structure to Ethan, also the characters seem to mirror each other's behavior in much of their individual story arcs)	Mistakenly believed to be one of the Others	"The Other 48 Days"

Frank Duckett	Reported alias of Frank Sawyer, the man who conned James Ford's/Sawyer's mother; man Sawyer seeks to kill; not the right man that Sawyer seeks, although Sawyer finds that out too late	"Confidence Man"
Frank Sawyer	Confidence man whom Sawyer wants to kill for destroying his family	"Confidence Man"
Francine	Young woman in Locke's anger management group	"Orientation"
Frank Heatherton	Father of Lucy Heatherton, Charlie's one-time girlfriend	"Homecoming"
Helen	Locke's phone-a-date	"Walkabout"
Helen	Locke's lover; a member of Locke's anger management group	"Orientation"
James Ford	Sawyer's real name	"Exodus"
Diego Reyes (Diego is Spanish for "James")	Hurley's brother's name	"Numbers"

Jason	Kate's boyfriend's name, her accomplice in a bank robbery in Taos, New Mexico	"Whatever the Case May Be"
Jason McCormick	The man who shoots Ana Lucia, the man she later kills	"Collision"
John Locke	Regional collections manager for a box company; the castaways' primary hunter; a believer in destiny; a challenger for leadership of the castaways	Recurring character
Jack Shephard (Jack is a nickname for John)	Spinal surgeon; the castaways' physician and leader	Recurring character
Joanna	Woman killed in the crash whose ID Kate steals	"Born to Run"
Zack although not a "John" name, rhymes with Jack	Child kidnapped by the Others shortly after the crash	"The Other 48 Days"
Johnny	Hurley's good friend and former co-worker at Mr. Cluck's Chicken Shack	Hurley's good friend and former co-worker at Mr. Cluck's Chicken Shack
Karen DeGroot	University of Michigan doctoral student; creator of the Dharma Initiative	"Orientation"

Karen Pace	Liam Pace's wife and Charlie's sister-in-law	"The Moth"
Kevin	Sarah's fiancé, who abandons her during her surgery	"Man of Science, Man of Faith"
Kevin	Kate's (now ex-)husband	"I Do"
Kelvin Inman	Man who, according to Desmond, ran from the jungle to drag Desmond into the Hatch; a "volunteer" who pushed the button	"Orientation"; "Live Together, Die Alone"
Marc Silverman	Jack's childhood friend and best man	"White Rabbit"
Mark Wickmund	Another name for Dr. Marvin Candle on a second orientation film	"?"
Michael	Walt's father	Recurring character
Mike	A leader of the commune where Locke lives	"Further Instructions"
Ray Mullen	Farmer who hires Annie (Kate) as a temporary worker; man who turns her in for the reward money	"Tabula Rasa"

Reyes (e.g., Hugo, Carmen, Diego)	Hurley's family name	First mentioned in "Numbers"; family members in "Numbers" and "Everybody Hates Hugo"
Sam Austen	The man Kate believed to be her biological father	"What Kate Did"
Sam Toomey	Navy buddy of Leonard Sims, who also heard the numbers; Australian who played the numbers and believed them cursed	"Numbers"
Sarah Shephard	Jack's (now ex-)wife	"White Rabbit"; "The Hunting Party"
Sarah	Alias given to Ana Lucia by Christian Shephard when they work together in Australia	"Two for the Road"
Steve	Survivor of Oceanic 815; background person who occasionally assists	Recurring minor character
Steve	Newlywed who, with wife Kristen, dies in the crash of Oceanic 815	Walkabout

Susan	Walt's mother	Recurring minor character
Suzanne	Kate's mother-in-law	"I Do"
Tom Brennan	Kate's best friend and love, who dies during a shootout when Kate escapes the law	"Born to Run"
Thomas	Biological father of Claire's baby, Aaron	"Raised by Another"
Tommy	Charlie's supplier and "friend"	"Homecoming"
Tom	Real name of Mr. Friendly (one of the Others)	"Live Together, Die Alone," recurring character in Season Three
Tom	Alias used by Christian Shephard when he works with Ana Lucia in Australia	"Two for the Road"

APPENDIX D

LOST EPISODE GUIDE

SEQ. #	EP #	AIR DATE	TITLE	WRITER	DIRECTOR
1	1.1	9/22/2004	"Pilot (1)"	J. J. Abrams & Damon Lindelof	J.J. Abrams
2	1.2	9/29/2004	"Pilot (2)"	J. J. Abrams & Damon Lindelof	J. J. Abrams
3	1.3	10/6/2004	"Tabula Rasa"	Damon Lindelof	Jack Bender
4	1.4	10/13/2004	"Walkabout"	David Fury	Jack Bender
5	1.5	10/20/2004	"White Rabbit"	Christian Taylor	Kevin Hooks
6	1.6	10/27/2004	"House of the Rising Sun"	Javier Grillo-Marxuach	Michael Zinberg
7	1.7	11/3/2004	"The Moth"	Jennifer Johnson & Paul Dini	Jack Bender

8	1.8	11/10/2004	"Confidence Man"	Damon Lindelof	Tucker Gates
9	1.9	11/17/2004	"Solitary"	David Fury	Greg Yaitanes
10	1.10	12/1/2004	"Raised by Another"	Lynne E. Litt	Marita Grabiak
11	1.11	12/8/2004	"All the Best Cowboys Have Daddy Issues"	Javier Grillo-Marxuach	Stephen Williams
12	1.12	1/5/2005	"Whatever the Case May Be"	Damon Lindelof & Jennifer Johnson	Jack Bender
13	1.13	1/12/2005	"Hearts & Minds"	Carlton Cuse & Javier Grillo-Marxuach	Rod Holcomb
14	1.14	1/19/2005	"Special"	David Fury	Greg Yaitanes
15	1.15	2/9/2005	"Homecoming"	Damon Lindelof	Kevin Hooks
16	1.16	2/16/2005	"Outlaws"	Drew Goddard	Jack Bender
17	1.17	2/23/2005	"...In Translation"	Javier Grillo-Marxuach & Leonard Dick	Tucker Gates

18	1.18	3/2/2005	"Numbers"	David Fury & Brent Fletcher	Dan Tallias
19	1.19	3/30/2005	"Deus Ex Machina"	Damon Lindelof & Carlton Cuse	Robert Mandel
20	1.20	4/6/2005	"Do No Harm"	Janet Tamaro	Stephen Williams
21	1.21	5/4/2005	"The Greater Good" (a.k.a. "Sides")	Leonard Dick	David Grossman
22	1.22	5/11/2005	"Born to Run"	Edward Kitsis, Adam Horowitz, & Javier Grillo-Marxuach	Tucker Gates
23	1.23	5/18/2005	"Exodus (I)"	Damon Lindelof & Carlton Cuse	Jack Bender
24	1.24	5/25/2005	"Exodus (II)"	Damon Lindelof & Carlton Cuse	Jack Bender
25	2.1	9/21/2005	"Man of Science, Man of Faith"	Damon Lindelof	Jack Bender
26	2.2	9/28/2005	"Adrift"	Leonard Dick & Steven Maeda	Stephen Williams

27	2.3	10/5/2005	"Orientation"	Javier Grillo-Marxuach & Craig Wright	Jack Bender
28	2.4	10/12/2005	"Everybody Hates Hugo"	Adam Horowitz & Edward Kitsis	Alan Taylor
29	2.5	10/19/2005	"…And Found"	Damon Lindelof & Carlton Cuse	Stephen Williams
30	2.6	11/9/2005	"Abandoned"	Elizabeth Sarnoff	Adam Davidson
31	2.7	11/16/2005	"The Other 48 Days"	Damon Lindelof & Carlton Cuse	Eric Laneuville
32	2.8	11/23/2005	"Collision"	Leonard Dick & Javier Grillo-Marxuach	Stephen Williams
33	2.9	11/30/2005	"What Kate Did"	Steven Maeda & Craig Wright	Paul Edwards
34	2.10	1/11/2006	"The 23rd Psalm"	Damon Lindelof & Carlton Cuse	Matt Earl Beesley
35	2.11	1/18/2006	"The Hunting Party"	Elizabeth Sarnoff & Christine M. Kim	Stephen Williams
36	2.12	1/25/2006	"Fire + Water"	Adam Horowitz & Edward Kitsis	Jack Bender
37	2.13	2/8/2006	"The Long Con"	Steven Maeda & Leonard Dick	Roxann Dawson

38	2.14	2/15/2006	"One of Them"	Damon Lindelof & Carlton Cuse	Williams
39	2.15	3/1/2006	"Maternity Leave"	Dawn Robertson Kelly & Matt Ragghianti	Jack Bender
40	2.16	3/22/2006	"The Whole Truth"	Christine M. Kim & Elizabeth Sarnoff	Karen Gaviola
41	2.17	3/29/2006	"Lockdown"	Damon Lindelof & Carlton Cuse	Stephen Williams
42	2.18	4/5/2006	"Dave"	Edward Kitsis & Adam Horowitz	Jack Bender
43	2.19	4/12/2006	"S.O.S."	Stephen Maeda & Leonard Dick	Eric Laneuville
44	2.20	5/3/2006	"Two for the Road"	Christine M. Kim & Elizabeth Sarnoff	Paul Edwards
45	2.21	5/10/2006	"?"	Carlton Cuse & Damon Lindelof	Dean Sarafian
46	2.22	5/17/2006	"Three Minutes"	Edward Kitsis & Adam Horowitz	Stephen Williams
47	2.23	5/24/2006	"Live Together, Die Alone, Part 1"	Damon Lindelof & Carlton Cuse	Jack Bender

48	2.24	5/24/2006	"Live Together, Die Alone, Part 2"	Damon Lindelof & Carlton Cuse	Jack Bender
49	3.1	10/4/2006	"A Tale of Two Cities"	J.J. Abrams & Damon Lindelof	Jack Bender
50	3.2	10/11/2006	"The Glass Ballerina"	Drew Goddard & Jeff Pinkner	Paul Edwards
51	3.3	10/18/2006	"Further Instructions"	Elizabeth Sarnoff & Carlton Cuse	Stephen Williams
52	3.4	10/25/2006	"Every Man for Himself"	Alison Schapker, Edward Kitsis, Adam Horowitz & Monica Owusu-Breen	Stephen Williams
53	3.5	11/1/2006	"The Cost of Living"	Monica Owusu-Breen & Alison Schapker	Jack Bender
54	3.6	11/8/2006	"I Do"	David Lindelof & Carlton Cuse	Tucker Gates

APPENDIX E

LOST'S AWARDS AND NOMINATIONS, 2004–2007

AWARD TITLE	ORGANIZATION/ AWARD NAME	NOMINEE(S)	DATE PRESENTED	NOMINEE/ WINNER
Best Network Television Series	Academy of Science Fiction, Fantasy, and Horror Films, Saturn Award	*Lost*	2005	Winner
Best Supporting Actor in a Television Series	Academy of Science Fiction, Fantasy, and Horror Films, Saturn Award	Terry O'Quinn	2005	Winner
Best Actress in a Television Series	Academy of Science Fiction, Fantasy, and Horror Films, Saturn Award	Evangeline Lilly	2005	Nominee

Best Actor in a Television Series	Academy of Science Fiction, Fantasy, and Horror Films, Saturn Award	**Matthew Fox**	2005	Nominee
Best Supporting Actor in a Television Series	Academy of Science Fiction, Fantasy, and Horror Films, Saturn Award	**Dominic Monaghan**	2005	Nominee
Best Network Television Series	Academy of Science Fiction, Fantasy, and Horror Films, Saturn Award	*Lost*	2006	**Winner**
Best Actor in a Television Series	Academy of Science Fiction, Fantasy, and Horror Films, Saturn Award	**Matthew Fox**	2006	**Winner**
Best DVD Television Release	Academy of Science Fiction, Fantasy, and Horror Films, Saturn Award	**Lost (Season 1)**	2006	**Winner**
Best Actress in a Television Series	Academy of Science Fiction, Fantasy, and Horror Films, Saturn Award	**Evangeline Lilly**	2006	Nominee
Best Supporting Actor in a Television Series	Academy of Science Fiction, Fantasy, and Horror Films, Saturn Award	**Adewale Akinnuoye-Agbaje**	2006	Nominee

Best Supporting Actor in a Television Series	Academy of Science Fiction, Fantasy, and Horror Films, Saturn Award	**Terry O'Quinn**	2006	Nominee
Best Supporting Actress in a Television Series	Academy of Science Fiction, Fantasy, and Horror Films, Saturn Award	**Michelle Rodriguez**	2006	Nominee
Outstanding Female TV Performance	Asian Excellence Award	**Yunjin Kim**	2006	**Winner**
Outstanding Male TV Performance	Asian Excellence Award	**Daniel Dae Kim**	2006	**Winner**
Outstanding Achievement in Television, Dramatic Series, Night (Pilot episode, Part 2)	Director's Guild of America	**J. J. Abrams**	2005	Nominee
Television Drama Multi-Episode Storyline (*Lost*— Charlie's Addiction)	Entertainment Industries Council, Prism Award	*Lost*—**"Pilot," "House of the Rising Sun," "The Moth"**	2005	**Winner**
Performance in a Drama Storyline	Entertainment Industries Council, Prism Award	**Dominic Monaghan**	2005	Nominee
Best New Series	Family Friendly Programming Forum, Family Television Award	*Lost*	2004	**Winner**

Best Drama	Family Friendly Programming Forum, Family Television Award	*Lost*	2005	**Winner**
Best Drama	Hollywood Foreign Press Association, Golden Globe	*Lost*	2005	Nominee
Best Drama Series	Hollywood Foreign Press Association, Golden Globe Award	*Lost*	2006	**Winner**
Actor in a Drama, TV Series	Hollywood Foreign Press Association, Golden Globe Award	**Matthew Fox**	2006	Nominee
Supporting Actor, series or miniseries	Hollywood Foreign Press Association, Golden Globe Award	**Naveen Andrews**	2006	Nominee
Best Drama Series	Hollywood Foreign Press Association, Golden Globe Award	*Lost*	2007	Nominee
Actress in a Drama, TV Series	Hollywood Foreign Press Association, Golden Globe Award	**Evangeline Lilly**	2007	Nominee
Actor in a Series, Drama	International Press Academy, Satellite Award	**Matthew Fox**	2005	**Winner**

Evangeline

Actress in a Series, Drama	International Press Academy, Satellite Award	**Lilly**	2005	Nominee
		Lost		
Television Series, Drama	International Press Academy, Satellite Award		2005	Nominee
		Lost		
Television Series, Drama	International Press Academy, Satellite Award		2006	Nominee
		Lost		
Best DVD Release of a Television Show	International Press Academy		2006	Nominee
		Lost		
Favorite Primetime Drama Series	Internet Entertainment Writers Awards		2006	**Winner**
		Matthew Fox		
Favorite Actor in a Primetime Drama Series Television Show	Internet Entertainment Writers Awards		2006	**Winner**
		Lost		
Outstanding Drama Series	NAACP, NAACP Image Award		2006	Nominee
		Jorge Garcia		
Outstanding Supporting Actor in a Television Series	National Council of La Raza, Alma Award		2006	**Winner**
		Michelle Rodriguez		
Outstanding Supporting Actress in a Television Series	National Council of La Raza, Alma Award		2006	**Winner**
		Lost		

Category	Award	Recipient	Year	Result
Best Television Drama	National Television Awards (UK)		2006	Nominee
Best Television Actor	National Television Awards (UK)	Matthew Fox	2006	Nominee
Best Television Actress	National Television Awards (UK)	Evangeline Lilly	2006	Nominee
Favorite New Series	People's Choice	*Lost*	2004	Nominee
Television Series: Drama	Producers Guild of America, PGA Award	J.J. Abrams, Damon Lindelof, Bryan Burk, Jack Bender, Jean Higgins, Carlton Cuse	2007	Nominee
Outstanding Performance by an Ensemble in a Drama Series	Screen Actors Guild, SAG Award	*Lost*	2006	**Winner**
Best Television Actor	Screen Nation Awards (UK)	Adewale Akinnuoye-Agbaje	2006	Nominee
Favourite Male Television Star	Screen Nation Awards (UK)	Adewale Akinnuoye-Agbaje	2006	Nominee
Best Television Show	Spike TV Scream Awards	*Lost*	2006	Nominee
Scream Queen	Spike TV Scream Awards	Evangeline Lilly	2006	Nominee
		Adewale Akinnuoye-		

Category	Organization	Recipient	Year	Result
Breakout Performance	Spike TV Scream Awards	Agbaje *Lost*	2006	Nominee
The Ultimate Scream	Spike TV Scream Awards	*Lost*	2006	Nominee
Best Television Series	SyFy Genre Awards	Matthew Fox	2006	Nominee and Runner-up
Best Actor/Television	SyFy Genre Awards	Evangeline Lilly	2006	Nominee and Runner-up
Best Actress/Television	SyFy Genre Awards	Terry O'Quinn	2006	Winner
Best Supporting Actor/Television	SyFy Genre Awards	*Lost*	2006	Nominee and Runner-up
Outstanding Drama Series*	Television Academy of Arts and Sciences, Emmy Award	*Lost*	2005	Winner
Outstanding Casting for a Drama Series	Television Academy of Arts and Sciences, Emmy Award	J. J. Abrams (pilot episode)	2005	Winner
Outstanding Directing for a Drama Series	Television Academy of Arts and Sciences, Emmy Award	*Lost*	2005	Winner
Outstanding Single-Camera Editing for a Drama Series	Television Academy of Arts and Sciences, Emmy Award	Michael Giacchino	2005	Winner

Outstanding Music Composition for a Series (Dramatic Underscore)	Television Academy of Arts and Sciences, Emmy Award		2005	**Winner**
Outstanding Supporting Actor in a Drama Series	Television Academy of Arts and Sciences, Emmy Award	Naveen Andrews	2005	Nominee
Outstanding Supporting Actor in a Drama Series	Television Academy of Arts and Sciences, Emmy Award	Terry O'Quinn	2005	Nominee
Outstanding Writing for a Drama Series	Television Academy of Arts and Sciences, Emmy Award	J. J. Abrams, Damon Lindelof, Jeffrey Lieber (*Lost*—Pilot episode, Parts 1 and 2)	2005	Nominee
Outstanding Writing for a Drama Series	Television Academy of Arts and Sciences, Emmy Award	David Fury (*Lost*— Walkabout)	2005	Nominee
Outstanding Sound Editing for a Series	Television Academy of Arts and Sciences, Emmy Award	*Lost* (Pilot episode, Parts 1 and 2)	2005	Nominee
Outstanding Special Visual Effects for a Series	Television Academy of Arts and Sciences, Emmy Award	*Lost* (Pilot episode, Parts 1 and 2)	2005	**Winner**
		Lost (Outlaws)		

Outstanding Single-Camera Sound Mixing for a Series	Television Academy of Arts and Sciences, Emmy Award	*Lost*	2005	Nominee
Outstanding New Program of the Year	Television Critics Association	*Lost*	2005	**Winner**
Outstanding Achievement in Drama	Television Critics Association	*Lost*	2005	**Winner**
Program of the Year	Television Critics Association	**Matthew Fox**	2005	Nominee
Outstanding Achievement in Drama	Television Critics Association	*Lost*	2005	Nominee
Outstanding Achievement in Drama	Television Critics Association	*Lost*	2006	**Winner**
Program of the Year	Television Critics Association	**Digital Dimension**	2006	**Winner**
Outstanding Supporting Visual Effects in a Broadcast Program (for the pilot episode's plane-crash sequence)	Visual Effects Society		2005	**Winner**
Outstanding Supporting Visual Effects in a Broadcast Program (Pilot episode, Part 2)	Visual Effects Society	**Kevin Blank, Mitch Suskin, Benoit Girard, Jerome Morin Kevin Blank, Mitchell**	2005	**Winner**

Outstanding Supporting Visual Effects in a Broadcast Program (Exodus, Part 2)	Visual Effects Society	ferm, Eric Chauvin, John Teska *Lost*	2006	**Winner**
Best Dramatic Presentation in Short Form	World Science Fiction Society, Hugo Award	*Lost*	2005	Nominee
Writing in a Dramatic Series	Writer's Guild of America	*Lost*	2006	**Winner**
Writing in a Dramatic Series	Writer's Guild of America	**"Two for the Road,"**	2007	Nominee
Writing in Episodic Drama	Writer's Guild of America	**Elizabeth Sarnoff and Christina M. Kim,** *Lost*	2007	Nominees

* Emmy Trivia: *Lost* is the first series since *The West Wing* to win an Emmy for best drama series in its first season.

BIBLIOGRAPHY

This bibliography directs you to some interesting interviews and tidbits about *Lost*. It includes information about the series in general, actors, creators, and crew. Of course, with a series as hugely popular with critics and fans worldwide, *Lost* generates many thousands of words in the press each year. The following bibliography by no means is an attempt to catalog all these articles. Online articles are not listed, simply because they are too numerous.

We've updated the bibliography with articles published between March 2006 and January 2007; with the exception of reviews of individual episodes, articles listed in the first edition remain in this bibliography so that you have a better reference list to the most interesting interviews and critical comments about *Lost* since its 2004 debut. The majority of these entries were published in the United States; a few articles from Canada and the United Kingdom are listed with country of publication.

"Action News Briefs." *Tomart's Action Figure Digest*, 2006, 146: 7.

Alter, Ethan, and Rich Sands. "An Unconventional Convention." *TV Guide*, August 7–13, 2006: 10.

Armstrong, Jennifer. "Love, Labor, Lost." *Entertainment Weekly*, September 9, 2005, 838/839: 28–32, 41 (poster 33–40).

———. "The Tailie's End." *Entertainment Weekly*, November 10, 2006, 906: 42–45.

Armstrong, Jennifer, Jeff Jensen, and Dan Snierson. "Lost Glossary." *Entertainment Weekly*, November 11, 2005, 849: 28–30, 33.

Ausiello, Michael. "The Ausiello Report: Who is *Lost*'s Latest Find?" *TV Guide*, August 7–13, 2006: 10.

"Behind the Scenes." *TV Guide*, October 16–22, 2006: 18–19.

Blackmoor, Eric, and Judy Ewens. "The Patient Englishman." *TV & Satellite Week*, August 20–26, 2005: 15. [UK publication]

Blasengame, Bart. "Josh Holloway." *Details*, June/July 2006: 186–190.

Bond, Jeff. "Finding *Lost*." *Cinefantastique*, September/October 2005, 37(6–7): 38–41.

Borow, Zev. "Josh Holloway: *Lost* in Paradise." *Men's Journal*, November 2006: 100–102, 104.

Brady, James. "In Step with Evangeline Lilly." *Parade*, October 23, 2005: 15.

Bried, Erin. "Reluctant Star: Evangeline Lilly of *Lost*." *Self*, November 2006: 22, 24, 26.

Byrne, Ciar. "Record Numbers Tune in to Channel 4 to See *Lost*, *Big Brother*, and cricket." *The Independent*, August 16, 2005: 3. [UK newspaper]

Cairns, Bryan. "Bear Everything." *Lost*, January/February 2006, 1(2): 25–27.

———. "Destination Boone." *Dreamwatch*, July 2005, 9: 42–43.

———. "Leading the Flock." *Cult Times*, August 2005: 14–17.

———. "Sail Away." *Lost*, January/February 2006, 1(2): 48–49.

———. "Sins and the Father." *Lost*, January/February 2006, 1(2): 14–21.

Calhoun, John. "Treachery in the Tropics." *American Cinematographer*, February 2005, 86(2): 44–48, 50–55.

Carrillo, Jenny Cooney. "Little Lilly Lost." *Dreamwatch*, May 2005, 7: 52–56.

———. "Lost Boy." *Dreamwatch*, February 2005, 4: 52–55.

"Catch-Up Guide: *Lost*." *Inside TV*, June 13–19, 2005, 1(8): 34–37.

Cimbalo, Guy. "Q&A: Dominic Monaghan." *Stuff*, October 2005: 78.

Cotton, Mike. "Fall Preview: *Lost.*" *Wizard 180,* October 2006: 72–75.

David, Greg. "Back to the Beach." *(Canadian) TV Guide,* September 30–October 6, 2006: 20–23.

———. "Paradise Lost." *(Canadian) TV Guide,* November 6–12, 2004, 28(45): 22–25.

DiLullo, Tara. "Agent Exposition." *Alias,* March/April 2005, File 9: 40–43.

———. "Falling From Grace." *Lost,* January/February 2006, 1(2): 14–21.

———. "In the Hands of Faith." *Lost,* January/February 2007, 8: 20–29.

———. "The Island and the Agents." *Lost,* January/February 2006, 1(2): 25–27.

———. "Leaders of the Pack." *Lost,* November/December 2005, 1(1): 20–27.

———. "Lost in Translation." *Dreamwatch,* June 2005, 8: 48–50.

———. "Lost Souls." *SFX,* September 2005, 134: 40–42, 44.

———. "*SFX* Profile: Josh Holloway." *SFX,* November 2005, 136: 32–33.

DiLullo, Tara, and Jenny Carillo Cooney. "The Lost World." *Dreamwatch,* September 2005, 132: 38–41.

Earp, Stephanie. "Lost Souls." *(Canadian) TV Guide,* March 26, 2005: 18–21.

Eden, Jenny. "Desert Island Disco." *TV Zone,* November 2005, 195: 20–22, 24, 26.

———. "Down the Hatch." *TV Zone,* June 2006, 202: 36–40.

———. "From Hobbit to Rock Star." *TV Times,* August 13–20, 2005: 16–17. [UK magazine]

———. "The Good Doctor." *TV Zone,* October 2005, 194: 20–23.

———. "It's a Battle to Keep My Clothes On." *Grazia,* August 15, 2005: 18–19. [UK publication]

———. "Life's Lottery." *TV Zone,* April 2006, Special 68: 54–58.

————. "The Mighty O'Quinn." *Xposé*, December 2005, 96: 38–41.

————. "Most Wanted." *TV Zone*, October 2005, 194: 24–26.

————. "To Tell a Tail: Cynthia Watros." *TV Zone*, April 2006, Special 69: 62–64, 66.

Edwards, Gavin. "Little Girl Lost." *Rolling Stone*, October 6, 2005, 984: 50–52.

————. "Lost Boy." *Rolling Stone*, February 10, 2005, 967: 45–46.

Elgar, Nick. "Dharma Chameleon." *Dreamwatch*, December 2006 (26): 46–49.

————. "Howdy, Girls . . . Josh Holloway: Sawyer, Son of a Bitch." *Dreamwatch*, November 2006, 25: 32.

————. "Locke Up. Terry O'Quinn: John Locke, Losing His Religion." *Dreamwatch*, November 2006, 25: 33.

————. "Love's Labour's Lost. Evangeline Lilly: Kate, Object of Affection." *Dreamwatch*, November 2006, 25: 31.

————. "The Others' Side of the Fence. Michael Emerson: Henry Gale, Leader of the Others." *Dreamwatch*, November 2006, 25: 34.

Elgar, Nick, Bryan Cairns, and Richard Matthews. "Full of Maggie Grace." *Dreamwatch*, November 2005, 13: 54–56.

Elgar, Nick, and Richard Matthews. "Medicine Man." *Dreamwatch*, November 2005, 13: 57.

Endelman, Michael. "Breakouts: Michael Emerson." *Entertainment Weekly*, December 29, 2006–January 5, 2007, 913/914: 86.

Eramo, Steven. "Make Room for Daddy." *Starburst*, September 2005, 327: 38–44.

Gross, Ed. "Mysterious Island." *SFX*, January 2005, 126: 60–61.

Gross, Edward. "Overview: Lost." *SFX*, January 2005, 126: 58–61.

Hatty, Michele. "Matthew's Moral Center." *USA Weekend*, May 6–8, 2005: 9.

Hayes, K. Stoddard. "Lost and Found." *Dreamwatch*, February 2005, 4: 22–23.

Hibberd, James. "'Lost' Planning End Date." TVWeek.com, January 14, 2007. http://www.tvweek.com/news.cms?newsId=11372.

Hockley, Ian. "Preview: *Lost*." *Cult Times*, Fall 2004, Special 32: 68–69.

Huddleston, Kathie. "By the Numbers." *SciFi*, October 2005, 11(5): 44.

———. "Down the Hatch." *SciFi*, October 2005, 11(5): 40–42, 44.

———. "TV in Focus: *Lost*." *SciFi*, June 2005, 11(3): 16.

Jensen, Jeff. "The Beach Boys." *Entertainment Weekly*, April 15, 2005, 815: 20–24.

———. "War of the Worlds." *Entertainment Weekly*, May 19, 2006, 877.

———. "When Stephen King Met the 'Lost' Boys." *Entertainment Weekly*, December 1, 2006, 909: 48–52.

Kempster, Grant. "Getting *Lost*." *The Works*, May 2006, 6: 40–46.

King, Stephen. "The Wonder of It All." *Entertainment Weekly*, Special Pullout Section, September 29, 2006, 899: 22–23.

Kizis, Deanna. "*Lost* and Found: Emilie de Ravin." *InStyle Weddings*, Summer 2006: 234-241."Ecce Eko." *TV Zone*, July 2006, 203: 60–62, 64.

Knoll, Corina. "*Lost* in Paradise." *KoreAm Journal*, October 2004, 15(16): 74–81.

Loeb, Jeff. "Loeb Gets *Lost*." *Dreamwatch*, June 2006, 20: 32–36.

"*Lost* Season One Episode Guide." *Cinefantastique*, September/October 2005, 37(6–7): 42–50.

"*Lost*: Everything You Need to Get Ready for Season 3." *Entertainment Weekly*, Special Pullout Section, September 29, 2006, 899.

Loudon, Christopher. "Lost and Found." *(Canadian) TV Guide*, November 19–25, 2005, 29(47): 17–19.

Lynch, Jason, and Monica Rizzo. "Fantasy Island." *People*, January 30, 2006: 73–74.

Malcom, Shawna. "Foxy!" *TV Guide*, January 16–22, 2006, 53(3): 22–27.

————. "*Lost*: Burning Questions." *TV Guide*, October 17–23, 2005, 53(42): 18–21.

————. "*Lost*: The Episode Guide." *TV Guide*, August 28, 2005, 53(35): 34–40. (with CD)

————. "*Lost*: The Ultimate Guide." *TV Guide*, January 30, 2005, 53(4): 22–28, 30–32.

————. "Lost Boy." *TV Guide*, April 3–9, 2005: 24–26, 28–29.

————. "*Lost* Catch-up Guide." *TV Guide*, January 9–15, 2006: 33.

————. "*Lost's* Sci-fi Roots." *TV Guide*, July 24–30, 2006: 24.

————. "RIP Boone!" *TV Guide*, April 17–23, 2005, 53(16): 8–9.

————. "Secrets of *Lost*." *TV Guide*, October 24–30, 2004, 52(43): 22–24, 26–28.

————. "Terry O'Quinn Unlocks Locke." *TV Guide*, July 24–30, 2006: 24.

Mallory, Michael. "Steve LaPorte Gets Lost in his Work." *MakeUp*, February/March 2005, 53: 42–47.

Miller, Kirk. "Evangeline Lilly." *Co-Ed*, Fall 2005, 1(3): 106–109.

Mitovich, Matt Webb. "*Lost's* Numbers Finally Add Up." *TV Guide*, September 18–24, 2006: 10.

Monaghan, Dominic. "Paradise Found: A *Lost* Photodiary." *Emmy*, 2005(1): 33–39.

Peyser, Marc. "*Lost*: TV's Coolest Show." *Newsweek*, May 22, 2006.

Poniewozik, James. "Why the Future of Television is *Lost*." *Time*, October 2, 2006.

————. "Welcome to His Unreality." *Time*, January 10, 2005.

Potts, Kimberly. "*Lost* Mysteries Revealed!" *Inside TV*, June 6, 2005, 1(7): 26–27.

Prato, Alison. "Paradise Found." *Giant*, June/July 2006: 80–88.

"Returning Favorites". *TV Guide*, September 18, 2005, 53(38): 42–43.

Roush, Matt. "Great Expectations: Can Last Year's Faves Live Up to Hype?" *TV Guide*, September 18, 2005, 53(58): 16.

————. "Matt Roush's Top 10 List for 2004." *TV Guide*,

December 19–25, 2004, 52(51): 40.

———. "Matt Roush's Top 10 List for 2005." *TV Guide*, December 19–25, 2005, 53(51): 40.

Rudolph, Ileane. "Evangeline Lilly." *TV Guide*, December 19–25, 2004, 52(51): 41.

———. Insider. "*Lost* Clues Revealed!" *TV Guide*, December 19–25, 2005, 53(51): 16.

———. "Matthew Fox." *TV Guide*, December 19–25, 2004, 52(51): 42.

Schneller, Johanna. "TV's Sexiest Men: Daniel Dae Kim." *TV Guide*, June 19–25, 2006: 32–33.

Sloane, Judy. "Jorge Garcia: Man of Action!" *Starburst*, February 2005, 319: 18–19.

———. "Land of the Lost." *TV Zone*, 2005, Special 59: 120–124.

———. "The Lost World." *Xposé*, April 2005, 93: 50–54.

———. "Nothing Lost." *Starburst*, November 2005, 329: 38–39.

———. "Terry O'Quinn: Locke Unlocked." *Starburst*, February 2005, 319: 20–21.

———. "Two Against Nature." *Starburst*, February 2005, 319: 16–21.

Sloane, Judy, and Paul Spragg. "Sun Shines." *Cult Times*, October 2005: 18–21.

Small, Jonathan. "Island Fever." *Stuff*, October 2006, 83: 70–75.

———. "The Women of *Lost*." *Stuff*, October 2006, 83: 76–77.

Snierson, Dan. "Spotlight: Elizabeth Mitchell." *Entertainment Weekly*, November 3, 2006, 905: 27–28.

Spelling, Ian. "The Adventures of Lost Sawyer." *Starlog*, June 2005, 335: 19–22.

———. "Calling Mr. Eko." *Starlog*, March 2006, 343: 73–75.

———. "Cuse Control." *Dreamwatch*, August 2005, 10: 50–52.

———. "Hurley Burley." *Starlog*, May 2005, 334: 73–75.

———. "Lost Soul." *Starlog*, March 2005, 232: 28–34.

———. "Ravin', I'm Ravin." *Cult Times*, Fall 2004, Special 32: 70–74.

————. "Tortured Soul: Naveen Andrews." *Starlog*, June 2006, 346: 32–35.

————. "Travels with Charlie." *Starlog*, November 2006, 350: 32–35.

Spragg, Nick. "Lost in *Lost*." *Cult Times*, January 2006, Special 37: 14–16, 18, 20.

Stein, Joel. "Matthew Fox." *Details*, September 2005, 23(10): 276–279.

St. Cloud, Marie. "*Lost* Again." *SFX*, June 2006: 62–65.

Terry, Paul. "Between a Rocker and a Dark Place . . ." *Lost*, November/December 2005, 1(1): 42–49.

————. "Meet Carlton Cuse." *Lost*, January/February 2006, 1(2): 50–54.

————. "Second Sight." *Lost*, September/October 2006, p. 34.

White, Cinday. "Road Map for the Fall TV Season. Fall TV '05. What You Are Watching: *Lost*." *Now Playing*, Fall 2005, 1(3): 44–45.

WORKS CITED

"2005's Sexiest Men Alive." *People.* November 21–28, 2005.
Retrieved November 20, 2005, from people.aol.com.

ABC-TV. Commercial. "Charlie. Redemption." September 2005.

ABC-TV. Commercial. "Locke. Destiny." September 2005.

Adams, Richard. *Watership Down.* New York: Macmillan, 1972.

Adventures of Brisco County, Jr., The. TV series. Exec. Prods.
Jeffrey Boam and Carlton Cuse. 1993–1994.

Ain't It Cool News. "Moonshine Has Seen the Museum of Radio
& Television *Lost* Event." Message posted March 14, 2005.
Retrieved November 27, 2005, from www.aintitcool.com.

Alias. TV series. Exec. Prod. J. J. Abrams. Bad Robot. 2001–2006.

Angel. Exec. Prod. Joss Whedon. Mutant Enemy. 1999–2004.

Armstrong, Jennifer. "Love, Labor, *Lost.*" *Entertainment Weekly* 9
September 2005: 28–32, 41.

Bianculli, David. *Dictionary of Teleliteracy.* New York: Continuum,
1996.

Bloom, Harold. *The Anxiety of Influence: A Theory of Poetry.* New
York: Oxford, 1973.

Bond, Jeff. "Finding *Lost.*" *Cinefantastique,* 37(6–7): 38–41.

Brennan, Richard P. *Dictionary of Scientific Literacy.* New York:
Wiley, 1992.

Buffy the Vampire Slayer. TV series. Exec. Prod. Joss Whedon.
Mutant Enemy. 1997–2003.

Burtt, Edwin A., ed. *The English Philosophers from Bacon to Mill.*
New York: The Modern Library/Random House, 1939.

Carroll, Lewis. *Alice in Wonderland.* Norton Critical Edition. Ed.
Donald J. Gray. New York: W.W. Norton, 1971.

Cast Away. Dir. Robert Zemeckis. 20th Century Fox. 2000.

Crichton, Michael. *Jurassic Park.* New York: Knopf, 1990.

Cuse, Carlton. "Save Our Show" *TV Guide.* Quoted on www.the11thhour.com.

Cuse, Carlton, and Damon Lindelof. "Podcast 1." November 8, 2005. Retrieved December 28, 2005, from abc.go.com/prime time/lost/podcasts/html.

Defoe, Daniel. *Robinson Crusoe.* Ed. Michael Shinagel. Norton Critical Edition. New York: W.W. Norton, 1975.

DeGroot, Samuel. Forum post. The Fuselage. Retrieved December 29, 2005 from thefuselage.com.

"Dharma." Retrieved October 1, 2005, from www.tiscali.co.uk.

"Dharma Initiative." Retrieved November 1, 2005, from thedharmainitiative.org.

DiLullo, Tara. "Deepening the *Lost* Mystery." *Dreamwatch,* March 2005, 5: 41.

Dilmore, Kevin. "Of Spies and Survivors." *Amazing Stories,* February 2005, 74(2): 20–24.

Dolan, Marc. "The Peaks and Valleys of Serial Creativity: What Happened to/on *Twin Peaks.*" *Full of Secrets: Critical Approaches to* Twin Peaks. Ed. David Lavery. Detroit: Wayne State University Press: 30–50.

Ebert, Roger. "Cast Away." Chicago Sun-Times, December 22, 2000, Retrieved from rogerebert.suntimes.com.

Edelstein, David. "Stand and Deliver: Cast Away Maroons a Bunch of Half-Baked Ideas on a Desert Island." Slate, December 22, 2000. Retrieved from www.slate.com.

Eng, Dinah. "Ten Writers Examine Life's Diverse Journey on *Lost.*" *Denver Post,* November 23, 2005. Retrieved November 26, 2005, from www.denverpost.com.

"Essential Elements and Doctrines." Retrieved October 1, 2005, from www.hindunet.org/quickintro/hindudharma.

Firefly. TV series. Exec. Prod. Joss Whedon. Mutant Enemy. 2002.

Fox, Matthew. (Interview.) *The View.* ABC Television. May 17, 2005.

Fury, David. "Q&A with David Fury" DavidFury.net. Retrieved December 28, 2005 from davidfury.net/qanda2004.html.

Gilbert, Matthew. "Getting Lost: Show Pursues TV's Most Elusive Genre—Mythology. Or Maybe That's Not It at All." *The Boston Globe*, October 27, 2004.

—"TV Characters' Names Often Say Something about Who They Are." *The Boston Globe*, February 22, 2005. Retrieved November 26, 2005, from www.northjersey.com.

Gilligan's Island. TV series. Exec. Prod. Sherwood Schwartz. Gladysya Productions. 1964–1967.

Golding, William. *Lord of the Flies.* Casebook Edition. Ed. James R. Baker and Arthur P. Ziegler, Jr. New York: Putnam's, 1954.

Grillo-Marxuach, Javier. Forum post. The Fuselage "Check Out." Retrieved December 29, 2005 from www.thefuselage.com.

—Forum post. The Fuselage. "Classification Video a Fake?" Retrieved December 29, 2005 from www.thefuselage.com.

Gross, Edward. "Man on a Mission." *Cinefantastique*, February/March 2005, 36(1): 34–36.

Grover, Ronald. "Has ABC Found Its Way with Lost? The New Drama May Have Broken the Ailing Network's Hit Drought. A Smart New Programming Exec and a Buzz-worthy Fall Lineup Also Helps." *Business Week Online*, September 29, 2004.

Hanso Foundation. Walt Disney Corporation. Retrieved November 1, 2005, from thehansofoundation.org/dharma.html.

Hatty, Michele. "Matthew's Moral Center." *USA Weekend*, May 6–8, 2005: 9.

Hibberd, James. "*Lost* Finds Top Spot." *Television Week*, 3 Jan. 2005: 19.

Hilton, James. *Lost Horizon.* New York: Pocket Books, 1939.

Hinman, Michael. "Lost Podcast #1." SyFy Portal. November 28, 2005. Retrieved December 29, 2005, from www.craveon line.com.

Hintz, Martin, and Kate Hintz. *Halloween: Why We Celebrate It the Way We Do.* Mankato, MN: Capstone Press, 1996.

"History of Halloween." Retrieved November 25, 2005, from www.redmoonhorror.com/halloween/the-history-of-halloween.htm.

James, Henry. *The Turn of the Screw.* Unabridged edition. New York: Tor Books, 1993.

Jayepmills. "DHARMA...DARPA and ARPA?" Discussion board post. September 29, 2005. The Fuselage. Retrieved November 20, 2005, from www.thefuselage.com.

Jefferson, David J. "Desperate? Not ABC. The network hasn't been able to buy a big hit in years. But with Desperate Housewives, Lost and Wife Swap, ABC has Found a Groove." *Newsweek,* October 25, 2004: 96.

Jenkins, Henry. "Do You Enjoy Making the Rest of Us Feel Stupid?" alt.tv.twinpeaks, the Trickster Author, and Viewer Mastery." *Full of Secrets: Critical Approaches to* Twin Peaks. Ed. David Lavery. Detroit: Wayne State U P: 51–69.

Jensen, Jeff. "The Beach Boys." *Entertainment Weekly,* April 15, 2005, 815: 20–24.

—"Treasured Islanders: The Cast of *Lost.*" *Entertainment Weekly,* 30 December 2005–January 2006: 43–44.

Kang, Sugwon. *The Philosophy of Locke and Hobbes.* New York: Monarch Press, 1965.

Keats, John. *Selected Poetry and Letters.* Ed. Richard Harter Fogle. New York: Holt, Rinehart, and Winston, 1969.

Keck, William. "She Shot Shannon; What's Ana Lucia's Next Target?" *USA Today.* November 15, 2005. Retrieved November 20, 2005, from www.usatoday.com.

King, Stephen. "*Lost's* Soul." *Entertainment Weekly,* 9 September 2005: 150.

—*The Langoliers.* New York: Signet, 1995.

—*The Stand.* New York: Gramercy Books, 1978.

King, Susan. "Stereotype not 'Lost' on Korean Actress." *Los Angeles Times.* May 1, 2005. E3.

Klein, Joshua. "X-Files Set Cherry-Picks Myth-Making Episodes." Chicago Tribune, June 10, 2005. Retrieved from metromix. chicagotribune.com.

L'Engle, Madeleine. *A Wrinkle in Time*. New York: Dell, 1963.

"Living Dharma." Retrieved October 1, 2005, from www. livingdharma.org.

Locke, John. *Two Tracts on Government*. Ed. Philip Abrams. London: Cambridge UP, 1967.

Lost: The Complete First Season. DVD. Buena Vista Home Entertainment, 2005.

"*Lost* Finds Another ABC Win Wednesday." Retrieved November 20, 2005, from tv.zap2it.com.

Malcom, Shawna. "Secrets of *Lost*." *TV Guide*, October 24, 2004, 52(43): 28.

Millenium. Dir. Michael Anderson. Live/Artisan, 1989.

Nelson, Resa. "Television: *Lost* Breaks Out as the Cult Hit with Mass Appeal." *Realms of Fantasy*, April 2005, 11(3): 8, 10–12.

O'Brien, Flann. *The Third Policeman*. Normal, IL: Dalkey Archive Press, 1999.

"Oceanic Air." Retrieved November 25, 2005, from www. oceanic-air.com.

Poniewozik, James. "Welcome to His Unreality." *Time*, January 17, 2005, 165(3), 61.

Ryan, Leslie. "Damon Lindelof." Television Week, 2 August 2004: www.tvweek.com.

Santino, Jack. *The Hallowed Eve: Dimensions of a Culture in a Calendar Festival in Northern Ireland*. Lexington: University Press of Kentucky, 1998.

Sellers, Patricia. "ABC's Desperate Measures Pay Off." *Fortune*, 15 November 2004: 40.

Smith, Andrew. Forum post. "Numbers." Retrieved December 29, 2005 from www.4815162342.com.

Snierson, Dan. "Almost Paradise." *Entertainment Weekly*, December 3, 2004, 795: 28–31, 34, 36.

Stafford, Nikki and Robyn Burnett. *Uncovering Alias: An Unofficial Guide.* Toronto: ECW Press, 2004.

Stam, Robert. *Film Theory: An Introduction.* Malden, MA: Blackwell, 2000.

Survivor. TV series. Exec. Prod. Mark Burnett. Castaway Television Productions. 2000–continuing.

Twilight Zone, The. TV series. Desilu Productions. 1959.

Twin Peaks. TV series. Exec. Prod. David Lynch. Lynch/Frost Productions. 1990.

Vargas, Elizabeth. Episode 1240. "*Lost* Special." *20/20.* ABC Television. May 6, 2005.

Varley, John. "Air Raid." *The John Varley Reader.* New York: Ace Trade, 2004.

Vaz, Mark Cotta. *Alias Declassified: The Official Companion.* New York: Bantam Books, 2002.

—*The Lost Chronicles.* New York: Hyperion, 2005.

Veitch, Kristin. "Secrets to TV's Hottest New Show: 'Lost' in the moment: E!s TV Expert Goes Beyond Plotlines to Find the Secrets to This Small Screen Megahit. Plus, the Show's Creators Reveal What's Next." *USA Weekend,* May 6–8, 2005: 8–9.

—Watch with Kristin. "*Lost* in Hawaii. Dominic Monaghan." *E!Online.* May 18, 2005. Retrieved November 26, 2005, from www.eonline.com.

Vowell, Sarah. "Please Sir May I Have a Mother?" *Salon,* 2 Feb 2000. www.salon.com.

"Wyrdology: The Halloween Pumpkin Head." Retrieved November 25, 2005, from www.wyrdology.com/festivals/halloween/pumpkin-head.html.

X-Files, The. TV series. Exec. Prod. Chris Carter. 1013 Productions. 1993–2002.

Zacharek, Stephanie. "Cast Away: Melancholy! Eternal Solitude! Tom Hanks and Robert 'Forrest Gump' Zemeckis Reunite for the Year's Most Unlikely Blockbuster." *Salon,* 22 December 2000. Retrieved from www.salon.com.

INDEX

A

Abrams, J.J. (*Lost* creator)
  experience, 19–20
  filmmaking knowledge, 20
  Lindelhof, collaboration, 22
  name recognition, 20–21
  quotes, 1, 13, 17
  scripts, success, 18–19
Abstract symbols, 131
Academia, impact, 257
Accent, differences, 117
Adolescents, dilemma, 57–58
Adults, parental troubles (outgrowth),
  67–68
Advanced technology, availability, 82
Adventures of Brisco County, Jr., The, 24–25
Advertising, usage, 266
Agape, 218–219
Airplanes, symbols, 130
Akinnuoye-Agbaje, Adewale (actor), 34,
  97
Alexander, Jesse, 22
Alias, 18–20
American Idol, ranking, 3
Andrews, Naveen (actor), 120
Angel, 18, 29
Apollo
  candy bars, features, 130
  Greek god, representation, 131
Armageddon, 18
Arzt, Leslie (character), 25
Audience, cultivation, 239
Austen, Kate, 36, 111–112
  animal cell, 64
  beliefs, 217–218
  character connections, 290
  character sketch, 275
  freedom, 85
  fugitive, 217
  handcuffs, 245
  personality, challenge, 58
  second change, usage (inability),
    216–217
  triangle. *See* Shephard-Austen-Ford
    triangle
  violence potential, 93–94
Awards (2004-2007), 311–320

B

Backstory. *See* Characters
  concern, 98
  unhappiness, 116
Beatles, reference, 107–108
Beechcraft, Locke/Boone discovery, 81
Beliefs, inclusion, 140
Bernard (character), 46
Biblical names, 167–169
Bibliography, 321–334
Black, symbol, 134–137
Black Rock, survivor arrival, 145–146
Black Smoke Monster, disappearance,
  207–208
Blogs, 247
Boam, Jeffrey, 24–25
Book, explanation, 8–10
Broadcast media innovations, 3
Buffy the Vampire Slayer, 18, 29, 45
Burial, Jack (charge), 169–170
Burke, Juliet (character), 9
  breakout character, 147
  Shephard dynamic, 118

C

Cancellation, potential, 241–242
Candle, Marvin (character), 4, 261
Cardiopulmonary resuscitation (CPR),
  usage, 224
Carlyle, Boone (character), 111, 114
  amputation, 86

blood transfusion, 85
character connections, 286
character sketch, 276
hallucination/vision quest, 194–195
money, 52
    cell phone, usage, 79–80
Cast
    Entertainment Weekly "Entertainer of
    the Year" (naming), 5
    size, advantages/disadvantages, 37
Cast Away, 19
Castaways
    dysfunctional family relationship, 68
    experiences, personal meanings,
        128–129
    formation, 78
    have nots, classification, 54–55
    lives, complication, 6
    medical technology, need, 88
    Others
        contrast, 71
        interaction, increase, 148
        rebirth. *See* Third season
        reluctance. *See* Technology
        responses. *See* Swan hatch;
        Technology
        stereotyping, reduction, 116–117
Casting, news, 241
Catholic Church, symbols, 188
Catholicism, 182–191
Cemetery, growth, 170
Characters
    actions, 104, 111–112
    backstories, unhappiness, 116
    body language/dialogue, 104
    changes, 35
    complexity, 70, 121
    connections, 285–293
    crisis, responses, 111–112
    death, impact, 272
    development. *See* First season; Third
        season
    growth, 62–63
    links, dialogue (usage), 125–126
    names, significance, 230
    pairings, possibilities, 119–120
    precrash connections, 122
    self-examination, honesty, 210
    similarities, 127–128
    sketches, 275–284

spiritual development, 144–145
traits/experience, sharing, 126
Charlotte (character), 199
Christian mythology, Garden of Eden,
    46–47
Church, symbols, 188–191
Clarity, moment, 80–81
Collective Consciousness/Big
    Brother/Implanted Memories
    Theory, 260
Colleen (character), wounding, 94
Colors, significance, 134–137
Comic Con convention, cast/creators
    (attendance), 243
Communication
    absence, 79–84
    technology, 82–83
Compasses, function/symbol, 133
Concept, network/producer skepticism,
    240
Concrete symbols, 129
Connections, meanings, 122–129
Conspiracy theories, 258–264
Conventions
    craze, 253–254
    Creation Entertainment (host), 4
    Lindelhof comments, 272–273
Corporation, control, 54–55
Cortez, Ana Lucia (character), 87, 115
    character connections, 285–286
    character sketch, 276
    funeral, attendance (Eko refusal),
        170–171
    Others, encounter, 215–216
Creation Entertainment
    host. *See* Conventions
Creation Entertainment, hiring, 253
Creative team, dangers, 39–40
Crisis, response, 79
Critics, *Lost* popularity, 4–5, 6–7
Critiques/essays, writing, 256
Cronenberg, David, 19
Crossing Jordan, 21, 22
CSI: Miami, ranking, 2
Cult
    audience, redefining, 240
    phenomenon, 28
    question, 268–269
    status, explanation, 8
Cuse, Carlton (executive producer), 13,

24–26, 149
collaboration, 26. *See also* Lindelof

D

Daniel, biblical name, 168
Dawson, Michael (character), 114
  character connections, 291
  character sketch, 276–277
  raft, sailing, 47
  rifle shooting, guidance, 94
Death, dealing, 169–175
Desperate Housewives, 15, 45
Destiny
  curse, relationship, 230–231
  relationship. *See* Fate
Destruction technology, 91–96
Dharma, Buddhist/Hindu spiritual con-
  cept, 231–234
Dharma Initiative, 4, 231–234
  change, Juliet observations, 54
  Locke, recruiter, 164
  logos, symbols, 130
  Others, connection, 53
  people, joining, 54
  testing facilities, usage, 53
  videos, 261
Dialogue. *See* Characters
  resonances, 128
Dick, Leonard (writer), 27
Dilmore, Kevin, 19
Discourse community, formation,
  256–257
Diversity, positive force, 77–78
Dolan, Marc, 27, 30–31
Dramatic irony, 108

E

Easter eggs
  distribution, 245
  offering, 262
Eko, Mr. (character)
  character connections, 291
  character sketch, 278
  death, 97, 171, 211
  dream, 184
  drug lord, 115
  epiphany, 183
  faith, 208–212
  faith, illustration, 182–185
  fate, valuation, 229–230

Monster encounter, 209–210
  pride, revelation, 211
  shadow, entrance, 209
  shoes, removal, 225
  spiritual enlightenment, 118
  spirituality, sincerity, 184–185
  spiritual path, rejection, 210–211
  story arc, 34
  storyteller/religious counselor, role,
    213
E.M.A. Fan Geek Productions, 253
Emotional strike, military tactic, 74
Encounters
  importance, 123–124
  results, 125
Episodes
  future, 271
  guide, 305–310
  writing, 22–23
Eugenics experiments, 263
Event interpretations, 155–158

F

Fabricated content, majority, 255
Faith
  battle. *See* Science
  concept, 205–212
  confidence, requirement, 208
  science, division (blurring), 158
Faithful, logical (contrast), 155–158
Family, separation, 65–69
Fans
  activities, 251–257
  base, listening/understanding,
    244–245
  behavior, 256–257
  community discourse/referral/specu-
    lation, 267–268
  culture, participatory nature, 239
  early followers, 239–247
  fiction, reading (prohibition),
    255–256
  formation, 242
  gatherings/conventions, 252
  influence, 243–244
  proliferation. *See* Second season
  relationship. *See* Merchandising
  show enjoyment, 7
  sites, 247–249
    increase, 248

support, 264–265
textual involvement, 245–246
Fate
destiny, relationship, 227–231
Muslim belief, 228–229
Firearms (regulation), Shephard (impact), 91
Firepower, reliance, 93
First season
character development, 35
highlights, Jack/Sun healing approaches, 86
meaning, 109–114
medical problems, 85
premiere, ratings, 244
Food
absence, 64
search, 146
Ford, James "Sawyer" (character), 36
character sketch, 277
triangle. *See* Shephard-Austen-Ford triangle
Forever Young, 18
Formal religion, usage. *See* Meanings
Fox, Matthew (actor), 84–85, 98
appearances, 252, 254
Funerals, ritual (momentum), 170–171
Fury, David (writer), 27, 29, 242
departure, 30
fandom, influence, 244
interview, 243

G

Gale, Henry (character), 6, 35
arrival, 73–74
control. *See* Others
literary character, 166–167
makeshift jail, holding, 74
mysterious realm, indicator, 50
sinister presence, 160–161
Them, Rousseau characterization, 73
torture/kill, inability, 216
Garden of Eden. *See* Christian mythology
Gathering, The, 259
Genres, hybridization, 18–19
Geographic lost feeling, 55–57
Giacchino, Michael (composer), 27
Gilligan's Island, 19
Global Health Organization (GHO), 263

Goddard, Drew (writer), 27
fandom, influence, 244
Gone Fishin', 18
Good/evil
contrast, 159–161
single-episode points, 32
Governments, ineffectiveness, 52–53
Grillo-Marxuach, Javier (writer), 26, 27, 239
Gross, Edward (questions), 19–20
Groups, identification, 71
Guilt by association (social theme), 74–75
Guns
availability/problems, 92
metaphor, 95
reverence. *See* Second season

H

Hanso Foundation, 51, 233, 262–264
Harmony, 232–233
Harry Potter books, role model, 13
Hatches. *See* Pearl hatch; Swan hatch
opening, theories, 260–261
references, 131
Hieroglyphics, 131
Hindsight, impact, 157
Hope, concept, 204–205
Horowitz, Adam (writer), 27
Hot-air balloon, presence, 166–167
Hume, David (philosopher), 163–165
Hume, Desmond (character), 9, 38
agape, demonstration, 218–219
Catholicism, 186–188
character connections, 287–288
character sketch, 278
fail-safe, operation, 165, 219
love, freedom, 56
sailboat, arrival, 229
sailor, 49
search, 46
self-sacrifice, Jin (understanding), 219–220
shipwreck, 56
suicide, plan, 155, 187
Hunting party, 91–92

I

I Ching, 130
Interactive experience, 136

Internet-based global fandom, 103
Isaac, biblical name, 168
Islam, 191–192
Island
    beauty, 47
    escape, impossibility, 49–50
    existence. *See* Second island
    guiding signs, 151–152
    help, avoidance, 50
    instructions. *See* Locke
    mapping, 47
    natural/unnatural world, transition,
        53–54
    sets/locations, impact, 51

J

Jarrah, Sayid (character), 47, 112
    character connections, 292
    character sketch, 279
    interrogator, interest, 139–140
    prisoner, 229
    refusal. *See* Locke
    transponder, function, 81
Jensen, Jeff (Juliet/Ethan hypothesis),
    97–98
Johnson, Jennifer (collaboration). *See*
    Lindelof
Jungle, perils, 52–55

K

Kelley, Malcolm David (actor), 18
Kelvin (character), keys (usage), 132
Keys, importance, 131–133
Killing
    ability, 95
    technology, usage (questions), 95–96
Kim, Daniel Dae (actor), 120
King, Stephen, 27–28
Kitsis, Edward (writer), 27
Knives, usefulness, 91
Knowledge network, formation,
    256–257
Kwon, Jin-Soo (character), 111, 114
    character connections, 289–290
    character sketch, 279–280
    father, rejection, 65
    fisherman, 117
    raft, sailing, 47
    Sun
        marital ups/downs, 220–221

    romance, 120
Kwon, Sun-Hwa (character), 111, 114
    character connections, 293
    character sketch, 280–281
    pregnancy, 118
    shooting, 94

L

Labeling, pattern, 114
Libby (character), 115
    character connections, 290
    funeral, attendance (Eko refusal),
        170–171
Lieber, Jeffrey (coauthor), 15
Life
    cyclicality, 86–87
    ups/downs, 59
LifeJournals, 247
Life-or-death situations, 96–100
Lilly, Evangeline (actress), 252, 254
Lindelof, Damon (executive producer),
    13, 21–24, 149
    concept, explanation, 15
    Cuse, collaboration, 23–24, 26
    Johnson, collaboration, 23
Linus, Ben (character), 6, 9
    control. *See* Others
    God, playing, 226
    Locke home/family, contrast, 154
    surgery, 85
Literary characters, 166–167
Litt, Lynne E. (writer), 29
Littleton, Claire (character), 37, 111
    character connections, 287
    dream, 134
    escape, 57
    father, knowledge (absence), 66–67
    independence, increase, 118
    Pace attraction, 189
    Rosemary (modern creation), 193
    surrounding, 91–92
Lives, significance, 99
Lloyd, Walter "Walt" (character)
    abduction, 35
    captive, 147
    character connections, 293
    character sketch, 281
    healing, facilitation, 173
    raft, sailing, 47
Locke, Jack (character)

character connections, 290–291
character sketch, 281–282
God, existence (question), 226
walking, ability, 224–225
Locke, John (character), 25–26,
    111–112
anger management sessions, 152–153
answers, need/desire, 152
arrival, destiny, 143
backstory (third season), 33
confession, 197–198
counselor/advisor, 195
destiny, belief, 151, 154–155
development, slowness, 34
direction, change (second season), 33
faith, 205–208
    crisis, 151–155, 205–206
    test, 153
fan complaint, 33
foster child, 65–66
hallucination, 196–197
Hatch entry, 194
home/family, contrast. *See* Linus
island, instructions, 154
mentor, role, 206
murder, Jarrah refusal, 92
mystery, reduction (first season), 32
mystical/symbolic character, 206
redemption/salvation, desire, 195
revelations, usage, 163–164
special label, 77
spiritual connection, Eko (assis-
    tance), 164
spiritual practices, 195–196
work habits, return, 61–62
Locke, John (philosopher), 163–165
Logical, contrast. *See* Faithful
Lord of the Flies, 19, 52
Loss
    occurrence, 98–99
    reality, facing, 172
Lost. *See* Geographic lost; Psychologic
    lost; Social lost
Lost, ABC (relationship), 14–15
Lost Wikia, 248–249
Love. *See* Parental love; Romantic love
    motivation, 218–223
    pain, 221

M
Madonna statue, religious symbol,
    190–191
Maeda, Stephen (writer), 27
Malkin, Joyce, 199
Malkin, Richard (character), 198–199
Marketing, 3–4
    usage, 266, 274
Mars, Edward (character) wounding,
    217
McPherson, Stephen, 14
Meanings, 43, 45. *See also* Connections
    derivation, 104–105
        example, 105–107
        opportunities, 135–136
    discernment, 108–109
    symbols, usage, 129–137
    unlocking, formal religion (usage),
        179
Medical technology
    absence, 84–88
    understanding, 87
    need. *See* Castaways
Merchandising, fans (relationship),
    265–268
Miniseries, conclusion/speculation, 14
Mission Impossible III, 15, 18
Mobile telephone game, 266–267
Mobisodes, 3
Monaghan, Dominic (actor), 108
Monster
    disappearance. *See* Black Smoke
        Monster
    Eko pride, nonacceptance, 213
    encounters, 146
    Locke sighting, 207
    menace, 47
Mother Nature, blessing, 193–194
Murders, 94
Mystery
    answers, clarity (increase), 30
    keys, 20
    self-discovery, 137
Mythology
    complexity, 39
    construction, correctness, 36–37
    deepening, 6
    development, assistance, 35–36
    Garden of Eden. *See* Christian
        mythology

N

Names. *See* Biblical names
  importance, 161–169
  significance. *See* Characters
  similarity, 295–303
Nash Bridges, 21, 24
Nature, 192–200
  blessing. *See* Mother Nature
New age, 192, 198–200
Nielsen Top 20, *Lost* placement, 2
Nikki (character), 119
Nominations (2004-2007), 311–320
Non-Christian practice, introduction,
  196
Number theory speculation, 252

O

Occupations, 60–63
  identification, 62
Oceanic 815, 9, 38
  crash, 46, 220
    planning, theory, 259
  seating chart, 262
Oceanic 815 survivors, 43
  captive, 48
  identification, 109–110
  meaning, 109–114
  Otherness, reference, 75
  punishment, 228
  visual impressions, 110–111
Odysseus, 51
Official *Lost* Fan Club, Creation
  Entertainment (host), 4
Online game, 245–246
Otherness
  conferring, 76–77
  creation, 75
  identification, impact, 77
  issue, 70–71
  malevolent form, 74
  perception, 77–78
  portrayal, 78
Others, The
  capture. *See* Tailies
  connection. *See* Dharma Initiative
  contrast. *See* Castaways
  depth, 148
  family, boasting, 69
  funeral, 171–172
  Gale/Linus, control, 56–57

haves, classification, 55
  inhabitants, 47
  naming, 72
  relationships, 118–120
  reputation, 71–72
  Sawyer/Austen murders, 174–175
  surgical unit. *See* Third season
  terrorists, perception, 72
Outside world, inclusion, 36

P

Pace, Charlie (character), 37
  Aaron dream, 189
  character connections, 286
  character sketch, 282
  dream sequence, 104–107
  drug use, 183
  entombment, 224
  epiphany, 183
  faith, illustration, 182–185
  father, problem, 67
  fire baptism, 190
  heroin, temptation, 188
  Hurley, friendship, 185–186
  music, importance, 61
  parental love, power (realization),
    222–223
  special label, 77
  spiritual enlightenment, 118
Paganism, 192–200
Pandora's Box
  opening, Hume assistance, 159–160
  religious metaphor, 160
Paradise Lost, 52
Parental love, 222–223
Patience, requirement, 39
Paulo (character), 119
Payoff, waiting, 38
Pearl hatch
  discovery, 152
  interpretation, 156
  visual communication technology, 83
Personal doubts/weaknesses, 63
Pharmaceuticals, hoarding, 88
Phenomenon, 2–8
  explanation, 257–258
Philanthropic agencies, ineffectiveness,
  52–53
Philosophers, 163–165
Pinkner, Jeff, 22

Plot, changes, 35
Polar bear, Locke battle, 153–154
Popularity, 1–2. *See also* Critics
Power, imbalance (Gale/Linus impact),
    55
Precrash connections. *See* Characters
Prime-time hit status, 3
Producers Guild of America nomina-
    tions, 5
Protestant Christianity, 180–182
Psychologic lost feeling, 55–57

Q

QUesting for Every Single Theory
    (QUEST), 259

R

Reality, expansion, 254
Real life, lost feeling, 58–59
Rebirth, 223–227
    Christian concept, 225
Redemption
    character search, 213–214
    concept, 212–218
    perils, 215–218
    power/possibility, 32
    story, 46
Redemptive stories (Lindelhof observa-
    tion), 203
Reeves, Matt, 18
Regarding Henry, 18
Religiosity, absence, 148–149
Reyes, Hugo "Hurley" (character), 112
    Catholic upbringing, 185–186
    character connections, 288
    character sketch, 283
    overeating, safety, 214
    problem, 118
    temptation, 214
Roebuck, Daniel, 25
Rom, Ethan
    burial, 170
    Pace shooting, 92
Romantic love, 219–221
Rose (character), 180–182
    character connections, 292
    science/faith, battle, 181
Rousseau, Alex (character), 56
    discovery, 47
    powerlessness, 57–58

teenage behavior, 57
Rousseau, Danielle (character), 81
    character connections, 287
Rousseau, Jean-Jacques (philosopher),
    163–165
Rutherford, Shannon (character), 111,
    114
    asthma attacks, 85
    behavior patterns, reliance, 172
    burial, Jarrah assistance, 192
    character connections, 292–293
    character sketch, 283–284
    father, death, 123
    money, 52
    Monster mutilation, Boone belief,
        207
    rescue boat, waiting, 80

S

Santoro, Rodrigo (actor), 120–121
Sarah (character), recovery, 124
Sawyer, James (character), 31, 111
    animal cell, 64
    character connections, 292
    crude behavior, 64–65
    hike, forcing, 87
    other behavior, 75–76
    otherness, high-status level (achieving),
        76
    parents, death/murder, 66
    positive role models, absence, 66
    raft, sailing, 47
    self-absorption, 173–174
Science, faith (battle), 149–161
Season One. *See* First season
Season Three. *See* Third season
Season Two. *See* Second season
Second chances, theme, 215
Second island, existence, 119
Second season
    catch-up episode, 81–82
    changes, 117–118
    characters, introduction, 96–97
    Claire/Charlie, romantic kiss, 68–69
    cliffhanger, 97
    fan proliferation, 254–255
    finale, political parallels, 52–53
    guns, reverence, 93
    Hatches, emphasis, 53–54
    imitation, 31

marketing approach, 104–105
meaning, 115–118
plot/characterization, additions,
   45–46
scheduling, frustration, 7
technology, ominous change, 89
Self-alienation, 63
Self-doubt, impact, 63–65
Separation, 59–60
Serial approach, benefits, 32
Serials, fans (addiction), 38
Serial storytelling, problems, 31–32
Sharks
   swimming, 63–64
   threat, awareness, 31
Shelters
   construction, 61
   search, 146
Shephard, Christian (character), 66–67
   character sketch, 284
   name, importance, 161–163
Shephard, Jack (character), 25, 26
   advance medicine/technology, belief,
      150
   character connections, 289
   crash, survival, 84
   cynicism (second season), 87–88
   doctor, identification, 60–61
   entombment, 224
   examination (under glass), 63
   facts, desire, 162
   father, death, 65
   impact. See Firearms
   medical supplies, stash, 88
   medicine, 245
   money, 52
   name, importance, 161–163
   plane cockpit location, 80
   revenge, 94
   survivor society, 48
   Tailies, merger, 48
Shephard-Austen-Ford triangle, 69, 117
Show
   creation, 17
   direction, 272
   elements, exclusion, 264
   future, 271
   teasers, 246
Simpsons, The, 22
Skin color, differences, 117

Social lost feeling, 55–57
Socially unacceptable actions, 75
Societies
   collision, 70–78
   technology, benefits, 96
Soprano, Tony (character), 17
Sorkin, Aaron, 18
S.O.S., 59
   construction, 46
Soul catcher hypothesis, 260
Spiritual concepts, 203
Spirituality, 139
   requirement, 149
Spiritual path, protection, 232
Spiritual perfection, impossibility,
   232–233
Spiritual practices, 143
Spiritual responses, 156
Stereotypes, variation, 120–121
Story
   arcs, projection, 272–273
   development, challenges, 28–29
   premise, 5–6
Studio 60 on the Sunset Strip, 18
Suicide, gunshot (usage), 95
Surprise/acceptability problem, identifi-
   cation, 30–31
Survival drama, 20
Survivors. See Oceanic 815
   lives, interconnection, 230
   societies, collision, 115–118
Suspense, sustaining (ability), 28
Swan hatch
   activity, monitoring, 156
   blast doors, food drop activation,
      50–51
   castaways, responses, 90–91
   destruction, 146–147
   knocks, sound, 157
   Locke discovery, 48
   opening, 36
   purpose, Jack/Locke opinions (differ-
      ences), 117
   targeting, 48
Sweat lodge, construction/usage,
   196–197
Symbolic level, 106
Symbols. See Abstract symbols;
   Concrete symbols

T

Tailies
  children, Others capture, 48
  experience, 81–82
  hike, 87
  merger. *See* Shephard
  story, 127
Tailies, arrival, 36
Taking Care of Business, 18
Team, examination, 21–26
Technology
  absence, 78–79. *See also* Medical
    technology
    survival, 83–84
  availability. *See* Advanced technology
  castaways
    reluctance, 89
    responses, 89–90
  function, 81
  usage/introduction, 88–91
Technology, interference, 54–55
Thelma and Louise, 93
Them, naming, 72
Third season
  castaway, rebirth, 226–227
  characters
    development, 36
    introduction, 96–97
  continuation, 273
  Gale/Ben/Jack, deal, 49
  hiatus, excitement, 13–14
  marketing phrase, 103
  meaning, 118–120
  Others, surgical unit, 82
  plot/characterization, additions,
    45–46
  promo, occupation statement, 62
  relationships, closeness, 68
  society, dispersion, 140–141
  understanding, second season
    (knowledge), 37–38
Troup, Gary, 4

Twilight Zone, 19, 27–28
Twin Peaks, mystery (answers), 29–30

U

Us/them mentality, 72–73

V

Vaz, Mark Cotta, 18
Virgin Mary statues, meaning, 129
Visual communication technology. *See*
  Pearl hatch

W

Watch with Kristin, gossip series, 242
Water, search, 146
Watercooler moments, 40
Weaponry, absence, 95
Websites
  ABC sponsorship, 264–265
  creation, 255
Whedon, Joss, 18, 242
Whispers, 249–251
  validity, 249–250
White, symbol, 134–137
Widmore, Penelope "Penny" (charac-
  ter), 46
  altruism, 51–52
  literary character, 166–167
  romantic love, Desmond demonstra-
    tion, 219
  search, continuation, 51
Widmore Corporation, 233
Widmore Industries, 51
William S. Paley festival, 252–253
Writers Guild of America nominations,
  5

X

X-Files, The, 13, 24, 27–28

Y

Yemi, Eko price (nonacceptance), 213

ABOUT THE AUTHORS

Lynnette Porter has authored or coauthored six books, including *Unsung Heroes of* The Lord of the Rings: *From the Page to the Screen*, a literary and film criticism of J. R. R. Tolkien's characters. She has presented more than 150 conference papers before the Popular Culture Association, Popular Culture Association in the South, Tolkien Society, Society for Technical Communication, and other professional associations in the U.S., U.K., Canada, Australia, and New Zealand. She also speaks at fan-related conferences such as the One Ring Celebration and Fellowship Festival. She teaches at Embry-Riddle Aeronautical University in Daytona Beach, Florida.

David Lavery teaches at Middle Tennessee State University. In the Fall of 2007 he became the chair in Film and Television at Brunel University, London. He is the author of over one hundred published essays and reviews and author/editor/coeditor of eleven books, including *Reading Deadwood: A Western to Swear By* and *Reading* The Sopranos: *Hit TV from HBO* in the Reading Contemporary Television Series. He co-edits the e-journal *Slayage: The Online International Journal of* Buffy *Studies* and is one of the founding editors of the new journal *Critical Studies in Television: Scholarly Studies of Small Screen Fictions.*